Beginning SVG

A Practical Introduction to SVG using Real-World Examples

Alex Libby

Apress®

Beginning SVG

Alex Libby
Rugby, Warwickshire, United Kingdom

ISBN-13 (pbk): 978-1-4842-3759-5   ISBN-13 (electronic): 978-1-4842-3760-1
https://doi.org/10.1007/978-1-4842-3760-1

Library of Congress Control Number: 2018955493

Managing Director, Apress Media LLC: Welmoed Spahr
Acquisitions Editor: Louise Corrigan
Development Editor: James Markham
Coordinating Editor: Nancy Chen

Cover designed by eStudioCalamar

Distributed to the book trade worldwide by Springer Science+Business Media New York, 233 Spring Street, 6th Floor, New York, NY 10013. Phone 1-800-SPRINGER, fax (201) 348-4505, e-mail orders-ny@springer-sbm.com, or visit www.springeronline.com. Apress Media, LLC is a California LLC and the sole member (owner) is Springer Science + Business Media Finance Inc (SSBM Finance Inc). SSBM Finance Inc is a **Delaware** corporation.

For information on translations, please e-mail rights@apress.com, or visit http://www.apress.com/rights-permissions.

Apress titles may be purchased in bulk for academic, corporate, or promotional use. eBook versions and licenses are also available for most titles. For more information, reference our Print and eBook Bulk Sales web page at http://www.apress.com/bulk-sales.

Any source code or other supplementary material referenced by the author in this book is available to readers on GitHub via the book's product page, located at www.apress.com/9781484237595. For more detailed information, please visit http://www.apress.com/source-code.

Printed on acid-free paper

This is dedicated to my family,
with thanks for their love and support whilst writing this book.

Table of Contents

About the Author

Alex Libby is a Digital Ops / MVT developer, working for a global distributor based in the United Kingdom. Although Alex gets to play with different technologies in his day job, his first true love has always been with the open source movement, and in particular experimenting with front-end frameworks and libraries. To date, Alex has written a host of books on subjects such as jQuery, HTML5 Video, SASS, and PostCSS. In his spare time, Alex can often be found putting on shows at his local theater, or out and about on his bike (and with his camera).

About the Technical Reviewer

Zach Inglis is a web design and developer hybrid. He started teaching himself design and programming 19 years ago and hasn't looked back since. As one-half of design agency Superhero Studios (`http://www.superhero-studios.com`), Zach takes care of web and print design, branding, and business strategy for a wide range of large and small clients. Zach was also co-organizer of HybridConf, an inclusive conference dedicated to bridging the gap between design and development.

Acknowledgments

Writing a book can be a long but rewarding process; it is not possible to complete it without the help of other people. I would like to offer a huge vote of thanks to my editors, but in particular Nancy Chen and Louise Corrigan, and with Zach Inglis as technical reviewer – all three have made writing this book for Apress a painless and enjoyable process, even with all of the edits!

My thanks also to my family for being so understanding and supporting me while writing – it requires a lot of late nights alone, so their words of encouragement (and also from Nancy and Louise) have been a real help in getting to the end and producing the finished result that you now have in your hands.

Introduction

Beginning SVG is for people who want to learn how to create and manipulate SVG content in the browser quickly, natively, or by using third-party tools such as Snap.js.

Originally released back in 2001, it has only gained real-world acceptance within the last few years, as an easy-to-edit, convenient format for displaying scalable content without loss of quality. Over the course of this book, I'll take you on a journey through using the format, showing you how easy it is to create and edit reusable shapes and text, using the format. We'll cover such diverse topics as animating content, creating custom filters, optimizing it for efficiency – right through to some real-world examples that you can use as a basis for future projects. This book will provide you will a solid grounding in using SVG as a format, with lots of simple exercises to help you develop your skills using SVG as a format.

Beginning SVG is for the website developer who is keen to learn how to use SVG to quickly produce dynamic visual effects in the browser, without the need to use or learn packages such as Adobe Illustrator. It's ideal for those in Agile development teams, where time is of the essence, and the pressure is on to deliver results rapidly. It's perfect for those developers who want to focus on producing great effects or content but who don't want to have to rely on using lots of external resources, or others to style content such as images when it can easily be done in the browser.

PART I

Getting Started

CHAPTER 1

Introducing SVG

Let me start with a question – *which image format should I use: bitmap or vector, PNGs, JPEGs...?*

If you spend any time developing content for the web, then I am sure you've asked yourself this question countless times: there is a whole array of different formats that we can use, all of which have their own particular qualities! There isn't a single image format that is ideally suited to the web, which encompasses the best qualities of all image types, although Google has tried to push this with the WebP format, which hasn't received widespread adoption among other browser providers.

In many cases, I suspect that either JPEG or PNG images would be favored; these are perfect for complex images where detail is essential (such as photographs). However, if you need to display clear line drawings, or 2D images, for example, then these formats aren't ideal. There are several reasons why, but one of the key weaknesses is maintaining quality – try resizing a schematic saved as a PNG, and the quality soon becomes very poor! There has to be a better way surely...?

Indeed there is – let me introduce you to the world of SVG, or Scalable Vector Graphics. Some people might associate them with applications such as Adobe Illustrator – it's a perfectly valid assumption; Illustrator is a market-leading product, even if it is something of a heavyweight application. However, there is a whole lot more to working with SVG images – over the course of this book, we'll see how easy it is to manipulate them using nothing more than just a text editor and a browser. There's lots to cover, so without further ado, let's make a start on exploring the benefits of using SVG images in our projects.

The Benefits of Using SVG

For anyone working with a new format for the first time, I am sure there will be one overriding question – what makes it so special? What makes this such a useful format to learn?

3

© Alex Libby 2018
A. Libby, *Beginning SVG*, https://doi.org/10.1007/978-1-4842-3760-1_1

There are several good reasons for exploring SVG as a format – it is not intended as a replacement for JPEG or PNG images; the formats work in different ways. SVG as a format really shines when used to display vector images on the web:

- SVG-based images do not lose quality when they are resized or zoomed in the browser;

- SVG images can be animated using JavaScript or CSS;

- SVG images integrate with the DOM very well, and they can be manipulated using JavaScript or CSS;

- SVG images can be indexed by search engines, which is perfect for SEO purposes;

- SVG images can be printed at any resolution.

This means we can create some really powerful designs that can be easily manipulated and which scale well. The question is – how do SVG graphics manage to retain such a level of clarity, compared to images that lose quality as soon as you try to resize them?

Well, I'll let you into a little secret: SVG images are not images. Yes, you heard me right – they are indeed not images! Instead, we're working with XML; to see what I mean, go ahead and view the kiwi.svg image that is in the code download that accompanies this book, in a browser. If you take a look at the source, you'll see something akin to the extract shown in Figure 1-1.

```
<?xml version="1.0" encoding="utf-8"?>
<!-- Generator: Adobe Illustrator 16.0.4, SVG Export Plug-In . SVG Ver
<!DOCTYPE svg PUBLIC "-//W3C//DTD SVG 1.1//EN" "http://www.w3.org/Grap
<svg version="1.1" id="Layer_1" xmlns="http://www.w3.org/2000/svg" xml
    width="612px" height="502.174px" viewBox="0 65.326 612 502.174" e
    xml:space="preserve">
<ellipse fill="#C6C6C6" cx="283.5" cy="487.5" rx="259" ry="80"/>
<path id="bird" d="M210.333,65.331C104.367,66.105-12.349,150.637,1.056
    c36.307,16.544,57.022,54.556,50.406,112.954c-9.935,4.88-17.405,11.
    c20.333,12.375,31.296,27.363,42.979,51.72c1.714,3.572,8.192,2.849,
    c-2.955-8.313,3.059-7.985,6.917-6.106c6.399,3.115,16.334,9.43,30.3
    c-1.864-7.522-11.009-10.862-24.519-19.229c-4.82-2.984-0.927-9.736,
    c-14.198-6.804-28.897-10.098-53.864-7.799c-11.617-29.265-29.811-61
    c-5.002,3.107-11.215,5.031-11.332,13.024c7.201-2.845,11.207-1.399,
    c3.739,3.303,8.413-1.718,6.991-6.034c-2.138-6.494-8.053-10.659-14.
    c13.849,0.396,22.886,8.268,35.177,11.218c4.483,1.076,9.741-1.964,6
```

Figure 1-1. *Source code for an SVG image*

It looks scary, but in reality, the numbers are just coordinates that trace the outline of the image (in this case a kiwi bird). Don't worry – you won't be expected to write code like that; instead, we would add an SVG image using the standard image tag:

```
<img class="mama" src="https://s.cdpn.io/3/kiwi.svg">
```

We can see the result as illustrated in Figure 1-2.

Figure 1-2. *An SVG image of a kiwi bird*

Clearly far easier to use and understand! It's important to get an understanding of what to expect though, as we can manipulate the contents of any SVG image (more on this later in the book).

For now, let's try a simple change, using the kiwi bird image.

CHANGING A COLOR IN AN SVG IMAGE

1. Go ahead and open up a copy of the kiwi image in a text editor.

2. Look for this line of code, on or around line 7:

    ```
    <ellipse fill="#C6C6C6" cx="283.5" cy="487.5" rx="259" ry="80"/>
    ```

3. Go ahead and change the color to a different HEX value – I've picked a random purple, using #834DCF;

4. Save the file, then preview the results in a browser – if all is well, you should see something akin to the screenshot shown in Figure 1-3.

Figure 1-3. *Updated image of a kiwi bird*

See how easy it was? Yes, the code may look archaic, but don't worry – as we go through some of the elements in more detail throughout this book, things will become clearer and easier to understand.

Try running through the steps again, but this time choose different colors – you will see that the image is updated but will also retain the same level of clarity throughout.

Okay – let's change tack: now that we've completed our first edit, it's time we took a look at how the SVG format stacks up against other image formats and see why there are occasions where SVG images will give a superior result compared to standard images.

Comparing Formats

When working on the web, we have a number of image formats we can choose from to display visual content. In many cases, it's likely that JPEG or PNG will be selected – these formats represent the best choice for size and support in today's modern browsers, when working with photo-based imagery. However, in a world where websites must be accessible on different devices, these formats do not scale well if we need to use line-based drawings; we've already covered how SVG can help in this respect.

To really understand how it can benefit us, it's worth taking a moment to see how the format compares to standard images; the key benefit is the ability to manipulate, but there are other reasons why SVG should be considered as a format:

- Resolution independence – with many image formats, we might have to download extra data or assets to fix resolution-based issues. A great example is when using retina screens, which require us to apply a @2x hack to force higher-resolution images to be displayed. This isn't the case with SVG images; these can be fully resized, irrespective of device or resolution used, and without the need for additional tags.

- Accessible DOM API – SVG elements can be manipulated using nothing more than standard JavaScript or CSS; this could be as simple as changing colors (as we saw back in the exercise "Changing a Color in an SVG Image") or as complicated as attaching event handlers to perform specific events.

- No unnecessary HTTP requests – unlike standard images, SVG images are created using XML and CSS. This avoids the need for the browser to request an image from the server, making it faster and more user friendly.

- Content can be indexed, scaled, searched, scripted, and compressed.

- We can create images using nothing more than a text editor – yes, it might be easier to create them in a suitable graphics application. However, let us not forget that the key principle I outlined earlier: Why download and install a graphics package if we can achieve the same result in a text editor that we already have?

With this in mind, it's worth summarizing what we should use SVG for – in summary, they are perfect where we need:

- Logos and icon with strong, geometric, vector-friendly designs;

- Graphics that need to be displayed in multiple sizes and screens;

- Graphics that respond to their device;

- Graphics that need to be edited, updated, and redeployed.

In comparison (and as a reminder), we can see how this stacks up against other image formats, as outlined in Table 1-1.

Table 1-1. *Comparison of Image Formats and Their Uses*

	Category	Palette	Used for
JPG / JPEG	Lossy	Millions of colors	Still Images, Photography
GIF	Lossless	Maximum 256 colors	Simple animationsGraphics with flat colorsGraphics without gradients
PNG-8	Lossless	Maximum 256 colors	Similar to GIFBetter transparency but no animationGreat for icons
PNG-24	Lossless	Unlimited colors	Similar to PNG-8Handles still images and transparency
SVG	Vector/lossless	Unlimited colors	Graphics/logos for webRetina/high-dpi screens
WebP	Lossless	Unlimited colors	Similar to PNGs, but typically 26% smaller in size – take-up isn't so extensive, with only Chrome and Opera supporting the format at present

> **Note**   Lossy images do not retain all of the data in an image, particularly when converted to JPEG; other formats retain data (i.e., are lossless), but do not offer capabilities such as built-in animation or clear scalability.

Okay – enough theory, methinks! Let's move swiftly on, and turn our attention to more practical matters.

We're at the point where we need to ensure we have the right tools in place – some of you may think this requires an array of different applications to be set up: as some might say, not if we can help it! True, there are some tools we can install if we decide to develop more advanced solutions, but for now, there is very little that we need to install. Let's take a look at what we do need, in more detail.

Setting Up a Working Environment

Now that we've been introduced to the SVG format, it's time to get stuck into developing code! We've already run through a basic edit using nothing more than a text editor; there are a few more tools we will need, though, in order to complete the exercises in this book.

Before we touch on what we need, there is a key principle I want to share: where possible, we will try to avoid downloading extra tools, and make use of what we already have available in our working environment. There's a good reason for taking this approach – I'm a great believer in keeping things simple, and not introducing extra tools unless they are needed. There is a trade-off in taking this approach, where some tasks may not immediately be possible, but hopefully we can keep this to a minimum!

With this in mind, let's take a look at the tools we need to avail ourselves of, to help set up our working environment. I suspect many of you will already have suitable alternatives in place, so feel free to skip steps if this is the case:

- We need a decent text editor – there are dozens available online. My personal preference is Sublime Text 3 (available from `http://www.sublimetext.com/3`), although feel free to substitute if you already have a favored editor.

- We will make use of Node.js later in the book – this is to automate some of the more menial tasks such as optimizing our images. This can be downloaded from `https://nodejs.org/en/` – you can use default settings where prompted during the installation.

- We need to create a folder for our code – for the purposes of this book, I will assume it is called `svgbook`; please alter accordingly if yours is different.

- In our project folder, we need to add a couple of extra folders – go ahead and create one called `css`, and another called `font`; both should be at the same root level.

- An optional extra is to download a font for our demos, to provide a little styling – we'll make use of PT Sans from FontSquirrel, available at `https://www.fontsquirrel.com/fonts/pt-sans`. Feel free to skip this step if you want to – the demos will work perfectly fine without it.

- Last, but by no means least, we need to stock up on SVG images that we can use (I would suggest that around six should be sufficient). There are dozens available on the Internet – here are a few links you can try, to help get you started:

  - `https://www.freesvgimages.com/`

  - `https://www.flaticon.com/`

  - `https://pixabay.com/en/`

  - `http://svgstock.com/`

Note   Where possible, I have included relevant source images in the code download; if this hasn't been possible, it will be noted in the text.

Hopefully you've managed to get everything set up, or have suitable tools in place – the key here is that we don't need anything complex when working with SVG images; it's all about simplicity, and working with what works best for your development environment.

Support for SVG

Okay – we've been introduced to SVG as a format, have tools in place, and touched on a basic edit of an existing image; what next? Ah yes – browser support!

SVG as a format has been available since 1999, although it is only in the last few years has it garnered support in recent browsers. A quick check on the CanIUse.com site (`http://caniuse.com/#search=SVG`) shows that most browsers support the format (as shown in Figure 1-4), although IE / Edge struggle to scale files correctly:

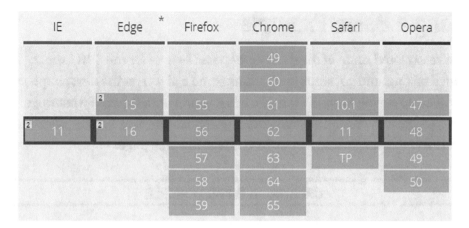

Figure 1-4. *Desktop support for SVG*

The only real concern we may have as developers is if we still have to develop for IE8 or older; the SVG format is not supported, so a fallback alternative will need to be used such as PNG images. Hopefully this isn't too much of an issue, as usage for IE8 is currently less than 1% – this will be one less headache when support for this browser is finally killed off!

In this age of portability, we must equally consider mobile devices – thankfully support for them is just as broad as for desktops, as indicated in Figure 1-5.

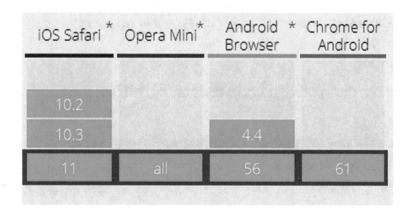

Figure 1-5. *Mobile support for SVG*

In short, support is widespread for most devices – where you might come unstuck is if you are still using anything older than Android 2.3, which doesn't support SVG as a format. This was introduced (in part) from 2.3 onwards, with more recent versions offering full support for the format.

Creating a Basic Example

So far we've explored some of the theory and possible uses for the SVG format – it's time we stopped talking, and got stuck into writing some code! Over the next couple of pages, we will knock up a really simple example; this will provide a taster of what to expect in Chapter 2, where we will look at some more in-depth examples. Let's explore what is involved in more detail, to add a basic SVG image to a web page:

CREATING A BASIC EXAMPLE
---

1. We'll start by opening a new file, then adding the following code, saving it as `simpleexample.html` in our project folder:

```
<!DOCTYPE html>
<html>
<head>
  <meta charset="utf-8">
  <title>Beginning SVG: Creating a simple example</title>
</head>
<body>
  <h2>Beginning SVG: A Simple Example</h2>
  <link rel="stylesheet" href="css/simpleexample.css">
</body>
</html>
```

2. Before the closing `</body>` tag, go ahead and add this code block:

```
<svg>
  <circle cx="60" cy="60" r="50" stroke="black" stroke-width="5"
fill="silver"/>
</svg>
```

3. The keen-eyed among you will spot that we've referenced a style sheet – for this, go ahead and copy the font file from the code download that accompanies this book, and save it into our project's font folder.

4. In a new file, add the following code:

```
@font-face { font-family: 'pt_sansregular'; src: url('../font/
pt_sansregular.woff') format('woff'); font-weight: normal;
font-style: normal;}

body { font-family: 'pt_sansregular', sans-serif; padding: 2rem;
}

circle { stroke: #000000; stroke-width: 4; fill: #cdc7c7; }
```

5. Save this as `simpleexample.css` in the `css` subfolder we've just created in the previous step.

6. We can now preview the results in a browser – if all is well, we should see something akin to the screenshot shown in Figure 1-6.

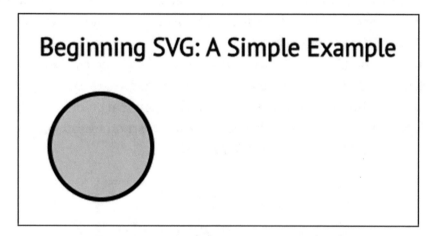

Figure 1-6. *A simple example of an SVG shape*

See how easy it is? Granted, this was a very simple example, but it proves that we only needed to use a standard text editor, with no graphics package in sight. The gray and black colors used were purely for the purposes of viewing the results in print, but we could easily have used different colors – this is limited only by your imagination. The key here is to understand how it works: let's take a quick look in more detail.

Understanding How It Works

At face value, our demo looks very simple – underneath though, it hides a few key principles that control how SVG images are displayed onscreen. Let's summarize each of these in turn for now – throughout the course of this book, we will explore these in more detail:

- The SVG **viewport** – this controls the size of the window, through which we may view a particular SVG element;

- We can restrict this by specifying a **viewbox** attribute – whereas the viewport can be enormous, the viewbox limits the extent of what we see.

In many cases, these two will be aligned – they work in a similar fashion to Google Maps, where we can zoom into a specific region. The visible, scaled-up area will be restricted to this region; the rest of it is still available but will be hidden as it sits outside of the boundaries of the viewport area.

Keeping this in mind, our code works on the basis of referencing a **coordinate** or grid system – it works in a similar fashion to many instances where we might draw elements, such as when using HTML5 Canvas. This means that point (0,0), or the **point of origin**, is considered to be the top left corner of our viewport (assuming both it and the viewbox are aligned), as indicated in Figure 1-7.

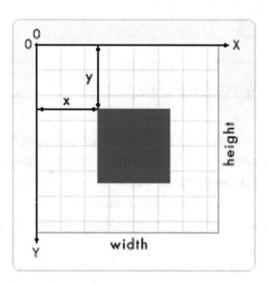

Figure 1-7. *Schematic of SVG coordinate grid*

So how does this work for our circle? If we examine our code as rendered in the browser (shown in Figure 1-8), we see this:

```
▶ <head>…</head>
▼ <body>
    <h2>Beginning SVG: A Simple Example</h2>
    <link rel="stylesheet" href="css/simpleexample.css">
  ▼ <svg>
      <circle cx="60" cy="60" r="50"></circle>
    </svg>
  </body>
```

Figure 1-8. *The code for our SVG circle example*

The cx and cy values indicate how far across to render the circle, with the r value controlling its radius. So, to translate our code into plain English, it will be rendered 60 units to the right (from top left), and 60 units down. The r value controls how big our circle will appear on screen – it goes without saying that the higher the number, the larger the circle!

One thing we must note – many values you will see in SVGs are often rendered with or without unit identifiers. If units have not been specified, then the value is assumed to be equivalent to the same value in pixels.

Adding Fallback Support

Our example is very straightforward, and will work in all recent browsers from the last two to three years. However, it won't work in old browsers such as IE8 – if we're working with a (in this case relatively) new format, how would we provide fallback support? This opens up a real can of worms – should one offer support? Or should we set the experience to degrade gracefully? How about displaying an alternative in PNG format, for example?

15

In this instance, there are several questions one must ask – these are all designed to help identify if fallback support is really necessary, or if an alternative must be provided. Let's take a look at some of the questions one might ask:

- The most important question is – how many visitors might this affect? If the analytics for our site shows a really small number, then we might decide to simply do nothing. This may seem harsh, but it is important to weigh up the economic benefits of implementing a solution, if we're only doing it for a small number of people. If that small number brings in a substantial amount of revenue though, then yes, we may be obligated to implement a solution!

- If the SVG content is merely a text label that can be displayed using an alt tag instead, then we may decide to do away with support; if necessary, we can add in standard CSS to provide some background styling instead.

- Should we degrade the experience gracefully, to encourage users to update browsers to more recent versions? This isn't always possible – some companies may require the use of older browsers for security reasons, which will have an impact on whether we can provide such a graceful exit.

- Do our processes allow for the automatic production of images in different formats? This might seem a little odd to ask, but if we can automate this process, then it reduces the manual effort required and makes implementing a solution easier.

- We might consider implementing a solution whereby any image link automatically includes the same image in two formats – if we happen to use a browser that doesn't support SVG, then it will automatically fall back to using the alternative format. The downside of this is that we may end up with some browsers downloading multiple versions of the same image, which has potential resource considerations.

If we do have to provide fallback support, then we have a number of options available to us, such as using background images or adding the code inline to our application. Each has its own merits, so let's take a look at some of these in more detail.

Types of Fallback

If we've determined that providing a fallback solution is essential for our project, then we must stop and think what *kind* of feedback we should provide. This can take any one of four different options – these are:

- No feedback – we've already touched on this, but if the content is visible without the SVG image (through an alt tag, for example) then we may find that a fallback isn't necessary.

- Text fallback – if we have an image or icon where an alternative text label could be used, then we should consider adding suitable text through the image's alt tag.

- Image fallback – in many cases, developers are likely to use this route when providing a fallback; a PNG or GIF image will work, but with the consequential trade-off in increased file sizes and poorer resolution.

- Interactive fallback – if we have to replace an interactive SVG, a PNG isn't likely to do it justice; we may have to resort to rewriting code using a library such as Raphaël (`http://dmitrybaranovskiy.github.io/raphael/`). It's an option to bear in mind, although working through it in detail will fall outside of the scope of this book

This leaves us with two viable options for implementing a fallback for any SVG image we use, namely text and image. What does this mean in practice? Well, let's take a look at the options:

Implementing a Fallback Image

With the wide support of SVG in recent browsers (certainly within the last two to three years), there should be little need for a fallback – in most cases, we can simply insert an SVG graphic in the same way as we would do for an image. If we had to swap out an image for a PNG equivalent, then we can use the `<picture>` tag, which not only swaps out the image, but can handle different fallbacks, based on what is in use:

```
<picture>
  <source type="image/svg+xml" srcset="image.svg">
  <img src="image.png" alt="">
</picture>
```

If we had to resort to JavaScript, then this nifty one-liner works very well:

```
<img src="image.svg" onerror="this.src='image.png'; this.onerror=null;">
```

The downside of using the JavaScript approach means we trigger multiple (unnecessary) requests for images that are not supported; we also have to use some workarounds to ensure images are displayed to the correct scale on screen.

Adding SVGs as Background Images

Instead of implementing SVGs as images using the `<img>` tag, we can make use of CSS error handling to correctly identify which image to display, if using older browsers:

```
body {
  background: url(fallback.png);
  background: url(background.svg), linear-gradient(
transparent, transparent);
}
```

If a browser supports multiple backgrounds, it will support SVG and therefore use the latter option; for those browsers that only support one background, the first `url(...)` value will be used, and the rest of the rule will be ignored.

It's worth noting that we could use `<object>` or `<embed>` to add SVG images, but this route has fallen out of favor – the near universal support of SVG makes this redundant for most browsers. If it has to be used, then it should be reserved for older browsers such as IE8 that do not support it natively without plug-in support.

Managing Inline Support

Although some might prefer the options we've just covered (for their concise approach), adding SVG images inline remains the most popular – it gives us the most flexibility in terms of controlling style and content using CSS and JavaScript.

However we lose the ability for a browser to simply ignore SVG content and treat it as HTML if it does not support the format – to work around this, one approach might be to simply include plain text within our SVG element, as highlighted in this (partial) example, where we can see fallback text has been added at the start of an SVG graphic:

```
<svg>
  <!--Text fallback-->
  I'm sorry, your browser does not support SVG images

  <circle fill="darkgrey" r="30" />
  <path stroke="forestgreen" ... />

  <!--Fallback with links-->
  <a href="#">Some link text</a>.
</svg>
```

This works very well, using the principle that if the SVG format isn't supported, then code will either be ignored or treated as plain HTML. This means that in our example, the plain text included at the start of the SVG will be displayed, along with the fallback link at the end.

Note that the text within `<text>` tags will not be displayed in a fallback – this is considered invalid by older browsers so will equally be ignored.

We can also develop our example to use either the SVG `<desc>` or `<use>` tags; for more details on how, I would recommend checking out the article on CSS Tricks by Amelia Bellamy-Royds at https://css-tricks.com/a-complete-guide-to-svg-fallbacks/. It's a couple of years old but still contains some useful tips! It's worth noting that we may also need to use JavaScript to test for support – the Modernizr library contains a neat example of how, although we can equally test using plain vanilla JavaScript.

The self-styled web spinner, Taylor Hunt, also has an intriguing article on the use of the SVG `<switch>` statement; this effectively uses the same principle, but varies content based on matching conditions. You can see the details on Codepen at https://codepen.io/tigt/post/inline-svg-fallback-without-javascript-take-2.

There is one more area we should cover – the SVG format is perfect for creating and managing icons. It's essential that we maintain an equally efficient fallback if we have to work on older browsers; this means simply switching formats within an `<img>` tag may not work so well. Let's round out our coverage of providing fallback support, by briefly covering the options available to us, when setting up a fallback for icons.

Supporting an Icon System

When adding images to a page, we clearly have to be careful about sizes, quantities, location and such – I need hardly say that poorly sized images will kill page speed! To help with this, we might decide to use sprites, particularly when using icons – combining multiple images into one sprite will indeed reduce requests for resources. The SVG format is perfectly suited to creating sprites – question is, how should we provide a fallback for them?

Any fallback solution needs to be equally as efficient as the sprite it is replacing – simply adding in single images would be a poor replacement for a sprite. To this end, there are a couple of avenues we can consider:

- We could simply use background images as fallback support, but these would need to be CSS sprites so we can maintain a "one request per image sprite" approach.

- An alternative might be to use an icon font as a fallback. We will need to provide an empty element, but support for `@font-face` in older browsers is more extensive than SVG, so might be a useful option to take.

- We could automate Use Grunticon (available at `http://www.grunticon.com/`), which starts with an empty element and progressively enhances up to SVG, while handling fallbacks (through a JavaScript test). We'll work on the concept of automating icon support for SVG in more detail, in Chapter 3, "Working with Images and Text."

Ultimately, it's up to us as developers to decide the most appropriate route to take – this will depend on the level of fallback support we need to provide, and whether we can reduce this by designing out those areas that will give cause for concern in older browsers.

We've covered a number of options available for maintaining fallback support – part of this will also entail optimizing content to ensure we make it accessible to older browsers. We'll cover this in more detail in Chapter 7, "Optimizing SVG."

Summary

The discovery of, and getting to grips with, a new technology opens up a world of possibilities when developing our projects – let's take a moment to explore what we've covered through the course of this chapter.

We kicked off our journey into the world of SVG with a gentle introduction to the format, to explore some of the benefits of using this format, and to see how it stacks up against other image formats. We then worked our way through a quick example of changing the color in part of an SVG image – this was to show that although we are working with XML code, it is still very easy to alter an image.

Next up came a look at setting up our working environment – we covered how we only need a minimal toolset to work with SVG, and that some of the tools we will use are optional extras, depending on our project requirements.

We then switched to exploring browser support for SVG images – we explored how most modern browsers will support this format natively, and that in the worked example, we can simply use an image tag to insert SVG images into the page without a problem. We also touched briefly on the SVG viewport and viewbox, to understand how these play a pivotal role in positioning SVGs on the page.

We then rounded out the first part of our adventure with a look at providing fallback support for the format. In many cases, we explored how this shouldn't be necessary, but in the event it is, we examined a few tips we can use to either degrade the experience gracefully, or provide an alternative on the page.

Phew – we've covered a lot, but we're just getting started! The next stage in our process is to understand how we can add shapes (both basic and more complex) to the page; we'll explore this and more in the next chapter.

CHAPTER 2

Adding SVG Content to a Page

Life is full of shapes. Square, round, oblong – it doesn't matter what: it's still a shape.

I don't know if there was someone famous who came up with that erudite comment, but it can equally apply to SVG images – even though we can create some intricate designs, at their core each will be made up of individual shapes.

These shapes might be any one of eight different types: we can create squares, rectangles, circles, ellipses, lines, polylines, polygons and paths, which when put together will form our final design. If we cast our minds back to the exercise we worked through in Chapter 1, "Introducing SVG", we created a simple circle with a silver color used to fill the center:

```
<svg>
  <circle cx="60" cy="60" r="50" stroke="black" stroke-width="5"
  fill="silver"/>
</svg>
```

This simple one-liner (for the purposes of this code I'm excluding the `<svg>` tags, which have to be present anyway), is all that is required to create a circle. Question is – is it that easy to create the other basic shapes?

Well, thankfully it is – with the exception of the multipoint shapes (polygons, polylines, and paths), it's a cinch to create these basic shapes, so let's dive in and take a look at the code to produce each one in turn.

© Alex Libby 2018

A. Libby, *Beginning SVG*, https://doi.org/10.1007/978-1-4842-3760-1_2

Implementing SVG Shapes

When working with SVG images, there are a number of basic shapes available for us to use – the purpose of many of these will be obvious from their names, although some less so! In all cases they are designed to help make it easier to read our code and ultimately keep the SVG documents as short as possible (avoiding duplication where practical).

Any shape we implement will be as an element – we touched on the different options for adding these to a page back in Chapter 1. Each has its own merits; for convenience we will add ours using the inline method, so that we can then manipulate them using standard CSS styling methods.

Do not feel constrained to use just one method when adding SVG images – most of the ones we touched on in Chapter 1 can be used, but some (such as iframe or embed) should be avoided if possible!

Enough talking – let's make a start and explore the shapes we can use, starting with the humble square and rectangle.

Creating Squares and Rectangles

The first of the basic shapes we will take a look at is the humble square (and it's cousin, the rectangle) – as someone once said, everything is made up of building blocks, so it seems only sensible to start with these two shapes!

The code to create both shapes is very straightforward, so without further ado, let's get cracking on our first exercise of this chapter:

CREATING SQUARES AND RECTANGLES

1. Let's begin by adding the following code to a new document, saving it as `squares.html` at the root of our project folder:

```
<!DOCTYPE html>
<html>
<head>
  <meta charset="utf-8">
```

```
    <title>Beginning SVG: Creating a simple example</title>
    <link rel="stylesheet" href="css/squares.css">
</head>
<body>

</body>
</html>
```

2. Next, we're going to provide a little styling – in a new file, add the following
    code, saving it as `squares.css` in the `css` subfolder of our project area:

```
@font-face {
    font-family: 'pt_sansregular';
    src: url('../font/pt_sansregular.woff') format('woff');
    font-weight: normal;
    font-style: normal;
}

body { font-family: 'pt_sansregular', sans-serif; padding: 2rem; }

span { width: 200px; vertical-align: top; }
svg { display: inline-block; height: 200px; padding-top: 20px; }
#squareID, #rectangleID { margin-left: -125px; }
```

3. In between the `<body>` tags, go ahead and add the following code:

```
    <h2>Beginning SVG: Drawing Squares and Rectangles</h2>
    <link rel="stylesheet" href="css/squares.css">

    <span>Adding a square:</span>
    <svg id="squareID">
      <rect x="10" y="10" width="100" height="100" stroke="darkgrey"
      fill="transparent" stroke-width="5"/>
    </svg>

    <span>Adding a rectangle</span>
    <svg id="rectangleID">
      <rect x="10" y="10" width="150" height="100" stroke="grey"
      fill="transparent" stroke-width="5"/>
    </svg>
```

4. Save this file, then go ahead and view the results in a browser – if all is well,
    we should see something akin to the screenshot shown in Figure 2-1.

Figure 2-1. *Drawing squares and rectangles*

See how easy that was? Creating simple SVG images is very straightforward – after all, our code uses standard HTML formatting, so there is no need to learn a specialist syntax when creating our images. The code, however, does introduce us to some unfamiliar keywords, so let's pause for a moment and take a look at these in more detail.

Understanding How the Code Works

At this point, some of you may be wondering why, if we look at the code closely, we appear to have two <rect> elements in use, when we clearly can see a square and rectangle on screen!

The truth is that although both clearly look different, they use the same element; this means they can share the same properties. If, for example, we were creating a square, then the values for width and height would be identical, as shown in our example – these would be different if we wanted to create a rectangle:

```
<svg id="squareID">
  <rect x="10" y="10" width="100" height="100" stroke="darkgrey"
  fill="transparent" stroke-width="5"/>
</svg>
```

We start with the standard <svg> tags to define our element – you will see these in use whenever you create an SVG image. Next, we have our <rect> element, which has a number of defined attributes that govern its size, position (x and y), fill color, and thickness (or stroke-width) of the border.

The key to this shape (and any other) is in the positioning – each shape is positioned using a defined grid position (as we touched on back in Chapter 1), where the top left corner of our viewport is point 0, 0. In our example, our boxes (although it isn't displayed as such in print), are displayed 10 pixels to the right and 10 pixels down, from point zero.

We will touch on stroke, stroke-width, and fill in more detail later in this chapter in the section "Painting elements."

We then simply pass suitable values for both width and height – the radius values are omitted, as we don't want curved corners on our shapes. These attributes are listed in full in Table 2-1.

Table 2-1. *Attribute Properties for Rectangles*

Attribute	Purpose
x	The x position of the top left corner of the rectangle.
y	The y position of the top left corner of the rectangle.
width	The width of the rectangle.
height	The height of the rectangle.
rx	The x radius of the corners of the rectangle.
ry	The y radius of the corners of the rectangle.

The remaining basic shapes are as straightforward to create, so let's continue with this theme, and take a look at how we can create SVG circles and ellipses.

Drawing Circles and Ellipses

The second basic shape we will now look at is the circle (and its cousin, the ellipse) – this kind of reminds me of the phrase "to be thrown a curveball." I don't know why, only except to say that there are no hazards to watch for when creating these shapes!

The code to create both shapes is very straightforward, so without further ado, let's get cracking on the next exercise of this chapter:

CREATING CIRCLES AND ELLIPSES

Much of the code that we need to use is already in place, so to make it easier, we can simply take a copy of the previous CSS and HTML files, then adjust as necessary:

1. We'll begin by taking a copy of `squares.html`, then renaming it as `circles.html` – go ahead and replace the code between the `<body>` tags with this:

    ```
    <h2>Beginning SVG: Drawing Circles and Ellipses</h2>

    <span>Adding a circle:</span>
    <svg id="circleID">
      <circle cx="60" cy="65" r="55" stroke="black" fill="transparent"
        stroke-width="5"/>
    </svg>

    <span>Adding an ellipse:</span>
    <svg id="ellipseID">
      <ellipse cx="75" cy="75" rx="70" ry="50" stroke="#a6a6a6"
        fill="transparent" stroke-width="5"/>
    </svg>
    ```

2. Go ahead and change the CSS style sheet link from `squares.css` to `circles.css`:

    ```
    <link rel="stylesheet" href="css/circles.css">
    ```

3. Next, take a copy of the `squares.css` file, then rename it as `circles.css` – remove the last rule, and replace it with this:

    ```
    #circleID, #ellipseID { margin-left: -125px; }
    ```

4. Save the contents of both files, then go ahead and fire up `circles.html` in a browser: if all is well, we should see two circular shapes, as indicated in Figure 2-2.

Figure 2-2. *Drawing circles and ellipses*

See how easy it is to create basic circular elements using SVG? There is very little different when compared to creating a square or rectangle – we use the same format of code, although some of the attributes will be different. Let's pause for a moment to review how our code works, and these attributes, in more detail.

Exploring How the Code Works

If we take a close look at the code we've just created, we can start to see some similarities – both to what we've just created in the previous exercise, and between how the circle and ellipse are created.

For example, we can use the same stroke, fill and stroke-width attributes as before – these have not changed. What is of more interest to us though are the attributes for sizing each element – both use the same cx and cy values to define the starting position of the circle. Unlike the circle where the radius is evenly defined (using the r value), an ellipse is clearly wider than it is taller – for this, we need to use the rx and ry values to define its size, as outlined in Table 2-2.

Table 2-2. *Attribute Properties for Circles and Ellipses*

Attribute	Purpose
r	The radius of the circle.
cx	The x position of the center of the circle.
cy	The y position of the center of the circle.
rx	The x radius of the ellipse.
ry	The y radius of the ellipse.

To put this in context of our example, our circle starts at point 60, 65 and has a radius value of 55. The ellipse is a little wider, so we must allow for this in our example – it starts at position 75,75: it has a x radius value of 70 and y radius value of 50. Note though that these values are from the center of the shape outwards; multiply both values by 2, to get the true size of the ellipse.

Okay – let's change tack: not every shape we need to create will be a simple square or circle; what about creating multisided shapes, for example? Thankfully it's just as easy to create these shapes, so let's dive in and take a look.

Drawing Lines, Polylines, and Polygons

At its heart, every SVG shape we create is made up of individual lines – I need hardly say that each goes from point A to B!

Okay – I confess: I am stating the obvious but with good reason. This next bunch of shapes relies on using this principle to work, so understanding which pair of values relates to which point in a shape is key to manipulating how they appear on the page. To see what I mean, let's dive in and create our next three shapes – a line, polyline, and polygon – as part of our next exercise.

DRAWING LINES, POLYLINES, AND POLYGONS

As in previous exercises, much of the code that we need to use is already in place, so to make it easier, we can simply take a copy of the previous CSS and HTML files, then adjust as necessary:

1. We'll begin by taking a copy of `squares.html`, then renaming it as `lines.html` – go ahead and replace the code between the `<body>` tags with this:

```
<h2>Beginning SVG: Drawing Lines, Polylines and Polygons</h2>

<span>Adding a line:</span>
<svg id="lineID">
  <line x1 = "20" y1 = "20" x2 = "175" y2 = "180" stroke = "black"
  stroke-width = "3"/>
</svg>

<span>Adding an polyline:</span>
<svg id="polylineID">
```

```
    <polyline points = "20,20 40,25 60,40 80,120 120,140 200,180"
      fill = "none" stroke = "black" stroke-width = "3"/>
  </svg>

  <span>Adding an polygon:</span>
  <svg id="polygonID">
    <polygon points = "60,10 140,10 190,70 190,130 140,190 70,190 10,
      130 10,70" fill = "gainsboro" stroke = "black" stroke-width = "3"/>
  </svg>
```

2. Next, go ahead and replace the link to lines.css at line 6, with this:

    ```
    <link rel="stylesheet" href="css/lines.css">
    ```

3. Now take a copy of the `lines.css` file, then rename it as `circles.css` – remove the last rule, and replace it with this:

    ```
    #lineID, #polylineID, #polygonID {
      margin-left: -116px;
    }
    ```

4. Save the contents of both files, then go ahead and fire up `lines.html` in a browser: if all is well, we should see three line shapes, as indicated in Figure 2-3.

Beginning SVG: Drawing Lines, Polylines and Polygons

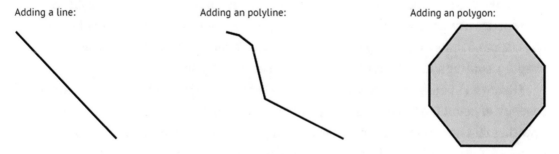

Figure 2-3. *Drawing lines, polylines, and polygons*

By now, some of the terms we've used should start to be a little more familiar – such as stroke, fill, and stroke-width. We will cover these shortly, but for now it's more important to understand how we've constructed our shapes, so let's dive in and take a look at our code in more detail.

Exploring How the Code Works

Creating polyline (or for that matter, polygon) shapes can be something of a paradox – the code may *look* more complicated, but in reality it is simpler, as we have fewer attributes that need to be configured. Those that do need to be configured are listed in Table 2-3.

Table 2-3. *Attributes for Lines, Polylines, and Polygons*

Attribute	Purpose
x1, y1	The x and y positions of point 1 (our starting point).
x2, y2	The x and y positions of point 2 (our finishing point).
points	A list of points, each separated by a comma, space, EOL, or line feed character. Each must contain an x and y coordinate – the drawing automatically closes the path, so a final line will be drawn from the last set of points to the starting set.
	Note: this applies to lines and polygons only; to see how it works for polylines, add a fill color to the shape.

If we take a look at our code examples, we can see the first two sets of attributes in use within the line example – these simply use the SVG grid position system to locate the starting and finishing points within our view port: x1 = "20" y1 = "20" x2 = "175" y2 = "180".

A little further down, the points attribute comes into play – again, we specify our coordinates using the x, y format. So for example, the starting point for our octagon is 60, 10, or 60 units in from top left, and 10 down. We then continue all the way round the shape, providing suitable coordinates to complete our shape.

Okay – let's change tack: we have one final set of shapes to explore; these open up a wealth of possibilities, although they will take a little more work to come to grips with how they can be configured! I'm talking about paths and markers, so let's dive in and explore the potential uses of these two elements in more detail.

Constructing Paths and Markers

So far, we've dealt with relatively simple shapes, which all follow a defined design – we can clearly recognize a circle as such, or a single line connecting two points! (Yes, it might sound like I'm really stating the obvious again, but yes, there is a point – stay with me on this...)

All of those shapes have one thing in common – they are made up of lines that connect two points; multiple lines together will create a shape. However, what if we wanted to create an *abstract shape, which is not a recognizable design, such as a square?*

Enter the world of SVG **paths** – we can provide a series of coordinates that when joined, form our final design. The beauty though is that we can apply all manner of different styles to it, just as we would do for a standard circle or square. We can really go to town on our design – to get a taster, try opening the gradients.html file that is in the gradients folder within the code download that accompanies this book....

I'll bet good money that your initial response will be something along the lines of *Yikes! What the...?* Does this sound about right? Don't worry – this wasn't meant to shock you, but to give you a flavor of what is possible when we work with SVG paths. Let's take it back a few notches and check out a simple example of what we can achieve, as shown in Figure 2-4.

Figure 2-4. *A simple example of an SVG path*

This curve example was taken from a useful Codepen of examples (available at https://codepen.io/chriscoyier/pen/NRwANp), created by the CSS expert Chris Coyier of CSS-Tricks.com fame; below is the code extract used to create our example:

```
<svg viewBox="0 0 10 10" class="svg-4">
  <path d="M2,5 C2,8 8,8 8,5"/>
</svg>
```

Clearly something a little easier to understand! The question is, what does it all mean? This is a really useful concept to learn when working with SVGs, so let's break it down into its constituent parts.

Understanding Our Code in Detail

The first line of code is the standard opening tag for any SVG shape or design; we've met this already in previous exercises, so should be a little more familiar by now. The real magic happens in line 2 – we have the (aptly named!) <path> tag, inside which we assign a series of numbers and or letters to create our design.

There is, however, method in the apparent madness of that string of characters – they are a series of commands to define how our shape should appear. To make sense of it, there is one important concept we should be aware of: the difference between **absolute** and **relative** commands.

What do I mean by this? Well – let's take the first command: M2,5. Put very simply, it means "move to the exact location 2, 5". The next command, C2,8 8,8 8,5, is a little more complex: we use this to create a Bezier curve. The starting point for it was defined with the initial command; the next three coordinates define the degree of curve and end point of our Bezier curve. Keeping this in mind, let's assign those coordinates to an edited version of the previous screenshot (Figure 2-5).

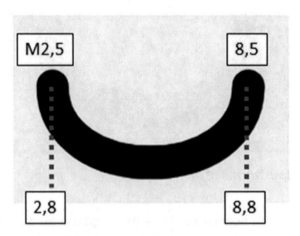

Figure 2-5. *An edited version of our Bezier curve SVG*

Note that in the above screenshot, I've only included the coordinates of the C command, to show how it matches with our original command.

We've touched on the need to understand the difference between absolute and relative commands – the key to making paths work is this: most commands come in pairs – either as uppercase characters, or as lowercase equivalents. The uppercase characters represent absolute commands, whereas the lower case ones are relative.

To put this into context, our example directed the starting point to be at the absolute location of 2,5. If we had made it relative (i.e., used a lowercase m instead), then it would read as "move 2 to the right, and 5 down," **from our current location instead**.

Working with paths can open a real minefield of possibilities – the d attribute we met at the beginning of this section has a mini-syntax in its own right! It's absolutely worth exploring what is possible; some people may say it's simpler just working with paths (as you can do just about everything we've already covered), but the key to remember is that using predefined shapes will make it easier to read the code in your final solution.

For a good in-depth tutorial, check out Chris Coyier's guide on using paths, which is available at `https://css-tricks.com/svg-path-syntax-illustrated-guide/`. This contains a list of the different commands we can use to create individual paths, in addition to a good explanation of how paths operate.

Let's move on – we can do a huge amount with the powerful path element, but to really take things up a level, how about adding markers to our design? *Mark...huh?* I hear you ask – what would that give us...?

Adding Markers to SVG Paths

Aha – let me explain: who hasn't used Google Maps in some form or other? You enter the zip code or name of a location, and up pops a little pointer to indicate the location, right?

That's a marker – trust me, it's nothing more complicated than simply identifying a point on our design! We use the same principle when working with SVG designs. There's a variety of different uses for markers – we could use them as indicators on maps, or for a wiring schematic we might create, where clarity is paramount, irrespective of the size of the design.

Let's put this to the test, and construct a simple SVG of a line that has a marker element at one end – this will be the subject of our next exercise.

DRAWING PATHS AND MARKERS

We're going to break with tradition, and create this as a Codepen (for variety), so go ahead and browse to `https://codepen.io`, then follow these steps:

1. We'll start by adding this block of code into the HTML section of our pen – this creates our basic line and marker:

```
<h2>Beginning SVG: Drawing Paths and Markers</h2>
<svg>
  <defs>
    <marker id="circle1" markerWidth="8" markerHeight="8"
            refX="5" refY="5" orient="auto">
      <circle cx="5" cy="5" r="3" fill="black"/>
      <circle cx="5" cy="5" r="2" fill="lightgray"/>
      <path d="M 4,3.5 L 6.5,5 L 4,6.5 Z" fill="slategray"/>
    </marker>
  </defs>
  <line x1="50" y1="120" x2="250" y2="50" stroke="black" stroke-
    width="5" marker-end="url(#circle1)" />
</svg>
```

2. In the CSS section, drop in these styles – they are not obligatory but will add a little variety to the title styling. You can leave these styles out if you prefer – the demo will work just fine without them:

```
@import url('https://fonts.googleapis.com/css?family=PT+Sans');

body {
  font-family: 'PT Sans', sans-serif;
  padding: 2rem;
}
```

3. Go ahead and save the pen by clicking on the Save button – if all is well, we should see something akin to the screenshot shown in Figure 2-6.

Beginning SVG: Drawing Paths and Markers

Figure 2-6. Drawing paths and markers

You can see a working version in a Codepen at `https://codepen.io/` `alexlibby/pen/goXbRJ`, or peruse a version available within the code download that accompanies this book (look for the `paths.html` file).

Our design is deliberately meant to look simple, but if you take a look at the code in more detail, you can see a few keywords we've not touched on to date. Let's dive in and take a look at them in more detail.

Understanding How Our Code Works

If we concentrate on the core part of our code, we can see this block – it kicks off with a `<defs>` element, which allows us to create an element for later reuse:

```
<defs>
  <marker id="circle1" markerWidth="8" markerHeight="8"
            refX="5" refY="5" orient="auto">
    <circle cx="5" cy="5" r="3" fill="black"/>
    <circle cx="5" cy="5" r="2" fill="lightgray"/>
    <path d="M 4,3.5 L 6.5,5 L 4,6.5 Z" fill="slategray"/>
  </marker>
</defs>
```

The <defs> element is not rendered immediately, but instead defines an object for later reuse – it's best to think of any object stored within a <defs> block as a template or macro created for future use.

Within our `<defs>` element, we create a `<marker>` tag, to which we apply an ID of `circle1`; the viewport size of our marker is defined by the `markerWidth` and `markerHeight` values, and will be attached using the `refX` and `refY` coordinates.

Inside our marker element, we define two circles – one is filled in with the color black, with the second placed inside it and colored light gray. (The final design looks like one circle with a thick border, but it is two circles that overlay each other). We then add a slate gray-colored arrowhead, which is applied using the path command; this is then completed with the closing `</marker>` and `</defs>` tags. Our marker is then applied to the line element we've drawn – we attach the marker at the end point of our line, using the marker-end attribute, as indicated in this code extract:

```
<line x1="50" y1="120" x2="250" y2="50" stroke="black" stroke-width="5"
marker-end="url(#circle1)" />
```

The value passed via marker-end references the object we created in our <defs> block, which we discussed earlier in this section.

We could have used marker-start to attach our marker at the start point of our line, but I don't think the final result would look quite as good! We've touched on some of the attributes that can be used – Mozilla has a useful article outlining each option in more detail, which is available at https://developer.mozilla.org/en-US/docs/Web/SVG/Element/marker.

Let's change tack and focus on something a little more complex – we've touched on using paths as a way of creating more abstract shapes, but there will be occasions where we need something a little more...practical! Thankfully we can use paths to achieve this; let's work on a more practical example of using this element in more detail.

Creating More Advanced Shapes

Up to this point, our examples have been relatively straightforward – it's time we took things up a level again and produced something a little more complex, to show what can be achieved with SVG.

A good example is the classic gauge – we can use this to measure and / or change any setting, such as opacity or measure broadband speed. Okay, perhaps a little contrived, yes, but the point being that if we need to measure a range of values, or quickly change them, then a gauge might be a useful tool to use.

The great thing about SVG is that we can easily create a basic gauge – it will automatically resize, without loss of function, and can later be animated if desired. Over the course of the next exercise, we're going to explore how to create such a gauge, using an example adapted from a Codepen created by Adao Junior.

CONSTRUCTING A CIRCULAR GAUGE

Let's make a start:

1. In a new file, go ahead and add the following code, saving it as advanced.
   html in our project area:

```
<!DOCTYPE html>
<html>
<head>
  <meta charset="utf-8">
  <title>Beginning SVG: Creating a more advanced example</title>
  <link rel="stylesheet" href="css/advanced.css">
</head>
<body>
  <h2>Beginning SVG: Creating a Circular Gauge</h2>
</body>
</html>
```

2. Go ahead and add the following code in between the <body> tags – this
   creates the gauge and accompanying text:

```
<svg id="gauge" x="0px" y="0px" width="176px" height="168px"
 viewBox="0 0 76 68">
<g>
  <text transform="matrix(1 0 0 1 22.9209 43.4141)"
   fill="#708090">45%</text>
</g>
<path fill="none" stroke="#222729" stroke-width="2" stroke-
 miterlimit="10" d="M16.652,65.29
  C8.984,58.838,4.112,49.171,4.112,38.366c0-19.424,15.746-
  35.171,35.17-35.171c19.424,0,35.17,15.747,35.17,35.17
  1c0,10.805-4.872,20.473-12.54,26.924"/>
<path class="completion" fill="none" stroke="#708090" stroke-width="5"
 stroke-miterlimit="10" d="M17.107,65.29
  C9.44,58.838,4.567,49.171,4.567,38.36
  6C4.567,20.6,17.74,5.911,34.852,3.532"/>
```

```
<text id="complete" transform="matrix(1 0 0 1 21.3916 51.7891)"
  fill="#000000">completion</text>
</svg>
```

3. We need to add a little styling to finish off the effect – go ahead and add the following to a new file, saving it as advanced.css within the css subfolder that is in our project area:

```
@font-face { font-family: 'pt_sansregular'; src: url('../font/pt_
sansregular.woff') format('woff'); font-weight: normal; font-style:
normal; }

body { font-family: 'pt_sansregular', sans-serif; padding: 2rem;
  font-size: 18px; }
#complete { font-size: 8px; }
```

4. Save both files – if we preview the results in a browser, we should see something akin to the screenshot shown in Figure 2-7.

Beginning SVG: Creating a Circular Gauge

Figure 2-7. *Creating a circular gauge*

You can see the original version of this demo in a Codepen at `https://codepen.io/junior/pen/RWQver`.

Although the code looks complex, we've touched on most of the key terms used within – in fact, the only terms we've yet to meet are <text> and <transform>! There are some useful concepts within this code we should be aware of, so let's pause for a moment to explore how the gauge was created in more detail.

Dissecting Our Gauge Code

For this demo, you might well be forgiven if an initial look at this code prompts a...shall we say...colorful response! It looks scary, but in reality it is easier to understand than it might first appear:

We begin with defining our SVG viewport, and set a viewport of around 50% its size – this will have the effect of zooming in the image when displayed. Inside our SVG, the first element we create is a `<text>` element, which displays the percentage completed in the gauge (in this case 45%).

The first of the two `<path>` elements creates the dark-colored back line, over which we show the 45% completed `<path>`, which is styled using a slate gray color. In both cases, we're setting stroke widths, which define the thickness of each `<path>` element, and which is drawn centered on the path. We then close out the SVG with a second `<text>` element, which contains the word complete, and uses a transform attribute to help center it in both the SVG and against the percentage value.

Note   To really understand the detail of how each path works, try breaking the `d=` attribute into separate lines, where you see an uppercase or lowercase letter. I would recommend taking a look at the excellent article by Chris Coyier at `https://css-tricks.com/svg-path-syntax-illustrated-guide/`; this shows you how to translate these letters (from any SVG), into something you can recognize as an action, such as M to move to an absolute point.

Let's move on – it's time to spice things up a little and go really abstract! Over the course of the next chapter, we will dive into how we can manipulate images and text when working with SVG. However, we can equally use them as a basis for creating abstract shapes using clip-paths; this tool is something of a special case, as it can be used both in a standard and SVG capacity. To see what we mean, let's dive in and see how crazy things might get...

Creating Unusual Shapes with Clip-Paths

Clip-paths – this is where we can really have some fun! This feature originated as part of the initial SVG spec from 2000, but has since been moved into the CSS Masking module, so it can be used in either a SVG or CSS capacity.

Put simply, we use clip-paths to specify a clipping path that can be applied to any element – this includes both text and images. This clip-path can take any shape we desire and can be created using the shape functions we've covered thus far in this chapter. Anything outside of the clip-path won't be displayed – in effect, a clip-path is a form of mask, which we can use to block out undesired content, without physically removing it from the original image.

The best way to understand how this work is to see it in action, so without further ado, let's put together a simple demo to show off the effects of applying a clip-path to an image. Our demo will use an image of houses in a sunset – you can see the original image on the publicdomainvectors.org site at `https://publicdomainvectors.org/en/free-clipart/Houses-on-the-horizon-vector/1525.html`.

CREATING AN UNUSUAL SHAPE

Let's make a start:

1. We'll start with add the following code to a new file, saving it as `clippath.html` in our project area:

```
<!DOCTYPE html>
<html>
<head>
  <meta charset="utf-8">
  <title>Beginning SVG: Creating a simple example</title>
  <link rel="stylesheet" href="css/clippath.css">
</head>
<body>
  <h2>Beginning SVG: Drawing unusual shapes with clip-path</h2>

  <svg height="0" width="0">
    <defs>
      <clipPath id="svgPath">
        <path fill="#FFFFFF" stroke="#000000" stroke-width="1.5794"
          stroke-miterlimit="10" d="M215,100.3c97.8-32.6,90.5-71.9,336-77.6
        c92.4-2.1,98.1,81.6,121.8,116.4c101.7,149.9,53.5,155.9,14.7,17
        8c-96.4,54.9,5.4,269-257,115.1c-57-33.5-203,46.3-263.7,20.1
        c-33.5-14.5-132.5-45.5-95-111.1C125.9,246.6,98.6,139.1,215,100.3z"/>
      </clipPath>
```

```
    </defs>
  </svg>
  <img src="img/houses.svg">
</body>
</html>
```

2. Next, go ahead and take copies of the `css` and `img` folders from `clippath` folder within the code download that accompanies this book. Store these in the project area – they contain some simple styling required for the demo, along with our source SVG file.

3. We're almost there – save the file, then go ahead and preview the results in a browser; if all is well we should see the weird image shown in Figure 2-8.

Figure 2-8. *Our crazy clip-path image...*

Okay – yes, perhaps describing this image as weird is a little over the top! However it does show that we can create some odd-shaped images using the clip-path property within SVG. The great thing about it is that we're simply using path values in a similar manner to that in the previous exercise – each is a set of commands that, when executed, draws our random shape as a series of connected points.

We open with our now familiar opening `<svg>` tags, inside which we've set up a `<defs>` element – this is to define our clip-path as a shape that can be reused. The shape itself starts at the absolute point of `215,100` and then simply moves around in a series of relative moves to various points in our viewport. The clip-path is then completed with the closing tags, ready for use in our page.

At the bottom of our HTML code, we've put a simple link into a SVG image – we tie this all together with the `img { clip-path: url(#svgPath); }` statement in our CSS file, which applies our SVG clip-path to our image.

We'll revisit working with images and SVG in the next chapter, "Working with Images and Text." To understand more of what is possible, please refer to the great article by Sarah Soueidan, available at `http://www.sarasoueidan.com/blog/css-svg-clipping/`.

Phew – we've come to the end of our journey through each of the different types of shapes available when working with the SVG format; it's up to us to choose the right ones to create our next killer design. A part of this though is adding color – we've touched on this at various points with attributes such as fill or fill-opacity in previous exercises, so let's take a moment to review this in a little more detail.

Painting Elements

Any SVG we create will look very dull if we simply created a line drawing – sometimes this may be necessary (in the case of an electronics schematic), but more often than not, we will need to add color. Question is – how?

Well, we've already done so in the examples we've created so far, but without realizing it! If you take a look at the examples we've worked through to date, you can't help but see code such as this example:

```
<path fill="#FFFFFF" stroke="#000000" stroke-width="1.5794" stroke-
miterlimit="10"...
```

These terms are just four of the options available for providing color – we start with the basics such as fill for painting shapes, through to stroke for defining the outline color of that shape, or stroke-linecap for determining how the ends of our segment lines will appear. There is a host of options we can use, so to bring all of the possibilities together from the various demos thus far, I've summarized the details in Table 2-4.

Table 2-4. *A summary of Painting Options for SVGs*

Attribute	Purpose
fill	Fills in the color of any SVG shape – can take any CSS color value, such as HEX, named colors, or RGB/a values.
fill-opacity	Used to set the opacity of the color specified in fill.
fill-rule	Determines how which side of a path is in a shape, and how the fill property paints that shape.
stroke	Defines the outline color of an element – accepted values can be none (default), or <paint>, context-fill, or context-stroke.
stroke-width	Controls the width of a border on SVG shapes.
stroke-linecap	Sets the starting and ending points of a border on SVG shapes – can take butt, square, or round as values.
stroke-linejoin	Controls how the joint between two segments is drawn – can accept the values miter, round, or bevel.
stroke-miterlimit	If two segments with miter joints meet at a sharp angle, this setting imposes a ratio of the miter length to the stroke-width. Exceeding this limit will change a miter joint to a bevel.
stroke-dasharray + stroke-dashoffset	Determines when and where to draw a dash array (a series of dashes instead of a continuous line).
stroke-opacity	Determines the opacity level of the outside border.

Some settings can be set using plain CSS, and not SVG-specific commands – it's best to test each in turn to find out what you can use.

These are just some of the options open to us when painting SVG elements – there is no secret recipe to creating a really stunning piece; that old adage of "practice makes perfect" comes into its own in this respect. The best way to learn is to choose an SVG and then open it up in a text editor and just change the values.

Granted we can learn what each does, but sometimes there really is no better way than to just go for it! And that just happens to be a perfect lead-in for our next exercise – let's put this into practice by adjusting colors in both radial and linear patterns.

Creating Gradients and Patterns

Up until this point, we've talked about painting (or filling) SVG elements with a chosen shade of color – there is one thing though: it doesn't matter what color we choose, it will always be just one color for that part of our design.

After a while this is likely to become a little dull – it might work if most of your projects focused solely on using single, bold colors, but this clearly won't suit everyone! What if we could include a *graduated* color into our designs though…?

Well, we can – in the same way as we might using standard CSS, we can apply gradient effects to SVG elements. Gradient effects come in two different types – linear (centered along one line), or radial (radiates out from a central point). A gradient is best explained with an example, so without further ado, let's crack on with our next exercise.

Constructing Gradients

When creating gradients, we can really have some fun and apply all manner of different effects – sometimes though just keeping it to a select few can create more of an impact! However many colors we decide to use, the fun is in trying out different combinations, and that taking a work-in-progress approach to this may pay dividends in the longer term (what you find now may be more useful later, and so on…).

For our next exercise, we're going to run with this work-in-progress approach and use it as a basis for starting to add gradients to an SVG image. I would absolutely encourage you to try different colors when creating gradients – the next exercise is all about illustrating the process of adding color gradients, rather than the final selected colors! We'll make use of an SVG image from the freesvgimages.com website; this is a good site to bookmark as a useful source of images for your projects.

CREATING A GRADIENT

Let's make a start:

1. We'll begin as always with a new document – go ahead and add the following code, saving it as `gradients.html` in our project area:

```
<!DOCTYPE html>
<html>
<head>
  <meta charset="utf-8">
  <title>Beginning SVG: Creating a simple example</title>
  <link rel="stylesheet" href="css/gradients.css">
</head>
<body>
  <h2>Beginning SVG: Adding linear gradients to SVG images</h2>
</body>
</html>
```

2. We are going to add a little extra styling for the title on our page – for this, extract a copy of `gradients.css` and drop it into the `css` subfolder of our project area. It will make use of the `fonts` folder we already have from previous exercises, and which should already be in this folder.

3. Next, go ahead and open up a copy of the `wip.svg` file from the code download that accompanies this book – copy the entire contents (yes, all 248 lines of it) and paste immediately before the closing `</body>` tag in our code.

4. We are now at the point where we need to add our gradient effect – for this, go ahead and insert a couple of blank lines after the `opening <svg>` tag, then add the following code as highlighted:

```
<svg id="message" x="0px" y="0px" width="612px" height="792px"
viewBox="100 150 612 792" enable-background="new 0 0 1212 1392">

  <defs>
    <linearGradient id="wip-gradient" x1="0%" y1="0%" x2="100%" y2="0%">
    <stop offset="0%" style="stop-color:#FF9133;" />
    <stop offset="100%" style="stop-color:#FF0015;" />
    </linearGradient>
  </defs>
```

5.   We have our gradient definition now in place, but for it to be applied, we need to make one final change to our SVG element. For this, look for this code, on or around line 19:

```
<path fill-rule="evenodd"...
```

Go ahead and insert this attribute after the opening `<path` element, as highlighted:

```
<path fill="url(#wip-gradient)" fill-rule="evenodd"...
```

6.   Save the file, then preview the results in a browser – if all is well, we should see something akin to the screenshot shown in Figure 2-9, which I hope might make you smile at the irony of it:

Beginning SVG: Adding linear gradients to SVG images

Figure 2-9. *A radial gradient applied to our SVG*

Hopefully you had a little chuckle at the irony of the image – you can see the original on the freesvgimages.com site at `https://www.freesvgimages.com/im-a-work-in-progress/`. Ultimately though the point being that as in life, nothing is ever finished; we should always consider things as merely evolving, so that we can strive to improve both ourselves and the projects we work on.

Using Radial Gradients

Our demo applied a linear gradient to the SVG image – it's a perfectly valid option and works just as well. Trouble is, there may be occasions where this might not work so well; the base image may suit a gradient that radiates from a central point in the artwork.

To understand what we mean by this, take a look at the source image used earlier in "Creating Unusual Shapes with Clip-Paths" – in a sense, I think the design would work better with a radial gradient than a linear one. In contrast, the image used in the previous demo has text that runs from left to right, so I suspect a radial one wouldn't work so well (Figure 2-10), and that a linear one would be more suitable:

Figure 2-10. *Using a radial gradient instead...*

Ultimately it is up to us to decide which fits our needs best – there is no hard-and-fast rule that determines which gradient should be used and when, so with that in mind, let's test that assumption:

Change the `<linearGradient` tag to `<radialGradient` and save the change – the code should look like this:

```
<defs>
  <radialGradient id="wip-gradient" x1="0%" y1="0%" x2="100%" y2="0%">
  <stop offset="0%" style="stop-color:#FF9133;" />
  <stop offset="100%" style="stop-color:#FF0015;" />
  </radialGradient>
</defs>
```

Save the change – if we refresh the demo, it shows a change, as indicated in Figure 2-10 on the previous page. Something in me says this doesn't look so good – it works, but the impact just isn't quite there! Leaving this aside, our code uses a number of new keywords, so let's take a moment to explore these in more detail.

Exploring How Our Code Works

Let's revisit the core part of our code, from the first part of the gradient demo:

```
<defs>
  <linearGradient id="wip-gradient" x1="0%" y1="0%" x2="100%" y2="0%">
    <stop offset="0%" style="stop-color:#FF9133;" />
    <stop offset="100%" style="stop-color:#FF0015;" />
  </linearGradient>
</defs>
```

Our code was set up in a `<defs>` block – this allows it to be reusable throughout the SVG image. A closer look at the content of the code for the image shows multiple paths in use – we've already applied our gradient(s) to one of them, so they can be applied to the remaining paths in the same manner.

Within our definition, we have our `<linearGradient>` tags – alongside the standard ID, we have our coordinates (`x1, y1` and `x2, y2`) and the `<stop>` attributes. The latter control the ramp of colors to use over the shape – in our case, we've specified 0% and 100%, so the gradient will run over the entire shape. If we had set something akin to 10% and 50% (for example), then the gradient will start from 10% in, and finish at 50% of the range.

I'd recommend changing the values as a test – this is the best way to experience the impact of changing the stop values on our design.

Taking It Further

It's at this point I would normally suggest taking things up a notch, and taking a look at more advanced examples, such as that of the flame animation created by Sarah Drasner, at `https://codepen.io/sdras/pen/gaxGBB`.

However, I have a confession to make – and with good reason: Remember how I suggested trying to change the `<linearGradient>` tag to `<radialGradient>`, but not change any other value? Well, this has worked, but I'm not convinced it's produced the best design – and not just because of the choice of colors!

The real reason is because of the coordinates we've specified in our shape – these are intended to be for linear gradients, whereas we should really be using `cx, cy,` and `r` to define the center and radius of the element. We should then use `fx` and `fy` values to define the focal point of our gradient – a mix of these values will very likely produce a gradient that has more impact than by simply replacing the tags as originally suggested at the end of the previous exercise.

To help gauge the impact of tweaking settings until you are more familiar with how they work, you may like to use an online gradient generator to help – there are several available online, such as the one available at the AngryTools.com website: `http://angrytools.com/gradient/`.

Enough of the confession – let's move on! We're not limited to simply creating SVG shapes to sit on a page; we can insert these into our page background as well. A good use case for this would be to create a company logo as an SVG image, then set the opacity to around 50%, and apply this as a fixed background image on our page. This is a really easy technique to get our heads around, so let's dive in and explore this in more detail.

Applying Pattern Effects to CSS Backgrounds

Throughout the course of this chapter we've created a variety of shapes which can easily be added as images to a page – this works very well, but what if we needed to create a *background* effect? Is this possible with SVG, you might ask....

Thankfully it is – Figure 2-11 shows that support for this feature in recent desktop browsers (last couple of years) is currently excellent:

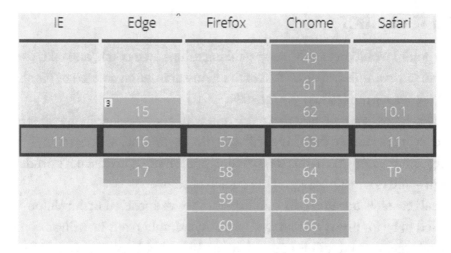

IE	Edge	Firefox	Chrome	Safari
			49	
			61	
	3 15		62	10.1
11	16	57	63	11
	17	58	64	TP
		59	65	
		60	66	

Figure 2-11. *Support for SVGs in CSS backgrounds – Source: caniuse.com*

If we were to check the CanIUse.com site, we will find that support among mobile devices is equally good, with only Opera Mini showing partial support in recent browsers. There is one question I do hear you ask though – why would we use a data-uri value to display our SVGs? There are several benefits for using data-uris, when working with SVGs:

- Data-uris can be stored within CSS files; this helps to reduce the number of calls to external resources, although this must be balanced against the size of our style sheet!

- We can perform micro-optimization on data-uris, to a greater degree than we might on a standard SVG; this is a more advanced topic that we will cover in Chapter 7, "Optimizing SVGs";

- SVGs stored as data-uris can be manipulated internally, unlike external images (more anon).

Leaving aside the reasons for using data-uris for the moment, how does the process work? We can implement an SVG as a background image directly, but it makes it harder to change the fill color easily. In many cases, this won't be an issue (or at least something we can live with), but there may be instances where we need to edit the color.

Fortunately, there are several ways to get around this: one such method is to use data-uris. Put simply, we convert our SVG image into a base-64 encoded string of characters, before adding it as a link within our style sheet.

Thankfully we don't have to manually convert our image – after all, the conversions involved would be horrendous! We can instead make use of a convertor such as the example at `https://codepen.io/elliz/pen/ygvgay`, to facilitate this process for us. We'll put this process to the test as part of our next exercise – this will make use of a pre-built SVG pattern, available from the Hero Patterns site, at `http://www.heropatterns.com`. Let's dive in to see what is required in action.

ADDING A PATTERN

1. We'll start by taking a copy of the `gradients.html` file from the previous exercise, then removing all of the code between the `<body>` tags – save this in our project folder as `background.html`.

2. Go ahead and add the following code in between the `<body>` tags of the file we've just created – don't forget to save it:

```
<div id="content">
    <h2>Beginning SVG: Applying SVGs to CSS Backgrounds</h2>
    <p>Lorem ipsum dolor sit amet, consectetur adipiscing elit. Vivamus
    consequat mattis risus. Ut magna quam, consectetur a consectetur in,
    rhoncus ut diam. Curabitur mauris lectus, malesuada quis viverra in,
    tristique at est.</p>

    <p>Vestibulum in felis vitae eros aliquam ornare. Nunc elementum
    risus non neque rhoncus malesuada. Curabitur ultricies tellus eu sem
    sollicitudin, vel bibendum sapien sagittis. Duis scelerisque urna
    nulla, vel accumsan massa gravida commodo.</p>
</div>
```

3. In a new file, add the following style code – this will format the text onscreen and provide a little styling for the panel containing the text. Save it as `background.css`, within the `css` subfolder of our project area:

```
@font-face { font-family: 'pt_sansregular'; src: url('../font/pt_
sansregular.woff') format('woff'); font-weight: normal; font-style:
normal; }
body { font-family: 'pt_sansregular', sans-serif; }
#content { border: 0.0625rem solid #000; border-radius: 0.3125rem;
width: 21.875rem; margin-left: auto; margin-right: auto; padding:
0.9375rem; background-color: rgba(255, 255, 255, .7); padding: 2rem; }
```

Don't forget to update the link to the CSS file in background.html!

53

Note the fonts folder should already be present in our project area from previous exercises.

4. Up next comes the real magic – we're going to incorporate an SVG image into our background. For this, browse to `http://www.heropatterns.com`, then click on the Jupiter pattern.

5. Copy the contents of the Generated CSS Code box, then paste it immediately after the `font-family:...` line within the body style rule in our demo style sheet.

6. Save the style sheet – we can now preview the results! If all is well, we should see something akin to the screenshot shown in Figure 2-12.

Figure 2-12. *Applying SVG effects to CSS backgrounds*

This little demo is meant to be very simple, but its simplicity belies the power of what we can achieve – the key lies in how we use a data-uri to display the image. Let's take a moment to explore how our demo works in more detail, and see how we can adapt it for our own use.

Exploring the Code in Detail

Remember how we talked about the different ways of implementing SVG images, back in Chapter 1? Well, for many occasions, we would simply use `<img>` tags, treating our SVG image as if were a standard PNG or JPEG image, for example. However, we can also use background images, although the trade-off is that we lose the ability to style individual elements with the SVG image.

Our code doesn't contain anything out of the ordinary, save for just one line – line 11. This is a call to background image: we treat our target image as if we are referencing one on available at a URL. However, instead of a URL, we have the code of our SVG as a string of characters; the code for this was provided by the Hero Patterns website, but it could equally have come from a convertor, such as the one available at `https://codepen.io/elliz/pen/ygvgay`. Once the code has been added to our style sheet, the results will be displayed when previewed within our browser.

Creating an Alternative Pattern

At this point, we've completed our demo – it looks great (at least for what it is) and works very well. This however is only part of the story: What about using some of the shapes we created right back at the start of this chapter?

Absolutely we can – the beauty of this is that we've already covered most of what we need to use to create it, save for one tag, the `<pattern>` tag:

```
<svg width=125 height=120>
  <defs>
    <pattern id="illustration" x="10" y="10" width="20" height="20"
     patternUnits="userSpaceOnUse" >
      <circle cx="15" cy="15" r="15" style="stroke: none; fill: dimgray" />
    </pattern>
  </defs>
  <rect x="10" y="10" width="100" height="100" style="stroke: #000000;
   fill: url(#illustration);" />
</svg>
```

To see how this works, go ahead and add this code to the background demo we've just created – it needs to go in immediately after the `<h2>`, on or around what will be line 12. We will also need to add in an `svg { float: left; }` to our style sheet, to allow text to flow around the SVG.

If we refresh the browser, we should see the updated version, as shown in Figure 2-13.

Figure 2-13. *Our updated SVG as a background image*

Notice the difference – this gives us the ability to add in SVGs as patterns to a page; if we wanted to, we can simply extract the contents of the SVG into a string and replace the existing background URL with this new code. Suffice to say that this gives us plenty of options when creating our projects!

It's time to change tack – we've almost come to the end of this chapter, but before we move onto exploring images and text, there is one more topic we need to cover. We've touched on a variety of different techniques for creating shapes; unfortunately, there is not enough space in this book to print all of the available configuration options we can use to manipulate these shapes. There are, however, plenty of good resources available, so let's take a moment to cover off some of the more useful ones as a starting point for developing your skills with SVG.

Setting Advanced Configuration Options

Over the course of this chapter, we've encountered a host of different attributes for manipulating different elements – such as the x1,y1 coordinates, or stroke-width for setting the width of the border on an SVG. Trouble is, we've only scratched the surface: detailing all of the possible options would easily fill a book by itself!

With this in mind, I would definitely encourage you to make use of available online resources that detail these and more advanced configuration options; some of them are listed below, to help get you started:

- https://developer.mozilla.org/en-US/docs/Web/SVG/Attribute

- https://developer.mozilla.org/en-US/docs/Web/API/Document_ Object_Model#SVG_interfaces

- http://devdocs.io/svg/attribute

- https://www.w3.org/TR/SVG11/

- The SVG color chart hosted at http://www.december.com/html/ spec/colorsvg.html – I've created a version of this chart as a PDF – you can view this from the code download that accompanies this book.

There are plenty more articles available online – note though that some are a few years old, so if in doubt, I would recommend checking the commands used against the MDN articles listed above, which are regularly updated and present a useful source of the attributes available when working with SVG elements.

Summary

Creating an SVG design consists of using a mix of different shapes – this might range from the humble square through to something that can perhaps only be described as being abstract. Clearly choosing the right mix of shapes to use will determine how easy or complex our final design is to create – we've covered a number of options throughout the course of this chapter, so let's take a moment to review what we've learned.

We kicked off this chapter with a review of the different types of shapes available, which included squares, circles, and lines; in each instance we created a simple example, before working through the different attributes that made up the code.

Next up came a look at creating more advanced or unusual shapes – we saw how paths can play a key part in rendering what is effectively a series of connected points in our design. We also took a look at how we might paint our designs: we covered how this has already been done in the examples thus far but also explored some of the other options available to us.

We then rounded out this chapter with a dive into exploring how SVG can be used to create patterns and gradients – this might be repeating a simple shape, through to something more complex such as a linear or radial gradients.

Phew – what a monster chapter! We're only just getting started though on our journey through the world of SVG: We've created shapes, but what about images and text? We can create some great effects using SVG in this respect, so stay tuned to see how in the next chapter...

PART II

In More Detail

CHAPTER 3

Working with Images and Text

One of the key benefits of working with SVG is the ability to resize an image with no loss of quality – to achieve this, we can use any one of several different core shapes (such as squares or circles), or even go freehand with paths, to create our design.

This is ideal for those instances where we can draw a relatively straightforward image – what if we needed to work with something more complex? This does not mean to say that SVG is limited to simple designs at all: other designers have produced some really complex SVG work, which includes animation, filters, transitions, and the like!

It does raise the question though as to what we can (or should) do if we need to work with standard images (i.e., not SVG). Can we include them in an SVG...? Would that even work...? Well, you can – let's dive in and take a look in more detail, starting with a recap on inserting images.

Inserting Images

Images – a vital part of any site; it goes without saying that a website without some form of visual content will clearly suffer. For example – images of products in an online store: customers will vote with their feet if they are anything less than perfect!

It goes without saying that we would use tried and tested code such as `<img src="....">` to add the image to a page; if we enter the world of SVG, this opens up some extra possibilities. Take for example this image of a close-up of one of my favorite plants, a moth orchid, as shown in Figure 3-1.

© Alex Libby 2018
A. Libby, *Beginning SVG*, https://doi.org/10.1007/978-1-4842-3760-1_3

Figure 3-1. *A Phaelenopsis orchid – Source: Flickr/pagonzales*

At first glance, it looks a perfectly ordinary image, right? It's a great shot of an orchid, close up; it has a title that's been added to confirm what type of orchid is in the image. What if I said this was a screenshot of an SVG element...*and not a standard PNG or JPEG image?*

No – I've not lost my marbles: Figure 3-1 is indeed an SVG image; to see it in action, try previewing the embedimage.html file in a browser from the code download that accompanies this book. How did we achieve this? Let's take a look at the code:

```
<svg viewbox="0 0 500 500">
    <rect x="10" y="10" height="500" width="500" style="fill: #000000"/>
    <image x="20" y="20" width="94%" height="94%" href="img/orchid.jpg" />
    <text x="23" y="75" font-family="Verdana" font-size="35"
      stroke="#ffffff" fill="#CC46BF">Phaelenopsis orchid</text>
    <line x1="20" y1="80" x2="440" y2="80" style="stroke: #ffffff; stroke-
      width: 3;"/>
  </svg>
```

We have a standard SVG element, set with a 500px square viewbox area – inside this we fill it with a black rectangle. The core of the code lies in the <image> element – this is set to start 20px in and to the right of point zero, and covers 94% of the rectangle (to provide the border effect). We then add a <text> element, which includes the name of the orchid; this is underlined by use of a <line> element that stretches across most of the image.

Understanding the Benefits

At this point I'm sure you will be asking one particular question – how would this work better than a simple PNG or JPEG (or even WebP) format image? Well, there are several benefits from using this approach:

- The SVG image can be made scalable without loss of quality – the downside is that our embedded image must be made large enough to suit the environment, so care needs to be taken over resource usage;

- We can add in text, which can be crawled for SEO purposes;

- If the SVG element is inline, then we can manipulate its contents using standard CSS and jQuery;

- If needed, we can export a fallback image automatically, for those browsers that don't support SVG – it has to be said though that they should have been put out to pasture a long time ago (yes, I'm looking at you, IE!).

Now – inserting images into SVG elements is just part of what we can achieve; there is a host of other tricks we can use, including embedding objects such as video! This opens up some interesting possibilities, but before we explore them, there is one topic we should cover: image fallback. Most modern browsers support SVG by default, but as in life, there always has to be the odd one out that people are still using...

Exporting Images

At this point, we've created some SVG images using the shapes we covered back in Chapter 2 – our design looks great, and can now be added to our page. Surely that's the next step...right?

Well, in some cases the answer may be no – there is one more step we should explore first: *Do we need to support older browsers, such as IE8...?* It's at this point we need to make that decision – according to the W3Counter website (`https://www.w3counter.com/trends`), there is a minority of users who are still using this browser. Irrespective of the reasons for not wanting or being able to update, it is nevertheless a group of users who we may need to cater for!

Leaving aside the reasons, let's assume for whatever reason that we need to provide this support. To take out some of the pain of providing this support manually (which doesn't add any value to the process), we can consider automating it; this is something that can be left to run in the background, allowing us to concentrate on more important tasks. It's an easy process to set up, but will come in two parts – let's dive in and take a look.

AUTOMATING EXPORT OF SVG IMAGES

This next exercise requires the use of Node.js and the svg2png NPM package (available from `https://www.npmjs.com/package/svg2png`). For now, we will use it in a basic capacity, but it does raise some interesting questions that may determine how you provide support. Let's take a look first at the technical steps:

Please note – the instructions will be for Windows (as this is the author's normal development platform). If you are a Mac or Linux user, there are plenty of articles online that will take you through the installation process, such as the one at `https://openclassrooms.com/courses/ultra-fast-applications-using-node-js/installing-node-js`.

1. First, we need some SVG images to work on – go ahead and extract a copy of the `img` folder from the export folder in the code download that accompanies this book. Inside this folder are some simple SVG images of credit card / payment methods.

2. We need to download and install Node.js, which is available from `https://nodejs.org` – for the purposes of this exercise, accept all defaults. Fire up Node.js command prompt as administrator.

3. In the Node.js command prompt window, change the working directory to our project folder, by entering `cd \svgbook` and pressing Enter. (If your project directory uses a different name, then please adjust to suit.)

4. At the prompt, enter this command then press Enter: `svg2png img/visa.svg -h=681 -w=974`

5. Verify that the image has been created (Figure 3-2) and can be opened using image viewer or in browser (it will appear at the root of our project folder).

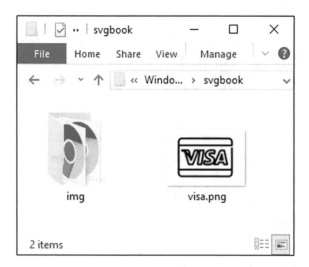

Figure 3-2. *SVG image exported in PNG format*

Exporting Images – an Epilogue

Perfect – we have a process in place to create our PNG fallback images: we can move onto more important tasks....

Not so fast my dear reader – can you spot a major flaw in our design? It's a deliberate gap – our process can only handle one image at a time, when run using the command line. This is fine if we're working on one image, but we may have hundreds – clearly this isn't something sustainable!

Thankfully the svg2png package can be used within a task runner such as Grunt (`http://gruntjs.com`), or Gulp (`https://gulpjs.org/`), to help automate the process if desired – I've focused more on the principles of conversion for this exercise, but if you browse to the NPM site, you will find details of how to implement the code required to fully automate conversion of images.

It should be said though that providing a fallback must be a considered decision: Is it worth spending time implementing this process if our target market only includes a tiny proportion of browsers that don't support SVG? If we don't provide PNG images, then what are the alternatives? It might be that we create a font that stores SVG icons for example (more anon), or that we convert images to data-URIs and store these in our style sheets. I would strongly recommend spending some time researching the options on the NPM package directory at `https://www.npmjs.com` – it's possible that you might find a package that provides a solution that better fits your needs!

For example, have a look at `https://www.npmjs.com/package/svg-to-png` – it's an older package that hasn't been updated for a while and doesn't provide command-line support; this may work just as well as svg2png.

One option we can explore though as part of exporting is to use data-URIs – these convert any images (including SVG) to long strings of random characters that can be inserted into our style sheet, as a replacement for calling a separate image. There are some benefits to using this process, so without further ado, let's dive in and take a look at the process in more detail.

Using SVGs as Data URIs

Do you remember the "Adding a Pattern" demo we created back in Chapter 2? We touched on the use of data-URIs, where we can convert images to seemingly random strings of characters, which can be set against a background-image property within our style sheet.

Well, it's worth revisiting this subject – if you take a close look at the code, you will see this within the body style rule:

```
background-image: url("data:image/svg+xml,%3Csvg xmlns='http...
```

This is the start of a data URI – or, to be more accurate, one of four different ways of writing such a data URI when working with SVG elements. Any one of these would replace the standard format when using background-image in a style sheet; the options available are:

```
<!-- base64 -->
background: url("data:image/svg+xml;base64,PHN2ZyB4bWxucz0iaHR0cDovL...

<!-- UTF-8, not encoded -->
Background-url("data:image/svg+xml;charset=UTF-8,<svg ...> ... </svg>

<!-- UTF-8, optimized encoding for compatibility -->
Background-url("data:image/svg+xml;charset=UTF-8,%3Csvg xmlns='http://...'

<!-- Fully URL encoded ASCII -->
Background-url("data:image/svg+xml;charset=US-ASCII ,%3Csvg%20...
```

The question is, which should we use? In short, the answer is the third one from the top; the reasons for this are a little complex (and involve getting into the depths of using gzip), but suffice to say that it provides the shortest string when converted into UTF-8 format. It is worth testing how many characters are required to create the data-URI strings in the remaining three options – data-URIs are known for producing lengthy strings, so we can choose which option gives us the shortest string, and therefore helps to keep code bloat to a minimum.

The developer Taylor Hunt has posted a useful article on Codepen, about optimizing SVGs in more detail – the article is available at `https://codepen.io/tigt/post/optimizing-svgs-in-data-uris`.

Leaving aside the choice of data-URI format to use, we should always work with optimized images where practical. Before we get stuck into our next exercise, let's quickly cover off a nice easy way to perform that task, with the minimum of fuss.

Optimizing Our Image

Our next exercise relies on using an optimized image to make it as efficient as possible and not clutter up our style sheet with irrelevant code.

This is a subject we'll cover in more detail, later in the book; for now, we'll work on the basics, using an online service.

To optimize our image, go ahead and follow these steps:

OPTIMIZING THE SOURCE IMAGE

1. We'll start by downloading the cart image – for this exercise, I've used the one available from linearicon.com, at `https://linearicons.com/free/icon/cart`; go ahead and click on Download SVG, then save the image to the `img` folder in our project area.

2. By default, the image will not be optimized, so it will contain extra XML code that should be removed before we convert it for use in our demo. For this, browse to `https://jakearchibald.github.io/svgomg/`, then click on Open SVG from the hamburger menu.

3. Find the `lnr-cart.svg` icon from within our project area then click on Open to load the SVG.

4. At the bottom of the window, look for a blue circular button, which has an arrow pointing downward – click on this to download an optimized version of our image. Save this as `cart.svg` into the `img` folder of our project area. You can now close the browser window.

Now that we have an optimized image, let's crack on with the main part of the demo:

CONVERTING SVG IMAGES TO DATA URIS

1. We'll start with opening a new document and then adding the following code – save this as `datauri.css` in the `css` subfolder of our project area:

```
@font-face { font-family: 'pt_sansregular'; src: url('../font/pt_
sansregular.woff') format('woff'); font-weight: normal; font-style:
normal;}

body { font-family: 'pt_sansregular', sans-serif; padding: 2rem;
  font-size: 18px; }

section > div { background-repeat: no-repeat; width: 20px; height: 20px; }
```

2. From the daturi folder that is in the code download that accompanies this book, go ahead and extract a copy of datauri.html – save this to the root of our project area.

3. We now need to prepare the URLs for each of our background images – we'll begin with the standard base-64 version. Browse to `http://b64.io/`, then drag and drop the `cart.svg` file into the green drop area – it will automatically display the base-64 encoded code in the window below.

4. Revert back to `datauri.css`, then leave a blank line. Take a copy of the code produced from step 2 and paste it into `datauri.css` – change the `.cart` class to `section > div.base64` and save the file.

5. Next up comes the UTF-8 version – for this, go ahead and leave a line in our CSS file, then add this code:

```
section > div.utf8 {
  background-image: url('data:image/svg+xml;charset=UTF-8,');
}
```

6. Open a copy of `cart.svg` in a text editor, and take a copy of the code – paste it immediately before the closing single quote mark shown in the previous step.

7. We can optimize this a step further – leave a blank line in the CSS file, then copy and paste the previous `section > div.utf8` style rule.

8. Rename this rule to `section > div.utf8opt`.

9. In the background-image attribute, look for these extracts of code:

```
charset=UTF-8,%3Csvg xmlns and 291z"/%3E%3C/svg%3E');
```

Go ahead and update as highlighted.

10. We have one more version left – that is to fully encode our SVG string, using a decoder such as the one by Eric Meyer at `https://meyerweb.com/eric/tools/dencoder/`. For this, copy the code from `charset=UTF-8`, to (and including) the last character before the closing quote, from the div.utf-8 rule created in step 5.

11. Paste this into the encoder window in the above URL, then hit Encode.

12. In the `background-image` attribute, look for the `charset=UTF-8`, then delete everything upto (but not including) the closing single quote. Replace it with a copy of the code created in step 11.

13. Save the file – if all is well, we should see four instances of our cart, as displayed in Figure 3-3.

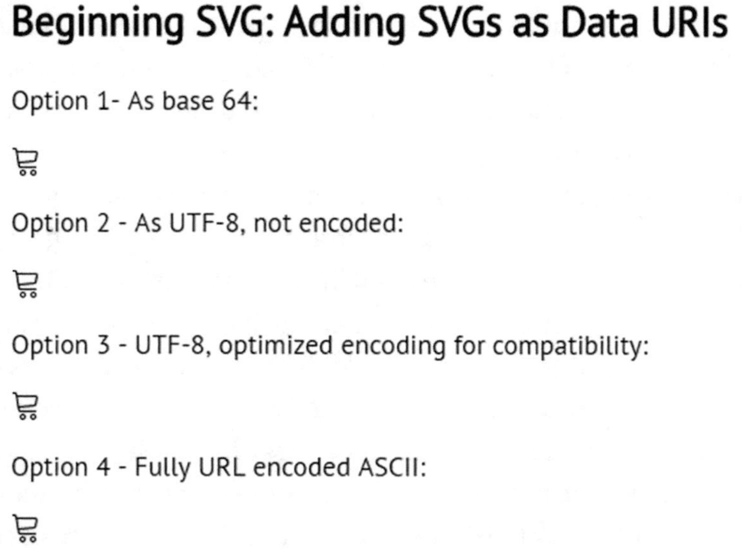

Beginning SVG: Adding SVGs as Data URIs

Option 1- As base 64:

🛒

Option 2 - As UTF-8, not encoded:

🛒

Option 3 - UTF-8, optimized encoding for compatibility:

🛒

Option 4 - Fully URL encoded ASCII:

🛒

Figure 3-3. *The different Data-URL options available*

Phew – that was a monster exercise! Some of you might ask how we can benefit from using this method: it is indeed a valid question! There are some benefits though to using this method (and some drawbacks too) – let's pause for a moment to consider them in more detail.

Understanding How Our Code Works

The basic principle of using a data URI has been around since 1998, when it was first defined in RFC2397, in August of that year. Put simply, we convert an image (of some description) into a string of characters, which can be inserted into a background-image property within a style sheet rule.

Sounds simple enough, right? Well, there are some pitfalls we should consider: The more complex the image, the longer the string of characters – this might make our style sheet page simply too large and cumbersome to navigate.

- Although we have four ways of creating data URIs, at least one of them isn't recommended (base-64). The other three will produce differing results, so we need to choose the right method carefully.

- We can't make changes to the styling of a SVG image that has been inserted as a background image; we can only do this if we put our code inline.

Leaving these aside for the moment, let's take a look at the code we created in more detail – we added in four different types of data URI as background images, which start with a `data:image/svg+xml;base64` tag, for base-64 images, or this tag for native SVG images: `data:image/svg+xml;charset=UTF-8`.

Within each data URI tag is our string of characters – this will either be a base-64 encoded text (option 1), or the optimized XML from within our SVG image (options 2 to 4). The last three examples all use the same basic XML from within our SVG, but the data URI has been progressively encoded to ensure compatibility with web browsers.

Okay – let's change tack: so far, our examples have focused on the basics of getting our image onto a page. In many cases, this will suffice, but what if we wanted to take it further? Traditionally we might do this using the likes of Photoshop – instead, how about using SVG to apply these effects? This opens up some real possibilities, such as using images to provide a color mask to SVGs – let's dive in and take a look to see what this means in practice.

Applying Image Masks

If someone were to mention the words "mask" and "image," then they could be forgiven for thinking that we're trying to hide a problematic part of that image – that is absolutely not the case!

Granted, that was a terrible attempt at humor, but using masks opens up a whole host of possibilities. Our next exercise just scratches the surface of what is possible; how about using a mask with a SVG filter over an image, to really give it curve appeal? Or perhaps have a background image to which we apply a filter (turning it a shade of blue, for example), and then animate on various elements, to provide a welcoming effect on an agency home page?

These are two example of what is possible – we're really only limited by the extent of our imagination. To get us started, and for our next exercise, we're going to use a landscape image, over which we will apply an overlay effect – it's a great effect if we want to provide some color to a background on a page, while still imparting relevant information to our visitor.

This demo is based on a Codepen example by Marco Barría with some slight tweaks – you can see the original at `https://codepen.io/fixcl/pen/CHgrn`

```
APPLYING MASKS
```

Let's dive in and take a look at the steps involved:

1. We'll start by extracting copies of the `css` and `img` folders from the masks folder in the code download that accompanies this book – save them to our project area.

2. Next, go ahead and take a copy of the datauri.html markup file, then delete the markup between the `<head>`...`</head>` tags, and the same within the `<body>` tags.

3. Add the following code between the `<head>` tags:

```
<meta charset="utf-8">
<title>Beginning SVG: Applying Masks to SVG</title>
<link rel="stylesheet" href="css/masks.css">
```

4. Go ahead and add the following in between the <body> tags:

```
<div class="overlay">
  <svg>
    <defs>
      <mask id="mask" x="0" y="0" width="100%" height="100%">
        <rect id="background" x="0" y="0" width="100%" height="100%"></
         rect>
        <text id="title" x="50%" y="100" dy="1.58rem">SVG Masks</text>
        <text id="subtitle" x="50%" y="0" dy="9.8rem">A quick demo</text>
      </mask>
    </defs>
    <rect id="base" x="0" y="0" width="100%" height="100%"/>
  </svg>
</div>
<section class="intro"></section>
```

5. Save the file as masks.html at the root of our project area – if we preview the
    results in a browser, we should see a landscape image, overlaid with a banner,
    as indicated in Figure 3-4.

Figure 3-4. *Applying an SVG mask to image*

Interesting effect, huh? It's a really simple one, but when used well it can make a page stand out. Most of the code within this demo focuses on styling the text and the background banner color; there is little in there that is unusual, with the exception of one rule. Let's take a moment to explore how this demo works in more detail, and why one rule brings everything together.

Exploring How the Code Works

Our demo has only touched the surface of what is possible when applying masks – a really great effect that I've seen in use is to blur a strip of text across a background image (such as in a carousel), and to then add suitably sized text over the top. I could go on, but suffice to say it's worth spending time on Google! But I digress...

Although we've used a fair number of rules in our style sheet, there are really only two parts that make the magic happen in our demo – the first is to apply a mask over our #base element:

```
svg #base { fill: black; -webkit-mask: url(#mask); mask: url(#mask); }
```

This particular property still hasn't been fully ratified for use, hence the use of the –webkit vendor prefix; hopefully this will disappear over the course of time. We can't have a mask without providing the content for that mask – this is taken care of within the <defs> block in our HTML markup:

```
<svg>
  <defs>
    <mask id="mask" x="0" y="0" width="100%" height="100%" >
      <rect id="background" .../>
      <text id="title" ...">SVG Masks</text>
      <text id="subtitle" ...">A quick demo</text>
    </mask>
  </defs>
  <rect id="base" x="0" y="0" width="100%" height="100%"/>
</svg>
```

So – what does a mask do? Put simply, it hides or "masks" an area specified using coordinates or an SVG shape; it has the effect of merging background and foreground images into one.

In this instance, the `#mask` reference in our CSS ties back to the mask defined in the `<defs>` block – we set a height of 100% square, starting at point zero. This contains a background element that we style with #666 (a very dark gray color); on top of this we add a main title and subtitle using `<text>` elements. Our mask is then applied to the `<rect>` element at the end of our SVG graphic, using the mask attribute provided in our style sheet.

Let's move on – we've covered the use of images, and explored how we can create shapes...what's missing? Ah yes: icons. There will be occasions where we might want to display some form of icon – credit card images, SSL security logos, and the like. We can of course display them individually – this will work, but as any good designer will say, it's not ideal. To get around this, we can use that age old principle of creating sprites; what works for standard images will also work for SVG graphics, so let's dive in and take a look.

Working with Icons

Icons have been around for decades – we use them to represent links to applications, buttons to click on, determine the state of a feature (aligning text, for example); the list is endless. They can be created in almost any format, although the universally accepted standard is the well-known .ICO format.

Irrespective of the format we use, there is a downside to using icons – the format does not lend itself to scaling well (if at all). The beauty of using SVG as a format though means this issue no longer exists - any icon we create in this format will scale perfectly, in the same way as their larger cousins.

There are dozens of different libraries available online that contain useful icons – two that come to mind are FlatIcon, available at `https://www.flaticon.com/`; and Simple Icons, from `https://simpleicons.org/`. These make a perfect base for creating icon sprites; we can create these using the image route, or by creating a custom font. We'll cover the latter method a little later in this chapter, but for now, let's explore the image route in more detail.

Creating Image Sprites with Icons

Creating sprites is nothing new – we can do this using most common image formats, although for convenience it's likely that most people will choose PNG or JPEG as their destination format. The same principles can be applied to SVG, although we have an extra route – for small projects, we can either manually create sprites by hand, or we can automate them using a technology such as Node.js. Let's look at each option in turn.

If we decide to create them manually, then our SVG image will look something akin to this extract of code:

```
<svg style="display:none;">
  <symbol id="visa" viewBox="0 0 62 51">
    <path fill="#000000" d="M38.9872..."></path>
  </symbol>
  <symbol id="amex" viewBox="0 0 60 64">
    <path fill="#000000" d="M15.9264..."></path>
  </symbol>
...
</svg>
```

All we need is a text editor and our images – provided we can open each image and extract the relevant code, we can put together our SVG sprite. The only changes we need to make are to use <symbol> as the element for each sprite image, and that we need to provide both a selector ID and a suitably sized viewbox attribute in our code.

Using the <symbol> Element

We've touched on specifying our viewBox, but what's this <symbol> element I see in our code...? Put simply, it's a way of grouping elements together, *for later reuse.*

This last part is key – when working with SVG graphics, we can group elements together using the <g> element, and perform actions on all elements in a group simultaneously. The <symbol> element takes it further by allowing us to instantiate an instance later (as if it were a graphical template), with a <use> statement. This is perfect if we have a shape that can be displayed in a range of colors; we don't need to implement separate SVG graphics for each, but instead reuse the base image multiple times.

To help with creating symbol elements, head over to `https://svg-to-symbol.` `herokuapp.com/` – this will convert an existing SVG to use <symbol> elements.

Let's move on – assuming our code has been added inline to the markup file, immediately after the opening `<body>` tag, we can then use the code thus, for the image to be displayed on screen:

```
<svg>
  <use href="#visa"></use>
<svg>
```

There are a couple of points we should be aware of though – notice how the SVG element has been styled with `display: none`? This is essential, otherwise we may find our images appear twice – once in the source file, and again as our sprite image. We can't avoid this, so it's something we have to get used to adding to our code!

The second drawback is size – creating a sprite manually really only suits small images, where the XML is manageable; this is really about being able to navigate through our code, than any speed issue! It's for this reason that a more automated approach is beneficial – we can complete the process using an online service such as Iconizr, or take the task runner approach and use Node.js and a runner such as Gulp or Grunt. Let's begin with a look at using an online service first.

CREATING AN SVG IMAGE SPRITE

There are a number of online services that allow us to create sprites, such as IcoMoon, or SpriteCow; my personal favorite is Iconizr, hosted at `https://www.iconizr.com`. Let's work through the steps to create our sprite:

1. We'll start by downloading our source images – browse to `https://www.flaticon.com/packs/credit-cards-4`, then pick five images at random; I'll assume for the purposes of this exercise that you've chosen `banktransfer`, `paypal`, `visa`, `mastercard`, and `amex`. Please adjust to suit if you decide to use different images.

2. Click on each icon in turn, then SVG | Download | Free download, to save the images to the `img` subfolder of project area.

3. We need to run through the optimization process for each – for this we'll use the same optimization service at `https://jakearchibald.github.io/svgomg/`, which we used earlier in this chapter.

4. Save optimized images to a new folder called svgo in our project area.

5. Next up comes the conversion process – for this, browse to iconizr.com, then drag and drop all five into "Drop your SVG icons here" box.

6. Enter css/ into the CSS resource directory input field, then click on Create & download icon kit, to begin the conversion process.

7. It takes a little time for the process to run – when it is completed, click on Download icon kit

8. Extract the css folder within to our project area, then run the iconizr-svg-sprite-preview.html file in a browser to preview the results (Figure 3-5).

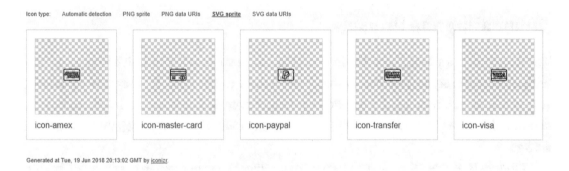

Generated at Tue, 19 Jun 2018 20:13:02 GMT by iconizr.

Figure 3-5. *Manually created SVG sprite*

9. If we check the code markup in the file from the previous step – you will see something akin to the extract shown in Figure 3-6.

```
.icon-amex, .icon-amex\:regular {
    background-image: url(icons/icons.svg)
    background-position: ▶ 0 0;
    background-repeat: ▶ no-repeat;
}
```

Figure 3-6. *Examining the sprite code in detail*

We can confirm that we're using just one image, by checking out the Icons.svg file that will be in the css/icons folder, along with a PNG fallback version.

Tip for a more in-depth look at creating SVG sprites, check out the article by Florens Verschelde at `https://fvsch.com/code/svg-icons/how-to/`. It's a little old but contains some useful tips!

We now have a useable sprite image, which can be referenced in code – this works perfectly well, but it is still something of a manual process that is dependent on demand on the Iconizr site. In this age of speed, we need something that removes this dependency – we can achieve this using Node and a task runner such as Gulp, so let's dive in and take a look.

Automating the Process

The use of sprites should be at the forefront of any developer's mind – it's easy to see that with a little extra styling, we can dramatically reduce the number of images we need to use, which in turn reduces the resources we must from the server. Creating them though can be a thankless task – it's one of those necessary evils, if we are to benefit from using sprites.

Trouble is, we've all got better things to do, right? I say better – in many cases, better is more likely to mean important, rather than interesting! This makes it all the more important for us to invest in automating this process if we can – it's very likely we would use a Node.js-based task runner such as Gulp or Grunt. There are plenty of Grunt or Gulp-based packages that can help; it's worth checking out the NPM Package Manager site at `https://www.npmjs.com` for ones you can try out.

As a start, you can take a look at `https://github.com/jkphl/gulp-svg-sprite` (for Gulp); or a Grunt equivalent, at `http://www.grunticon.com/`.

For our next exercise, we will use Gulp to create our sprite, and the gulp-svg-sprite package – if you prefer to use a different task runner (such as Grunt), then this is fine; the process will be very similar. In any case, we will assume that Node.js has already been installed – if you didn't install it earlier, then go ahead and do it now.

AUTOMATING THE CONVERSION

Assuming Node.js is installed and ready to go, let's work through the steps involved:

1. We'll start by installing Gulp – for this, fire up a Node.js command prompt, then enter this command and press Enter:

   ```
   npm install --global gulp-cli
   ```

2. When this has completed, go ahead and enter npm init at the prompt, then press Enter – this creates a package.json file, which is used by Gulp to store package dependencies. Enter the details as shown in Figure 3-7.

   ```
   See `npm help json` for definitive documentation on these fields
   and exactly what they do.

   Use `npm install <pkg>` afterwards to install a package and
   save it as a dependency in the package.json file.

   Press ^C at any time to quit.
   package name: (svgbook) exportsvg
   version: (1.0.0)
   description: Task to export SVG images to PNG
   entry point: (gulpfile.js)
   test command:
   git repository:
   keywords:
   author: Alex Libby
   license: (ISC)
   About to write to C:\svgbook\package.json:
   ```

Figure 3-7. *Details for the package.json file*

3. Next, we need to install Gulp itself – for this, enter npm install --save-dev gulp@next at the prompt, then press Enter.

4. We can now install the gulp-svg-sprite package – at the prompt, enter npm install gulp-svg-sprite --save, then press Enter.

If you get an issue with phantomjs not installing, then run this command at the prompt, and rerun step 5: npm install phantomjs -g

---

With the gulp-svg-sprite package now installed, we can prepare a quick demo to test that our sprite works:

5.   In the Node.js command prompt window, enter gulp svg at the prompt, then press Enter. The sprite will be created – you will find it in the \output\ symbol\svg\ folder, which is created automatically.

6.   Go ahead and add the following code to a new file, saving it as autosprite. html within the \output\symbol\svg folder:

```
<!DOCTYPE html>
<head>
  <meta charset="utf-8">
  <title>Beginning SVG: Creating SVG Sprites</title>
  <style>svg { background-color: transparent; fill: slategrey;
    width: 140px; height: 140px; }</style>
</head>
</head>
<body>
  <svg style="display:none;"></svg>
  <svg><use href="#american-express"></use></svg>
  <svg><use href="#bank-transfer"></use></svg>
</body>
</html>
```

7.   We need to add in the XML from our SVG file – open sprite.symbol.svg, which is in the same folder, then replace the first <svg> tag with the contents of this file.

8.   We need to make one small tweak to hide the core SVG file (our code will show the relevant sprite image later). For this, look for line 17, then edit it as indicated:

```
<svg style="display:none;" xmlns="http:...
```

9.   Save the file – if all is well, we should see something akin to the screenshot shown in Figure 3-8.

Figure 3-8. *SVG images created from sprite*

See how easy it was to convert to using sprites? Our demo uses just the one image; we instead make use of the <use> tag to insert the selected sprite image into our page. It is worth noting though that in case you're wondering, the pure svg-sprite Node module does not read or write to the filesystem, so extra work is required to configure it; using a package for Grunt or Gulp will take care of this step automatically for us.

Use of Icon Fonts and SVG

At this point, I'm going to just touch on a different subject, but related to SVG icons: there are online services available that allow us to convert icons into a font file, for use in our pages. However, this is not without its issues; it is no longer a recommended practice. If you are interested in knowing more, then please check out the *Working with Icon Fonts and SVG* PDF I've created, and put in the code download that accompanies this book.

Okay – let's move on: we've covered the use of images in SVG in some detail; how about we take a look at using text within an SVG graphic? There are some interesting options available to use, of which we'll cover some of the more interesting ones later in this book. For now though, let's look at the basics of using the <text> element within SVG.

Adding Text with the <text> Element

So far, all of our content has been largely visual – it goes without saying that "a picture paints a thousand words," but there are occasions when we must use text to get across our message. Thankfully it is really easy to add text to an SVG element – take a look at this example:

```
<svg xmlns="http://www.w3.org/2000/svg" width="600" height="160">
  <text x="50" y="100">SVG text styling</text>
</svg>
```

Look familiar? Although we're working with a new element, we've already touched on using it; remember the embedded image of a moth orchid at the start of this chapter? The text displayed was added using such a <text> element.

The great thing about using a <text> element is that we can style it the same way as we would for normal text. Let's put this into practice, and add a little color to the example markup as a new online pen using Codepen.

ADDING COLOR TO SVG TEXT

Let's make a start:

1. Head over to https://www.codepen.io – in the HTML window, copy and paste the markup from the start of this section.

2. Next, go ahead and add the following styles to the CSS window:

```
@import 'https://fonts.googleapis.com/css?family=Oswald:700';
text {  font-family: 'Oswald', sans-serif;  font-size: 72px;
stroke: rgb(117, 109, 106);
   stroke-width: 3px;  fill: rgb(240,213,184); }
```

3. Click on the Save button – if all is well, Codepen will automatically update, to display the text shown in Figure 3-9.

Figure 3-9. Styling SVG text

Go ahead and try changing the colors or stroke-width – any changes you make will be automatically reflected in the pen.

I've created a version of this demo, which you can see at https://codepen.io/
alexlibby/pen/mpQNWQ.

If we take a look at our code, we can see that most of it should be self-explanatory; attributes such as x and y are common to many SVG elements. However, this isn't the extent of what is possible with the <text> tag; it's a great opportunity to have a look at the key attributes for <text>, which are summarized in Table 3-1.

Table 3-1. *SVG Attributes for <text>*

Attribute / element	Purpose
`x, y, dx, dy`	The starting (x, y) and finishing (dx, dy) coordinates for a `<text>` element.
`text-anchor`	Used to align a string of text with reference to a given point (using the properties `start`, `middle`, or `end`).
`rotate`	One of several transforms that can be applied to an element and its children. Examples also include `skew()`, `scale()`, and `translate()`. **Note**: this is dependent on browser support for MathML – if this is not supported, then a CSS fallback will be used instead.
`textLength`	Specify the width of the space into which text will be drawn.
`lengthAdjust`	Controls how a specific string of text should be drawn into a `<text>` or `<tspan>` element, using `spacingAndGlyphs` or `spacing` to control the appearance.
`<textPath>`	Used to place text along any arbitrary path, using coordinates referenced from a defined `<path>` element.
`<title>`	Specifies a description string that is displayed when the description is text only. The `<title>` element is not rendered n graphics, but can sometimes be rendered as a tooltip, depending on the browser in use.

Our example worked very well, but I can't help wonder if we can do more – after all, SVG is perfect for creating graphics that have been drawn, so why not do something bigger with text? Well, we can – let's step it up a gear and create something a little more complex using the `<text>` element as part of our next exercise.

Applying Different Effects to Text

If someone posed the question, "What can one do with text when working with SVG graphics…?," then the only answer must be "How long is a piece of string…?"

It might sound odd to answer a question with one, but the truth is – we are only limited by our imagination! If you search online, Google will return hundreds of results, where others have created all manner of examples of styled text. To really push the boat out though, and add some extra sparkle, animation may be required - SVG is a great format for animating elements; for inspiration, take a look at a post by Henry Wijaya at http://bashooka.com/coding/20-cool-svg-text-effects/, or the collection on Codepen by Julia Buhvalova at https://codepen.io/collection/DPYwYN ?

We will cover animating SVG elements in more detail in Chapter 6, "Animating Content" – if we bring it back to reality though for now, we can still apply different patterns to our text within SVG. Our previous example touched on simply adding color and thicker edges to our text, but what about using *images* to style our text?

APPLYING SVG EFFECTS TO TEXT

This is an interesting effect – for it to work, it relies on using the right type of font, and in some respects the choice of image can also have an impact on our overall design. Let's dive in and take a look:

1. In a new file, go ahead and take a copy of autosprite.html, then delete the markup between the <head> and <body> tags.

2. Next, add the following code in between the <head> tags:

```
<meta charset="utf-8">
<title>Beginning SVG: Adding Effects to Text</title>
<link rel="stylesheet" href="css/texteffects.css">
```

3. We now need to add our SVG graphic – for this, paste the following code in between the <body> tags. There are a few steps involved, so I'll break it down, starting with the opening <h1> and <svg> container tags:

```
<h1>
  <svg viewBox="0 0 800 800" class="heading">
```

4. Go ahead and save this file as texteffects.html, at the root of our project area.

5. Next up comes the definitions block – we're using this to define our pattern, which is a landscape image:

```
<defs>
  <pattern id="img-pattern" patternUnits="userSpaceOnUse"
  width="800" height="800">
    <image href="img/landscape.png" x="0" y="0" width="900" height="900" />
  </pattern>
  </defs>
```

84

6. We then create our text element in a similar fashion as previously, before closing out our demo with the appropriate tags:

```
    <text text-anchor="middle" x="50%" y="20%" dy=".25rem"
     class="headingtext">
       Text Effects with SVG
    </text>
  </svg>
 </h1>
</body>
</html>
```

7. Our demo won't be complete without some styling – for this, go ahead and add the following code to a new file, saving it within the css subfolder in our project area as texteffects.css:

```
@import url('https://fonts.googleapis.com/css?family=Oswald');

body { font-family: 'Anton', sans-serif; background: #3C3928; }

.heading { font-size: 4.5rem; }
.headingtext { stroke: rgba(255,255,255,.5); stroke-width: 0.1rem;
    fill: url(#img-pattern); letter-spacing: 0.1rem; }
```

8. Go ahead and save both the HTML markup and CSS files – if all is well, we should see this text, against a very dark grayish yellow background, as shown in Figure 3-10.

Figure 3-10. *Applying text effects*

A beautifully simple demo, which can add some real sparkle if we apply it the right way – the irony though is that it only requires one line of code to bring it all together and make it work! Sure, our choice of font and image will play a part, but it all hangs on just one line:

```
fill: url(#img-pattern);
```

Let's take a look at the code in more detail, to see how this simple but effective style works, and why we must choose the right font, color, and image for maximum impact.

Exploring How the Code Works

Our code begins with creating what should now be a familiar SVG container – we've applied a class of heading that we use to control the font size of our text (set at 4.5rem). We then set a definition block, into which we create our `<pattern>`, using the landscape image from earlier in the chapter. This pattern is set to 900px by 900px – this `patternUnits` value of `userSpaceOnUse` means it will adapt in size if it's calling element (the `<text>` tag) changes in size.

We then create the all-important `<text>` tag – this is set to be centered in the middle of the screen, with the start point being set as 50% in, and 20% down. We've applied a class of `headingtext`, which is used to set the `stroke`, `stroke-width` and `letter-spacing` values – and of course our pattern! We then tie off our design by setting the background color to #3C3928, or a very dark grayish yellow color.

Embedding Other Content

Adding images and SVG graphics a page is a start, but we can take things even further – how about adding video? It has to be said that with the current state of HTML5 video, this might not immediately make sense; most recent browsers will play MP4 format natively, without the need to embed it within a container.

However – embedding it as part of a SVG does open up some interesting opportunities for us: any `<text>` elements within can be crawled for SEO purposes; we can add subtitles for different languages without having to edit the original video, and can also overlay elements with ease. Above all, though, we can make our video responsive – provided we don't set static size values for the video within, then it will automatically resize if our SVG container element changes size.

How does it work? To embed our video, we make use of the `<foreignobject>` element – this can contain almost any element that is not native SVG, such as HTML video, or longer texts, where the HTML format is easier to manipulate and manage than the SVG equivalent. Adding in our content is very straightforward, so let's dive into our next exercise to find out how it all works in practice.

Adding Videos

For our next exercise, I'm going to revisit a favorite haunt of mine – anyone remember the *Big Buck Bunny Project*?

No – don't worry: this is not a reference to some wild animal-based website! It's one of several movies created by the Blender Foundation, created using the open source Blender tool. We're going to use another of their videos for our next exercise – *"Sintel"*, which was premiered in September 2010. The original movie is still available from `https://durian.blender.org/`; we'll make use of the MP4 version in our next demo.

ADDING VIDEO TO SVG ELEMENTS

Let's make a start:

1. We need to download some assets first – go ahead and extract copies of the `css` and `video` folders from the `foreignobject` folder in the code download that accompanies this book, and save them to our project area.

There is a font folder also in the code download – it contains the same font file from previous demos, so you only need to download it if you don't already have it in your project folder.

2. Next, take a copy of the `texteffects.html` file, and delete the content from within the `<head>` tags, then the content from within the `<body>` tags. Save this as `foreignobject.html` at the root of our project area.

3. Add the following code in between the `<head>`...`</head>` tags:

```
<meta charset="utf-8">
<title>Beginning SVG: Creating SVG Sprites</title>
<link rel="stylesheet" href="css/foreignObject.css">
```

4. Next, add the following SVG markup in between the `<body>` tags:

```
<svg xmlns="http://www.w3.org/2000/svg">
  <g>
    <rect x="0" y="0" width="300" height="200"></rect>
    <foreignObject x="-151" y="-104" width="500" height="400">
      <video controls="">
        <source src="video/sintel.mp4" type="video/mp4">
      </video>
      <p>Trailer for "Sintel"</p>
```

```
        </foreignObject>
      </g>
    </svg>
```

5. Go ahead and save the file – if all is well, we should see (and be able to play) our video, as shown in Figure 3-11.

Figure 3-11. *"Sintel" video embedded as SVG*

Although our code may look complicated, in reality it isn't – we start with defining a standard SVG graphic. Inside this, we create a `<rect>` of 300px by 200px, followed by our `<foreignObject>` element.

It's inside this we set up our video tags – for the purposes of our demo, we're referencing a single MP4 video, but we could easily add in links for other formats such as OGG or WebM if needed. We then include a standard `<p>` tag for our text, before closing the SVG element – when using a `<foreignObject>` tag, the one thing we can't include inside it is SVG elements!

Okay – let's move on: many of the examples we've used have been somewhat theoretical; we're going to round out this chapter with one more example of a practical example, making use of an online tool that...well, if I had a dime for every time I used it, I might have retired somewhere warm and sunny, and lived off the proceeds....

Implementing a Real-World Example

Cast your mind back to the "Adding Markers to SVG Paths" demo we created back in Chapter 2, "Creating Shapes" – remember how we touched on creating markers, the basis of which we might use to create suitable indicators for Google Maps?

Well, it's time for a little trip down memory lane – our next exercise, in case you hadn't already guessed – is going to be about one of my favorite tools: Google Maps! Yes, it may have only been around since 2005, but it has become one of the most popular tools on the web; it allows use of SVG, so it seems fitting to explore this in more detail.

ADDING MARKERS TO GOOGLE MAPS

Now, before we get started, there is an important point to be aware of – Google Maps will only accept SVGs if they contain a single path. That makes anything more complex than a simple image impossible, so how can we get around this?

Fortunately there is an option: the developer John Hoover has created the SVG Marker overlay object (available from `https://github.com/defvayne23/SVGMarker`) that allows us to use more complex SVGs with Google Maps. It's really easy to use, so without further ado, let's make a start:

1. We'll begin by downloading copies of the `css` and `img` folders for this demo, from the svgmarkers folder in the code download that accompanies this book – go ahead and store these in our project area.

2. Next, add the following code to a new file, saving it as `svgmarkers.html` at the root of our project folder:

```
<!DOCTYPE html>
<head>
  <meta charset="utf-8">
  <title>Beginning SVG: Adding SVG Markers to Google Maps</title>
  <link rel="stylesheet" href="css/svgmarkers.css">
  <script src="https://maps.google.com/maps/api/js"></script>
  <script src="js/SVGMarker.min.js"></script>
  <script src="js/markers.js"></script>
</head>
```

```
<body>
  <h2>Location of Apress Media:</h2>
  <div id="map"></div>
</body>
</html>
```

3. With our markup in place, we now need to make our map work – for this, go ahead and download the SVGMarker library from `https://raw.githubusercontent.com/defvayne23/SVGMarker/master/SVGMarker.min.js`, and store this in a new `js` subfolder within our project area.

4. The SVGMarker library allows us to convert an SVG image into something that Google can use – we now need to tie it into our map. For this, go ahead and add the following code to a new file, saving it as `markers.js` in the `js` subfolder from the previous step:

```
window.addEventListener('load', function() {
  var map = new google.maps.Map(document.getElementById('map'), {
    zoom: 19,
    center: new google.maps.LatLng(40.7255945,-74.0051243)
  });

  var marker = new SVGMarker({
    map: map,
    position: new google.maps.LatLng(40.7255945,-74.0051243),
    icon: {
      anchor: new google.maps.Point(90, 90.26),
      size: new google.maps.Size(120,90.26),
      url: 'img/apresspin.svg'
    }
  })
});
```

5. Save all of your files, then try previewing the results in a browser – if all is well, we should see the location map for Apress Media in New York, as indicated in Figure 3-12.

Location of Apress Media:

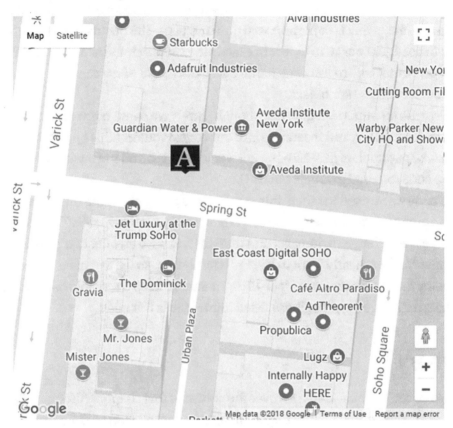

Figure 3-12. *Location of Apress Media in New York*

This opens up some great possibilities – we could of course create our marker(s) using a format such as PNG, but at the risk of losing sharpness if the image were to be resized. SVG is perfect for this format, although there are a couple of considerations – let's dive in and explore the practicalities of using this format with Google Maps in more detail.

Understanding How It Works

At face value, if we were to compare the code used to create our map with that provided by Google, we wouldn't notice any real change. Sure, the configuration options may be in a different order, but it will still have the same effect.

So how does it work? The magic lies in the SVGMarker.min.js file – it's too large to reproduce here in full, but in a nutshell, it takes a copy of the icon we've specified, and draws it as an image that is superimposed onto the map. The beauty of this solution is that we can configure our map object in exactly the same way as for a standard PNG or JPEG image, as the work to translate it into a format Google Maps can understand, is handled by the SVGMarker object.

It does raise an important question though: surely we could convert all of our SVG graphics into data URIs, and insert this into our code. Wouldn't this be better – allowing us to resize or manipulate it? Well – the answer is both yes and no: it will depend on the size of the code required to create our SVG.

If the code we've used to create this graphic is large, then adding this (and other images) to our markup will clearly make it larger and less manageable. There will come a point where it is too large to manage, and that this will have an effect on page load times. This is something we clearly want to keep to a minimum, so we just need to be mindful of how many images we turn into data-URIs, so that we keep a sensible balance between calling external images, against those listed inline within our code.

Summary

Phew – we've certainly covered a lot over the course of this chapter! Although SVG graphics are ideally suited for creating 2D images, it doesn't stop us from using the format to host other media, such as images and videos. We can create some great effects when working with images and SVG – let's take a moment to review what we've covered over the course of this chapter.

We kicked off with a quick look at embedding an image within a SVG graphic, before starting with a look at exporting images, so that we have both SVG and PNG versions available as source images. We then moved onto covering the different formats of data URIs, and saw how the level of optimization can have a beneficial effect on the resulting code. We then moved onto understanding how we can use image masks to add a simple but effective overlay to an image, and saw how we can use it to provide a title or header effect to a background image.

Next up came a look at working with icons – we explored how easy it is to create image sprites, before making use of the icons from within SVG graphics. We covered both the manual route and how to set up an automated process; we covered how the former route may suit occasional use, and that for anything more than the odd icon, the automated route may be a better option.

We then moved onto learning how to apply effects to text elements within a SVG graphic – we covered a couple of simple examples, as a taster for what is possible, and that this is only limited by our imagination.

We then rounded out the chapter with a look at incorporating videos – we saw that in this day and age of social media, there is still a use for SVG and video, even though the latest HTML5 video standards are more than capable of displaying content. Last, but by no means least, we finished with a real-world demo, where we added an SVG marker to a Google Map – we saw that although this is really easy, current limitations prevent anything more than a simple marker, and that with some trickery, we can work around that limitation!

Right – onwards we go: there is never any rest for the wicked! One of my favorite topics in web development is making content responsive; with more and more people viewing the web on mobile devices, it is so important to have a site that works well for this platform. SVG has a number of features that makes it suited to Responsive Web Design (and by default, sizing content easily), so go ahead and turn that page to find out more...

CHAPTER 4

Sizing SVG

In Chapter 3, we worked our way through creating different types of SVG elements – this includes the humble square, through to a circle and finishing up with more complex paths. Yet one key feature remains, upon which we've touched, yet not really discussed in any detail – scaling. If we have to scale up a standard image, then this becomes tricky; in most cases we end up with a picture that...well, looks rubbish!

SVG graphics are different: we can take any SVG element and resize them with ease and without loss of clarity. How? Well, it all hangs around the SVG coordinate system and the SVG viewport; it's key to how SVG graphics work. A good analogy would be a well-known online map application – no prizes for guessing which one! With that in mind, let's kick off with a look at the basic principles in more detail.

Understanding Scalability

A question – what might Google Maps and your browser have in common with SVG, I wonder? No, I've not completely lost the plot; this is a very good analogy for how SVG elements work. Let me explain more:

If you ever look at a Google Map, you're only looking a small part of what is an infinite-sized canvas – clearly our browser could never be wide enough to view everything! In this instance, our browser acts as a viewport (or window) to the canvas; the content on that canvas is our SVG graphic. We can use controls provided by Google to pan around the map, or zoom in; no matter how much we move, we will only ever see a small part of that canvas.

Still with me so far? Good – let's hold that thought for a moment and turn our attention to a small demo: in it we will see some of the effects that moving the canvas around will have on our SVG elements.

© Alex Libby 2018
A. Libby, *Beginning SVG*, https://doi.org/10.1007/978-1-4842-3760-1_4

SCALING SVG GRAPHICS

Okay - let's make a start:

1. In a new document, go ahead and add the following code, saving it as
    `scaling.html` at the root of our project area:

```
<!DOCTYPE html>
<head>
  <meta charset="utf-8">
  <title>Beginning SVG: Scaling an SVG Graphic</title>
  <link rel="stylesheet" href="css/scaling.css">
</head>
<body>
  <svg width="500" height="100">
    <circle r="25" cx="25" cy="25" fill="dimgrey" />
    <rect x="500" y="100" width="50" height="50" fill="#933" />
  </svg>
</body>
</html>
```

2. Next up, we need to add a couple of styles to our demo – although the core part
    of the demo has most of them, there are a couple we need to finish it off. Add
    the following rules to a new document, saving it as `scaling.css` within the
    `css` subfolder of our project area:

```
@font-face { font-family: 'pt_sansregular'; src: url('../font/
pt_sansregular.woff') format('woff');
  font-weight: normal; font-style: normal; }

body { font-family: 'pt_sansregular', sans-serif; padding: 2rem;
  font-size: 18px; }

svg { outline: 5px solid #000; }
```

3. Go ahead and save the files – if we preview the results, we'll a circle within a
    box, as indicated in Figure 4-1.

Beginning SVG: Scaling Elements

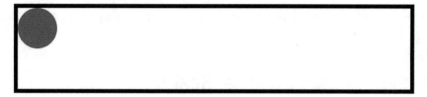

Figure 4-1. *Our initial SVG, before scaling*

At this point, we're going to alter how the circle looks, by changing our code – we'll start by adding a viewBox parameter to our code:

4. Go ahead and add the following code in, immediately after the <height> parameter for our SVG element:

    height="100" **viewBox="0 0 500 100"**

5. What happens if we alter the viewBox attribute to this: viewBox="25 25 500 100"?

6. Let's focus on one of the shapes – go ahead and remove the <rect> line from within our SVG, then set the viewBox values to "0 0 250 50". Notice how the circle has increased in size?

7. As a final change, go ahead and update the opening SVG tag as indicated:

    <svg width="500" height="100" **viewBox="0 0 50 100"**
    preserveAspectRatio="none">

    We will see the circle expand to fit the SVG container, as indicated in Figure 4-2.

Beginning SVG: Scaling Elements

Figure 4-2. *Scaled SVG of a circle*

Over the course of this exercise, we've not made any changes to our circle element, yet you will have noticed that after each change, it has altered shape. What gives? Unlike ordinary images, SVG images don't resize in quite the same way – let's take a breather to explore this in more detail.

Understanding the Impact of Scaling

At this point I'm sure you will be asking just how we managed to make our SVG graphic change shape and position, without changing its sizes. The key to it lies in the viewport – we're not moving our SVG, but *moving the viewport* instead:

We initially don't see any change once we've run step 3 and added in the `viewBox` attribute – our `viewBox` is 500px by 100px, which is identical to the viewport. Notice though that we've specified both a circle and a square in our SVG, yet only the former is showing? If we change our `viewBox` values to 25 25 500 100, this shifts our canvas up and to the left; this aligns it to the origin (25, 25), hiding part of the circle and revealing the top part of the square.

When we remove the square element and change the `viewBox` values, we don't shift the canvas this time, but set the `viewBox` to only cover half the width and height of our viewport. This has the effect of scaling our `viewBox`, so that all four corners align with the viewport – this doubles the size of the canvas, scaling the circle to twice the size to fit.

If we had doubled the size of our viewBox values, then this would have had the opposite effect of shrinking our graphic — there is twice as much to cover in the same space, so the elements are shrunken to fit.

Our final change completely alters the aspect ratio of our circle – the `viewBox` is set as 1:2, against the viewport, which has a ratio of 5:1. This means that the circle's `height` is stretched by a factor of 10, but its height remains constant; the stretching comes from the presence of `preserveAspectRatio` to none.

Okay – let's move on: over the course of this exercise, we've touched on some of the key concepts for scaling SVG graphics. At the heart of this scaling lies the SVG coordinate system, which controls where our canvas is displayed. Each time we create a new SVG element, we also create a new coordinate system; let's take a look at how it works in more detail.

Getting to Grips with SVG Coordinates

If you recall from the start of this chapter, we talked about our SVG canvas as being of infinite size – our viewport on this canvas being akin to a window through a wall that covers the entire size of our canvas.

Each time we create a new SVG element, we also create a new coordinate system, with an infinite canvas where point zero (0,0) is at the top left of our parent element (such as a div). Specifying positive values on either axis will move an element down or to the right. Negative values will move it in the opposite direction, or upwards and to the left of our canvas.

We can see this in more detail, in Figure 4-3.

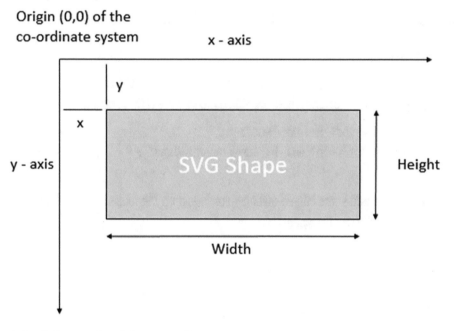

Figure 4-3. *Schematic of the coordinate system*

By default, the coordinate systems of each canvas and viewport will align with each other, although (as we saw in the previous exercise), this does not have to be the case; we can change the alignment to suit our needs. This includes the unit of measure we use to position elements; we can use any unit, with the exception of percentage values, and then we can mix and match which units are used in each system, within our projects.

Applying Coordinates to an SVG

Enough of the talk – let's get stuck into some code! As any teacher will say, there is no substitute for practice, so over the course of the next couple of pages, we will work our way through some examples of creating and positioning SVG elements, so we can see the effects of setting values as coordinates for an SVG drawing.

For this exercise, we're going to make use of Codepen as an interactive demo – this means we will see the results of our change immediately, without having to manually refresh the screen:

MOVING SVG ELEMENTS

Let's make a start:

1. We'll start by creating a simple demo in a Codepen – head over to `https://codepen.io`, then add this code into the HTML section:

    ```
    <svg width="600" height="300">
      <rect x="0" y="0" width="200" height="100" />
    </svg>
    ```

2. We need to add some simple styling – for this, drop the following code into the CSS section of our Codepen:

    ```
    svg {
      outline: 5px solid #000;
      overflow: hidden;
    }

    rect {
      fill: slategray;
    }
    ```

At this point, we've created a viewport of 600px by 300px, with a silver gray rectangle inside, measuring 200px by 100px. At present, as no units of measure have been specified, it assumes a default of pixels; we could easily have specified a different unit as desired.

Our SVG demo also has an outline, so we can see where our rectangle is – everything inside the outline forms our viewport. The lone rectangle is in the top left corner, which aligns with the viewport; if values are not specified for the starting point, then it assumes a default of 0,0, or zero point.

It's worth noting that if we had not specified values for the size of our `<rect>`, then most browsers will use a default of 300px x 150px. It's not consistent, so it is better set values if you can!

Let's return back to our exercise –

3. Try changing the starting points for our rectangle, as indicated:

   ```
   <rect x="10" y="10" width="200" height="100" />
   ```

   Notice how it moves away, down and to the right, by 10px? Changing the x and/or y coordinates in this manner will move the element on our canvas – it's important to note that our neither our canvas nor our viewport have moved; only the rectangle has been displaced.

4. This time, try changing the values as shown in this example:

   ```
   <rect x="-100" y="-50" width="200" height="100" fill="#f00" />
   ```

This time, only part of our rectangle is visible – the rest has been drawn, but falls outside of our viewport. In this instance, we've only moved it by a few pixels, but there is nothing stopping us from drawing our SVG anywhere on our canvas (which could be measured in billions of pixels – yes, *billions of pixels!*).

5. What happens if we needed to see outside of our viewport? This is normally set to be hidden by default, but no problem – go ahead and make this change to our CSS, to reveal our (hidden) SVG:

   ```
   svg { outline: 5px solid #000; overflow: visible;   margin: 50px
   0px 0px 150px; }
   ```

   We can see the results of our change (including the displacement), in this extract, shown in Figure 4-4.

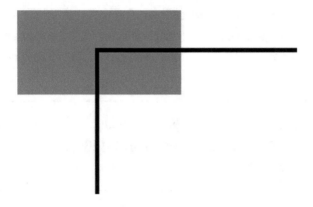

Figure 4-4. *Our (exposed) overlapping SVG*

The changes we've made in our exercise have been very straightforward, yet we've only scratched the surface of what is possible! Trouble is, we're still a little limited in what we can do: How can we take things further? Well, the answer comes in the form of a useful little toolkit – it may be small, but it will help earn its keep when working with SVG: let me introduce the SVG Scaling Toolbox.

We've already used parts of it in previous exercises, but as scaling SVGs can be tricky, it's worth spending some time to get to know it in more detail. It comes in several parts – we'll kick off with a look first at setting heights and widths of SVG elements.

Introducing the SVG Scaling Toolbox

At this point, I can already hear the next question coming – what is this Toolbox all about…? Well, to answer this very pertinent question, I need to step back for a moment:

If we resize any image, we have an idea about how they should scale, correct? After all, raster format images such as JPEGs or PNGs have a clearly defined size, and that we can include an option to automatically scale a particular dimension if we only provide height or width, but not both.

SVGs don't operate in the same way – they are not images but documents that require a different mindset when scaling. It means that not only do we need to control the size of our canvas, *but also the elements within*. It means that scaling considerations increase: we need to be mindful of the size of the canvas, whether the image should maintain a height to width ratio, should the image scale uniformly, or can we allow for some distortion?

This is where the Scaling Toolbox comes into play – its assorted attributes will help retain some sense of order when it comes to scaling images. The first tool to understand is the height and width attributes – but there is a sting in this tale…

Setting Height and Width Attributes

When adding SVGs to a page (assuming we use one of the methods we touched on back in Chapter 1), we can set both height and width sizes directly in code, using something akin to this:

```
<svg width="500" height="300"></svg>
```

This seems pretty reasonable, right? We can use any one of several different units of measure, such as ems, rems, picas, or even millimeters (mm) – SVG can use standard CSS units when referring to dimensions of an image.

In our example, the `<svg>` element doesn't specify any units though; by default, this equates to pixels, unless we specify a named unit. Now – assuming we have set suitable values: at first glance, one would expect any set on an SVG container, to implicitly set an aspect ratio, so that an SVG will scale in the same way as normal images. Sound reasonable, right…?

Unfortunately, this is not the case – setting height and width on an SVG can end up being counterproductive:

- If your SVG is embedded using `<img>` tags, then setting values will make the element scale as predicted in most browsers, save for Internet Explorer. It's likely that you will see the SVG element automatically scaled to maintain a constant aspect ratio in IE, but that the content within will not be scaled.

- Although their use has fallen out of favor, setting heights and widths on an `<object>`, `<embed>` or `<iframe>` will not change the frame size; you will end up with scrollbars if the SVG is too large.

- If you have set your SVG inline, this will control both the image area on the page, and the content within. So, any CSS we set on the `<svg>` element, such as `svg {width: 100%; height: auto;}`, will override anything set within the SVG code. In this case, setting these dimensions will set a default height of 150px or 100vh, depending on the browser we use.

There's one word that comes to mind – ouch! The safest way to control width and height is to not set it in code. Instead, set it within your CSS; this will allow the SVG to scale accordingly. To be sure that we set a suitable aspect ratio, and that the drawing scales to fit, we need the second tool in our kit – the viewBox. We've already used it a few times, so let's take a moment to explore this in more detail.

Implementing a viewBox

Until now, we're using a canvas that could be of any size, and that we've applied something called a viewBox to define the extent of what we can see at any one point. But – what *really* is a viewBox, and how does it work when we apply it to our code?

Well, the viewBox is what makes the S of SVG – it makes our vector graphics scalable. Consider this example, where the viewBox attribute has been highlighted:

```
<svg width="400" height="300" viewBox="0 0 40 30">
  <rect x="20" y="10" width="10" height="5" style="stroke: #000000;
  fill:none;"/>
</svg>
```

This little example creates an `<svg>` element with a width of 400 pixels and a height of 300. We've applied a `viewBox` attribute to the `<svg>`, which contains four coordinates, to define the view box of the `<svg>` element. These coordinates start with the x and y starting points ("point zero"), with `width` and `height` controlling its size.

It's worth noting that if we were to work with other non-SVG elements, then the CSS properties `object-fit` and `object-position` work in a similar manner to the `viewBox` attribute.

If we set a `viewBox` attribute (as in our example), we can use this to control the following:

- The aspect ratio of our image.
- How all the lengths and coordinates used inside the SVG should be scaled to fit the total space available.
- The origin (or point zero) of the SVG coordinate system, where x and y equal 0.

We've already seen in several code examples that the viewBox settings are a list of four numbers, separated using commas or spaces, which control the starting position and size of our viewBox. These values will default to pixels, unless we specify a different unit of measure.

- The first pair of values set the starting point (or point zero) of our viewBox, in a similar fashion to setting it in JavaScript. For simple scaling, we can set both to zero; centering the coordinates will make it easier to define and transform shapes (as opposed to performing these actions from a corner), or to crop an image to a smaller size than its original definition.

- The second pair of values represent the width and height of the content that should be scaled to fit the area into which we're drawing our SVG. It's worth noting that if our SVG uses a different unit of measure (such as centimeters), then it will be scaled to match the overall scale set by the viewBox.

Okay – with that in mind, let's take a look at a couple of example viewBox values, to see how this works in practice:

- Imagine we had set a viewBox="0 0 100 100": this defines a coordinate system which is 100 units wide and 100 units high. If we had placed a circle in the center of our graphic, with a radius of 50px, then this will fill the whole screen, even if we tried to resize our browser window! If we'd set a <rect> element instead, with a height of 1in, this would almost fill the screen – 1 inch equates to 96px in CSS, and each side would be scaled to the same length.

- If however we had set a viewBox="5 0 90 100", then we would have had almost the same view. This time though, it would be cropped in by 5px on the left and right, so that the total width equates to 90 pixels.

When we've set a viewBox in our code, our SVG graphic will scale to fit its size, without loss of quality. However, we should note that it will not by default stretch or distort the image if the dimensions we've given it do not match the aspect ratio that has been set. Instead, the scale will change to preserve the aspect ratio that has been set – this is set using the preserveAspectRatio attribute, so let's dive in and see what this in means for us in more detail.

Preserving the Aspect Ratio

Ask anyone to think of famous double acts, and one might get a variety of answers – *Cagney and Lacey, Smokey and the Bandit*...the list is endless! How does this relate to SVGs, I hear you ask...?

Well, leaving aside the reference to well-known films, one might say that the `viewBox` parameter is but one half of a double act (if you excuse the pun!) – It's partner in crime is `preserveAspectRatio`. By itself, it has no effect on our SVG, but when teamed up with viewBox, its role is to define how an image should be scaled, if the `viewBox` doesn't match our viewport's aspect ratio.

In most cases, we can simply set it with default behavior, which works well in most cases – our image will be scaled until it fits the available space, allowing for any extra space around the image.

If, however, we need to tweak its behavior, `preserveAspectRatio` comes with two parameters that we can adjust:`<align>` and `<meetOrSlice>`. Let's take a look at these properties in more detail, beginning with the compulsory `<align>` attribute; the details of which are listed in Table 4-1.

Table 4-1. *Attributes for Aligning the viewBox*

Value	Description
xMin	Align minimum x of view box with the left edge of the viewport.
xMid	Align midpoint on the x-axis of view box with the center of the viewport on the x-axis.
xMax	Align maximum x of view box with the right edge of the viewport.
YMin	Align minimum y of view box with the top edge of the viewport.
YMid	Align midpoint on the y-axis of view box with the center point of the viewport on the y-axis.
YMax	Align maximum y of view box with the bottom edge of the viewport.

> For a full list of options, please refer to `https://developer.mozilla.org/en-US/docs/Web/SVG/Attribute/preserveAspectRatio`.

Although the properties are listed individually in Table 4-1, they are designed to be combined into one value, such as in these examples: xMaxYMax and xMidYMid. They look very similar (and yes, the change in case is deliberate), but their behavior on our SVG will be different. The first example aligns the right edge of the viewBox with the right edge of the viewport, whereas the second aligns the middle of the viewBox with the middle of the viewport. These are not the only comnbinations we can use – the full list is shown in Table 4-2.

Table 4-2. *Possible Combinations of Alignment Keywords*

	Left	Center	Right
Top	xMinYMin	xMidYMin	xMaxYMin
Center	xMinYMid	xMidYMid	xMaxYMid
Bottom	xMinYMax	xMidYMax	xMaxYMax

The second parameter, `<meetOrSlice>`, is optional; it can be included if needed, but should separated by a space as indicated in this example:

`preserveAspectRatio="xMidYMid meet"`

For this parameter, we can specify any one of the following three values – `meet`, `slice` or `none`; the role each plays is detailed in Table 4-3.

Table 4-3. *Values for preserveAspectRatio*

Value	Description
`meet`	Preserves aspect ratio and scales view box to fit within viewport.
`slice`	Preserves aspect ratio and slices off any part of the image that does not fit inside the viewport.
`none`	Does not preserve aspect ratio. Scales image to fit view box fully into viewport. Proportions will be distorted.

An interesting point worth noting that this second attribute works in a similar fashion to standard CSS for background images – the closest equivalent for meet is `background-size: contain`, and for slice, we could use `background-size: cover`. The only thing to be aware of is that when using slice, it will scale the image to the largest dimension, and may or may not slice off the rest – the latter depends on how we have (or have not) set the value of the `overflow` property!

We may of course decide not to specify a value at all, and rely on it simply using the default of none. This allows the SVG to scale more like a raster image (but clearly with better resolution) – it will stretch or squash the image to fit the height and width values specified in our code.

To really understand how the coordinate system works, and the impact of changing viewBox or preserveAspectRatio properties, I would recommend trying out the interactive demo by Sarah Soueidan, at `https://www.sarasoueidan.com/demos/interactive-svg-coordinate-system/` – this is a great eye-opener!

Right – enough chitchat: time we got physical with some code! Although the Scaling Toolbox attributes may *look* straightforward enough, their simplicity belies the strength of their power; let's put some of that to use, with a quick demo to see the impact of setting these values in code.

Putting the Toolbox to Use

Over the course of the last few pages, we've talked in detail about the Scaling Toolbox – although the settings within are not complex, it's all about the interaction and finding the right balance for our needs.

There's no better way to get accustomed to achieving that balance, than in a demo – for our next exercise, we'll use a simple graphic of an apple, to explore how setting the various properties of the toolbox can have an impact on the appearance of our image.

PRESERVING SIZE

Before we start our exercise, there is a simple task we need to perform – we need an SVG; for this, I will use one of an apple that I've sourced from `https://openclipart.org/detail/183893/simple-red-apple`. You can of course use any for this, although I would recommend keeping it as simple as possible!

Okay – assuming we have our graphic, let's make a start:

1. We'll begin with setting up our markup – in a new file, go ahead and add the following code, saving it as `preserve.html` at the root of our project folder:

```
<!DOCTYPE html>
<head>
  <meta charset="utf-8">
  <title>Beginning SVG: Setting preserveAspectRatio</title>
  <link rel="stylesheet" href="css/preserve.css">
</head>
<body>
  <h2>Beginninng SVG: Preserving Aspect Ratio</h2>
  <div class="center"> </div>
</body>
</html>
```

2. We need to add a couple of styles – for this, download a copy of the `preserve.css` file, and drop it into the `css` subfolder that's in our project area.

3. Next, we need to add our SVG – for this, I will use a graphic of an apple (which is available in the code download). Go ahead and extract a copy and save it to the `img` folder, which is in our project folder.

4. As good practice, we should ensure it is optimized – we can do this quickly using the SVGO online service, available at `https://jakearchibald.github.io/svgomg/`. Browse to the site, then drag and drop the image file straight over the top; once optimized, you can save a copy of the results by clicking on the white arrow and saving the file to our `img` folder.

I would suggest saving it as a different name – we don't link to the file directly from our demo, but copy the contents into our markup. Saving a copy means you can then compare images, to see how optimization can remove redundant code.

---

5. We now need to add the content of our SVG – go ahead and open the SVG in your text editor, then copy and paste the contents in between the `<div class="center"></div>` tags.

6. Next, add in this attribute to the SVG code, as indicated:

   ```
   viewBox="0 0 442.23 482.04" preserveAspectRatio="none">
   ```

7. Save the file – if we preview the results, we will see something akin to the screenshot shown in Figure 4-5.

Figure 4-5. *Effect of not setting preserveAspectRatio*

8. Try changing the `preserveAspectRatio` value to `meet`, as indicated: `prese rveAspectRatio="`**xMidYMax meet**`"`, then refresh the screen – you should see a smaller apple, as shown in Figure 4-6.

Figure 4-6. *Shrinking our apple*

This time, let's take a different tack: keep the `slice` attribute, but alter the `viewBox` values as highlighted: `viewBox="`**`0 0 430 250`**`"` `preserveAspectRatio="xMidYMax `**`slice`**`"` – what do you get? You should see our apple zoomed in, as shown in Figure 4-7.

Figure 4-7. *Zooming in on our apple*

Phew – see what a difference changing just one word or digit can make, to our SVG? It's all about where we want to position our graphic, and whether we need it to all display as much as possible within the viewport, or are happy for parts to be sliced off (hidden) as needed. This is an important concept to master, so let's pause for a moment to explore how our demo works in more detail.

Understanding How It Works

So – what did happen in our demo? The key to understanding it is that we have not changed the image itself (even though it may appear so), but we have *changed how we view that image.* Let me explain what I mean:

If we list all three viewBox examples, then we have the following code:

- viewBox= "0 0 442.23 482.04" preserveAspectRatio="none"

- viewBox= "0 0 442.23 482.04" preserveAspectRatio="xMidYMax meet"

- viewBox= "0 0 430 250" preserveAspectRatio="xMidYMax slice"

Notice how in two out of the three cases, our `viewBox` doesn't change size; in the third example, we reduce the size, which has the effect of zooming in on our image, so it becomes more enlarged.

Our first example sets `preserveAspectRatio` to `none` – this tells our `viewBox` to scale to fit the size of our viewport, effectively (in this instance) aligning both to the same set of coordinates as each other. The net effect of this is that the image itself is not scaled accordingly but squashed into whatever dimensions we specify: this results in something of a distorted image!

In comparison, setting `xMidYMax slice` tells our `viewBox` to scale our graphic; we align the smallest value of our `viewBox` (point zero) with the smallest value of our viewport. The key here is the use of `meet` – this tells the `viewBox` to scale up to, but not over the edge: in other words, "Align the image to be horizontally centered, but push it towards the bottom edge of our view box."

Our third and final example takes a different tack – this time, our `viewBox` does not have a uniform size; it follows the same principle of alignment as our second example. This time though, we've set our second attribute to `slice` – this scales the SVG to the point that no empty space is left; it makes it look like we've really zoomed in on our image! If we were using standard CSS, then the equivalent would be `background-size: cover`.

Okay – time for a change of subject: as a developer, I'm sure you will be familiar with the need to make content available on multiple devices, right? We live in an age where more people access the Internet through devices other than a standard desktop PC; this will only increase over time!

At this point, I'm sure you will be asking what does this mean for SVG images – how easy is it to make an image responsive? Thankfully it is easy enough to do, and in fact we can use many of the same principles we might use for other content. Let's take a moment to explore what is required in more detail.

Making SVG Content Responsive

Just over 20 years ago, when I first started using Windows PCs, I'd have never imagined browsing the Web from anything other than a standard PC – granted, that might later have included Apple Macs, but a PC is still a PC!

Today, it's possible to view web-based content over dozens of different devices, from the humble smartphone through iPads, gaming consoles and of course standard PCs. This makes it harder for us developers, as we need to ensure our content is available on multiple devices; this does include how much (if it is not core to a strategy for mobile use for our site, for example, then why display it?)

Leaving aside the vulgarities of what should and should not be displayed, making an SVG graphic responsive is very easy – there are three some simple steps we can take:

1. Optimize our code – this should be treated as a given for every SVG we work with, but in many cases optimizing it will remove many of the elements that make an image non-responsive!

2. Add a `preserveAspectRatio` attribute and a class as a minimum – you may prefer to also surround the `<svg>` block in a `<div>`, although this isn't always necessary:

```
<div class="container">
  <svg version="1.1" viewBox="0 0 500 500"
preserveAspectRatio="xMinYMin meet" class="content">

    ...
  </svg>
</div>
```

3. Add in a CSS style rule for your content class (and container class, if you've used one) – the container code should look something like this:

```
.container { display: inline-block; position: relative;
  width: 100%; padding-bottom: 100%; vertical-align: middle;
  overflow: hidden; }
```

...and for the content, we can use this:

```
.content { display: inline-block; position: absolute; top: 0;
  left: 0; }
```

The key to making it work is to use percentage values where possible – in many cases this is sufficient to make our image responsive, although we may need to use media queries for edge cases which have to be treated differently (more on this in a moment).

In our (theoretical) example, not only would our SVG graphic be responsive as an element, but the content within too – we've used padding in our case to ensure our content is correctly positioned, in a similar fashion to making responsive videos.

Adding code isn't the only thing we need to do though – to create really effective responsive SVG, there are a number of steps we should follow. I've termed these the Golden Rules – this makes them sound a little formal, but they are really meant as guidelines to help you get the best out of your responsive SVG images. Let's take a look at them in more detail, beginning with the setup of your tools.

Introducing the Golden Rules

If there is one thing in life I've leared, it is never to be too prescriptive – there are frequently times when flexibility is very much the order of the day! With that in mind, the following shouldn't be interpreted as gospel, but more as a "checklist of inspiration" – something to help encourage optimal development:

- Make sure you set your tools up correctly – this is where diligence can really pay off! It's not something we've gone into detail, but I would recommend checking the following:

    - Consider using unitless values where possible, such as percentages; this helps to define proportional sizes, rather than specifying absolute values such as pixels. Pixels, ems and rems will work but can cause issues with accessibility, and don't always display consistently across different devices.

    - Make sure your canvas is not set too big, with lots of empty space. Do allow some for anti-aliasing, if you want the edges of your SVGs to blend smoothly into the background (this will add extra pixels, to reduce the effect of sharp edges).

    - If you are using decimal precision, then two places is sufficient; anything larger will add bloat to our code and increase file sizes.

    - Try to use as few points as possible – this will provide greater control over the element, and keep file sizes down.

- Remove any height and width attributes – many vector applications will add a lot of unnecessary code when exporting SVG images. In most cases, all we need at the start of our SVG files is the following, assuming a 500px by 500px viewBox is sufficient for your needs:

```
<svg xmlns="http://www.w3.org/2000/svg" viewBox="0 0 500 500">
<!-- SVG code here -->
</svg>
```

- Absolutely make sure your SVG code is at least optimized, if not also minified – this can typically save anywhere from 20 to 80 per cent in our file size, so it is absolutely worth the effort!

- Where necessary, make sure you test your SVG images and code in IE9-11. SVG files (added using img tags) do not scale properly in these browsers, when viewBox, width and height values have been set. A quick fix is to take out height and width values from your SVG, and manipulate it using CSS only – you can see an example of how at `https://stackoverflow.com/a/27971005`.

- Consider using SVG for text within a banner – standard text can indeed be used, but SVG text has the added benefit of resizing automatically.

- Use vector effects to keep hairlines thin – when working with SVGs, we can use stroke-width to set the thickness of lines. It is possible they might increase, depending on the size of the drawing; we can set vector-effect to prevent this from happening:

```
path {
  ...
  stroke-width: 2;
  vector-effect: non-scaling-stroke;
}
```

- Don't forget that we can embed other image formats within our SVG elements, such as JPEG, BMP, or even WebP. As long as we've followed the rules outlined so far, then these will become responsive if they have been added using the `<image>` tag.

- Any media queries you create for manipulating the contents of your SVG should be stored within the SVG itself; SVG can only see these queries, when stored internally. If however the media query relates to positioning on the page, or whether it is displayed or hidden, then this can be applied to the container and stored externally.

- There is a risk that at extremes our image may appear very small on a large canvas – try scaling up the image to fill the space, and avoid the need for extra code to fix the issue!

Ouch – it looks a little scary, but many of these guidelines can be automated: for example, we can use Node.js to automate tasks such as optimizing and minifying our code. These guidelines are not just about pure coding, but also about the creative thought and testing processes – after all, there's more to just producing code, right?

Okay – let's move on: time, I think, for a demo! We've talked a lot about how to make images responsive, so why not put this into action and see what it looks like in practice? With that in mind, let's take a standard image and run through the steps to make it responsive, before applying media queries to help make our image truly responsive.

Updating SVG Images

For our next exercise, we'll use a standard SVG image – this time it will be of my favorite drinks, coffee! Yes, I'm sure this will be something many developers can relate to – long nights of coding, regular bouts of caffeine to keep going…not healthy I know, but sometimes needs must…

But I digress – we'll use an SVG from the `openclipart.org` site; our one can be found at `https://openclipart.org/detail/293550/coffee-to-go`. I've already included a copy in the code download; please feel free to substitute if you want to use a different image.

MAKING IMAGES RESPONSIVE

Okay – let's make a start:

1. We'll start by downloading a copy of the `responsive` folder from the code download that accompanies this book – go ahead and store this at the root of our project folder.

2. Next, we need to optimize our SVG file – for this, go ahead and browse to `https://jakearchibald.github.io/svgomg/` – this is the online SVGO optimizer tool we've already used earlier in this book. Drag and drop a copy of the `coffee-to-go.svg`, that is in the img folder from step 1, onto this page – this will automatically optimize the image for us.

3. Save the optimized image as `coffee.svg` into the `img` folder – we need the contents of that file shortly.

4. Go ahead and open up a copy of the `responsive.html` file from within the folder we stored back in step 1 – you will see a blank line at line 10.

5. We also need to open a copy of the `coffee.svg` file we've just saved, in our text editor – copy and paste the contents of that file into line 10 of `responsive.html`.

6. We're almost there – there is one change we need to make to this content. Find this line:

    ```
    <svg xmlns="http://www.w3.org/2000/svg" width="157" height="211">
    ```

    …and replace it with this:

    ```
    <svg version="1.1" viewBox="0 0 300 500" preserveAspectRatio="xMinYMin
    meet" class="content">
    ```

    …this adds a class which we make use of, sets the SVG to maintain an aspect ratio, and removes static size values.

You can see a finished version of the markup in the code download – it's stored as `responsive - finished version.html`.

---

7. Save the file – if we preview the results in a browser, we'll see something akin to the screenshot shown in Figure 4-8, when resized smaller.

Beginning SVG: Making Images Responsive

Figure 4-8. *Our responsive SVG image*

Go ahead and try resizing your browser window – what happens? Hopefully you will see that the image resizes automatically, without any loss of quality. The key here is that we've used the code we outlined in "Making SVG Content Responsive"; this proves that it is very easy to resize a basic SVG image. Granted, it might not work for some images, but it should be enough to cater for most standard SVG images.

Take a look at the CSS file used for this demo – you will see some of the code commented out. This is with good reason: you may find occasions when we don't need to specify **all** of the code we used earlier, and that you can get away with just the attributes that have not been commented out.

Okay – what's next, I wonder? We've touched on the basics of making images responsive, but there may be occasions when we find that simply adding max-width values isn't enough. This might be for images that become unreadable on small screens, or where it isn't necessary to display some content on particular devices. This is a perfect opportunity to use media queries, so let's dive in and take a look at how we can set these up to work with SVG images in more detail.

Using Media Queries with SVG Content

Creating content that responds to a particular device can be a real minefield – there are so many decisions to make! What do we display? Do we hide X, and show Y instead...?

With standard formats such as JPEG or PNG, it's simply a case of showing or hiding them, or perhaps resizing them to allow for the change in size of their location. But with SVG, this opens up some real possibilities – instead of changing the whole image, how about affecting *a part of it*? Yes, you heard me right – it's easy to do, and adds a degree of flexibility to what we can achieve. It's a perfect opportunity for a quick demo, so let's dive in and see how easy it is to remove elements from an SVG image.

APPLYING MEDIA QUERIES TO SVG IMAGES

Let's get cracking:

1. We'll start by extracting a copy of the media folder from the code download that accompanies this book – it contains our markup, semi-prepared for our demo.

2. Open up the file media.html, then look for this comment, on or around line 28:

    ```
    <!-- label and badge on sleeve -->
    ```

3. Go ahead and edit the next two path statements – we need to add in IDs, as highlighted, which we will reference within our media queries:

    ```
    <path fill="#EDF1F9" id="badge" d="M80 ... />
    ...
    <path fill="#014463" id="label" ... />
    ```

4. Save the file, then preview the results in a browser – if we resize the browser window to its smallest width, we will see the badge and label on the sleeve disappear, as shown on the left in Figure 4-9.

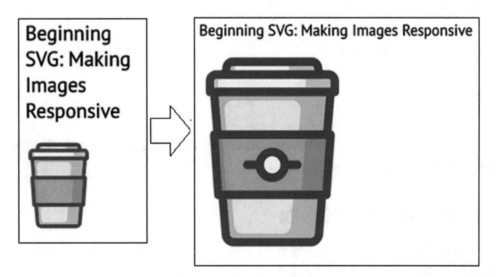

Figure 4-9. *Applying a media query*

See how easy that was? All we're doing is applying a technique that will be familiar to anyone who has developed responsive sites before; the trick (if anything) is where to apply the media query. As we've seen in our demo, the query must be inside the SVG; placing it outside might make better sense from an architectural perspective, but this is one of those occasions where we're obliged to keep the rules within the SVG!

There is indeed a benefit to this approach – as media queries have to be stored internally, they will only ever react to the viewport of the image, not of the browser; it means that we can control how images look, independently of how they will be used.

In this instance, we've added in a simple style sheet inline - notice that it is encapsulated in <defs> tags; these definition tags help identify entries that are then applied to the core part of our code:

```
<defs>
 <style>
  @media all and (max-width: 300px) {
   #sleeve { opacity: 0; }
   #badge { opacity: 0; }
  }
 </style>
</defs>
```

The code within these <defs> tags is just standard media query code, to hide the two elements identified earlier in our code.

Understanding the Pitfalls

Up until now, I've painted what might seem a rosy picture – in that all we need to do is add a little code, and that all will be well, right...?

Well, if truth be told, making SVG images responsive isn't always as easy as it might look – there are some pitfalls we should be aware of, when adding responsive capabilities to SVG graphics; some of these include the following:

- Specifying fixed values for dimensions will clearly prevent our SVG from scaling – removing them is a must, but we might have to use the padding-bottom hack to ensure images are correctly displayed (in a similar fashion to responsive videos).

- Testing is a must – most browsers will display SVG images correctly, but IE always likes to play the odd one in the pack, so to speak!

- Planning what changes to make and when is essential – there is a temptation to work on desktop first, when mobile devices should be given preference. This will depend on the use cases for your project, so don't assume desktop should always take priority!

- Sprites can be used, but this requires two separate files: SVG and CSS, so what we gain from using sprites in a responsive capacity, is cancelled out by using multiple external resources.

- There is a question around portability between different platforms when working responsively. Traditionally we may have simply hidden or displayed images based on the available screen width, but this is very limiting. Instead, we can easily manipulate individual elements of a SVG graphic, and this is a more efficient means.

- Although we can set our own presentation attributes within a SVG file, these can be overridden by style declarations from outside of our SVG, such as in external style sheets.

In many cases, it would seem that the 80:20 rule would apply, but in reverse – the easy (20%) part is to add the code, but the harder, "bigger picture" part is making sure our site works as we expect!

Let's change tack – we've almost reached the end of our journey through scaling SVG, but I want to leave you with some parting comments on one particular subject: Do we make our images responsive, or adaptive? Is there a right or wrong answer, or is it just a case of choosing one we prefer...?

Making SVG images Adaptive or Responsive?

Do I make my image responsive...? Adaptive...? What's the difference...?

Making images responsive can be a double-edged sword – while the code required can be very easy to implement, I'll bet there are still questions being asked as to how images should be made "responsive" in the first place, right?

In truth, there are lots of different options we could use – many date from some years ago, and have either fallen out of favor, or been superseded by techniques that are cleaner and simpler to implement. This isn't helped by some of the terms that we may hear – it can get very confusing!

To start with, you might have heard of the phrase "adaptive" – what does that mean, and how does it differ? Well, if you were referring to standard images, it's about caching various sizes of an image, then serving the most appropriate size based on the detected screen size in use. This method relies on server-side code, which isn't ideal – it's a dated approach, and there are definitely better alternatives available. But – some people may treat the adaptive approach as referring to the use of media queries, which is a perfectly valid approach: perhaps you can understand why it might seem confusing! This isn't helped by the fact that we can nest SVG images inside each other – not only is our main SVG now responsive, but the ones inside will also be too...

To really add to the mix, we can use a fluid approach – this is similar to responsive, but we instead calculate what proportion of screen estate an image should use. With the responsive approach, we will likely set a value such as `max-width: 100%;` with fluid, we will calculate the percentage to use, based on the width of an image as a percentage value of our document. Let's say we have a 400px wide image, in a document that is 950px wide. The calculation would be:

`(430 / 950px) x 100 = 45.26%` (rounded to 2 pixels)

If we use this approach, we may need to set a max-width value to be sure that our image remains visible at extremes, but our image will always remain in scale with the rest of our document.

There is no one single right or wrong answer to solving this conundrum – the easy answer is that it will depend on individual circumstances. The technology is such now that we should not need to rely on server-side solutions to display images; we can use markup such as `<picture>` and the `srcset` attribute to render the appropriate image for the desired screen width. This should remove the need for media queries for all browser except IE; for this browser, we can use a polyfill such as Scott Jehl's picturefill library, available at `http://scottjehl.github.io/picturefill/`.

As a good starting point though, we can specify percentage values in place of static sizes; this will cover most scenarios, although there may be occasions where a more complex solution is required. Part of what we do will depend on which browsers we support – it may be a case of using the `<picture>` element, which does support a form of media query; I personally think this approach is cleaner than using media queries, but that is just personal preference! Whichever route we decide to use, I think that old adage of "test, test and test again" is so apt – any method we use should be tested to ensure maximum compatibility for the browsers we choose to support when using our site.

Summary

Scaling SVG content is a useful skill to master, along with making it responsive – many of the tricks we can use work in a similar fashion to CSS, although there are some key differences: enough to keep us on our toes. We've covered a lot of useful content in this chapter, so let's take a moment to review what we've learned.

We kicked off with a quick introduction into scalability within the world of SVG, before moving onto exploring the SVG coordinate system, and how to apply it to SVG graphics. We then moved onto cover the Scaling Toolbox, before putting it to good use in a quick demo.

Next up came a brief journey through the steps needed to make SVG content responsive – we covered the basic principles of using CSS, before taking a look at how media queries can be used to manipulate more complex content. We then rounded out our journey through the world of scaling with a look at some of the pitfalls of making SVGs responsive, and covered some of the wider thoughts on how we might make our content responsive, or whether an adaptive approach might suit our needs.

Phew – onwards we go: there is never any rest for the wicked, I always say! Thankfully our next stop on this whistle-stop tour of SVG is one of my favorites: How many times have you played with filters in applications such as Photoshop? Well – that time may be coming to an end, as we can achieve a great deal within the browser, without the need for big heavyweights such as Photoshop – turn the page over if you want to learn more!

CHAPTER 5

Creating Filters

Introduction

Take a look at this Codepen by the front-end developer Sean Free at `https://codepen.io/seanfree/full/eBppyE/`. It paints an idyllic picture of a calm, barely shimmering lake, with snow-covered mountains rising in the background and forests in the distance. No signs of other people, no boats, no noise: sounds like the perfect advert for a travel brochure!

I'll bet that, at first glance, you'd think that this is some sort of animated GIF image, or even a little trickery with video, right? After all, how could we achieve this animated effect…?

Well, what if I said there isn't a single animated GIF or video being used? Yes, you heard me correctly – the only trickery we're using is *SVG filters*. This is a great example of what we can achieve when working with SVG: granted, this demo uses a little JavaScript and the GSAP library, but it is still nevertheless a wonderful example of the art of possible with SVG filters. We'll explore how to use GSAP later in Chapter 9, "Incorporating SVG Libraries," but for now let's wind things back and take a look at why we can benefit from using SVG filters.

The Benefits of Using SVG Filters

So – why would we want to use SVG filters, if many of the effects we might need, can be provided using standard CSS filters? This question is particularly valid, as most CSS filters are merely shortcuts derived from SVG – why go to all that extra effort?

Well, the answer is simple – control. Yes, using an SVG filter gives us far more control over how an image or SVG graphic will look, than with using standard CSS filters. Sure, applying a filter such as `sepia(50%)` will give an image a more vintage look and is more concise – but what if we don't like the shade of color used? If we were to expand the standard `sepia(X)` filter, it would equate to this:

```
<feColorMatrix type="matrix" values="X..."/>
```

125

© Alex Libby 2018
A. Libby, *Beginning SVG*, https://doi.org/10.1007/978-1-4842-3760-1_5

...where X... is the matrix of color channel values that represents how much of an effect we should apply. The great thing about using SVG filters is that we can manipulate our filter at a color channel level to obtain exactly the right effect we want for our project.

An added bonus is that support for using SVG filters has been excellent for some time now, with only one exception – yes, you guessed it: IE! SVG filters don't work in IE9 or below but are fully supported for (IE10 and) IE11, as indicated in Figure 5-1.

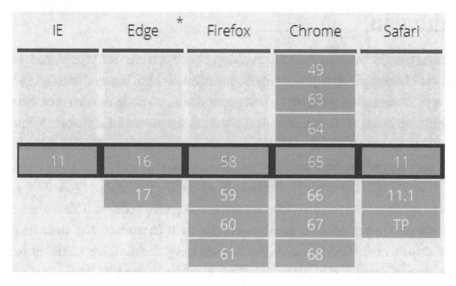

Figure 5-1. *Big Web support for SVG filters*

The same applies for the mobile platform – Figure 5-2 shows support is just as good.

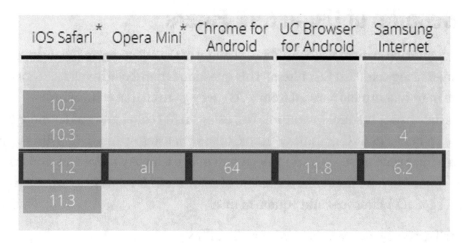

Figure 5-2. *Mobile support for SVG filters*

Okay – let's move on: assuming that we're using relatively modern browsers (at least IE10 or above, plus the rest of the usual suspects), what types of filters are there available that we can use? There are a whole host available – I suspect you may be familiar with some of them, such as blur() or sepia(), so without further ado, let's quickly cover off the full list, as a precursor to converting them to their SVG equivalent versions.

Exploring Existing Filters

In our introduction, we've briefly touched on some examples of current CSS filters that are available for us to use. Although the collection looks somewhat diverse, it's possible to divide them into two groups – the first covers those which adjust the colors used (such as brightness() and sepia()), while the others relate more to the physical appearance (such as drop-shadow() and opacity()). The full list of filters is summarized in Table 5-1:

Table 5-1. *List of Available Standard CSS Filters*

Name of filter	Purpose of filter
blur()	Applies a Gaussian blur to our image: the value we provide controls the amount of standard deviation to the Gaussian function, or how many pixels on the screen blend into each other. The larger the value, the more blur is created: if a parameter is not provided, then a value of zero is used.
brightness()	Applies a linear multiplier to the image, to change the brightness levels – values should be 0% (completely black), or a multiplier; if no value is specified, then it is assumed to be 100% by default.
contrast()	Adjusts the level of contrast on the specified image – values should be 100% (completely untouched), or a multiplier; if no value is specified, then it is assumed to be 100% by default.
drop-shadow()	This applies a drop-shadow effect to an image – this is a blurred, offset version of the image's alpha channel, which is drawn in the chosen color, offset to the parent image.
grayscale()	Converts a chosen image to its grayscale equivalent – the value can be from 0 to 100% or a number; 0% is completely unchanged, to 100% which applies a full grayscale effect.

(continued)

127

Table 5-1. (*continued*)

Name of filter	Purpose of filter
hue-rotate()	This applies a hue rotation on the chosen image – the value provided defines the number of degrees around the color circle. This value can be anything from 0° (untouched, or assumed if the value is missing), to a maximum of 360°.
invert()	Inverts the colors within the chosen image, by a given value – the amount specified defines the proportion of conversion. Values can be in the range of 0% to 100% and cannot be negative – if this is not specified, the default of 100% is assumed.
opacity()	Adjusts the level of transparency within the specified image – the value can be from 0 to 100% or a number; 0% is completely transparent, to 100% which leaves the image unchanged.
saturate()	This saturates the image – this can be 0% (where the image is completely unsaturated), to 100% (where the image is unchanged), or provided as a number. Values over 100% can be provided, which will super-saturate the image.
sepia()	Applies a sepia effect to a chosen image – the input value determines the amount of conversion: 0% leaves the image untouched, to 100% which applies a complete sepia effect.

The odd one out (and not in the list), is url() – this is not a filter as such, but is used to apply any of the other filters to an element within our style sheet.

If we use any of the filters listed in Table 5-1, then we can start to apply effects to our images; this will really start to come alive if we mix and match these effects. This becomes a little cumbersome though, if we're applying more than just a couple of filters at the same time - what can we do? Well, how about being able to mix and match filters at a more granular level, while at the same time applying custom values?

Introducing SVG Primitives for Filters

Over the last few pages, we've explored what filters are available, and the role they play in modifying an image - to really customize how these filters work, and provide those custom values, it's time to introduce filter **primitives**.

These primitives make up the building blocks of any filter we can use in our projects. Take, for example, the standard blur() filter: this makes use of the feGausianBlur primitive. Oh – and yes, before you ask: the fe in each name? It stands for "filter effect"; the full list of primitives is summarized in Table 5-2.

Table 5-2. *List of SVG Primitives*

Name of Primitive	Function – can be used to...
feBlend	Apply a blend mode, similar to CSS, to change how an image or text appears, such as making it lighter or darker.
feColorMatrix	Modify colors used in an image – think of this as changing the color channels using an application such as Photoshop, while retaining the original image.
feComponentTransfer	Alter a specific color channel (red, green, or blue), so an image may appear with a green hue, for example.
feComposite	Uses a set of mathematical algorithms to combine two sources based on their alpha channels at a pixel level, with the alpha channel controlling the shape.
feConvolveMatrix	Apply emboss or beveled type effects to text.
feDiffuseLighting / feSpecularLighting	Add special lighting effects to an image or shape, to give it a gloss or reflective effect.
feDisplacementMap	Move or displace pixels in an image – great for creating warp-effect filters.
feFlood	Completely fill the filter subregion using a specified color and alpha level, without having to create extra SVG elements – this is useful for compositing or merging filters.
feGaussianBlur	Blur an image.
feImage	Load an external image, for later use within other use within other filters (such as feBlend or feComposite).
feMerge	Create a new filter effect, based on applying two or more source filters together concurrently, such as the watercolor filter we create in "Applying a Watercolor Filter," later in this chapter.

(continued)

Table 5-2. (*continued*)

Name of Primitive	Function – can be used to…
feMorphology	Make the lines of a source image or text appear thinner or fatter (depending on settings).
feOffset	Create a drop-shadow effect.
feTile	Fill a target shape with a repeated, tiled pattern, using an image specified in the filter.
feTurbulence	Allows the creation of synthetic textures using the Perlin Noise turbulence function – it's perfect for creating artificial textures such as clouds or marble.

We have access to 15 filter primitives in total, which can be used to create anything from the humble drop-shadow effect, through to mimicking shimmering water on a lake – the latter with not a single video or animated GIF in sight!

They open up a world of possibilities, limited only by our imagination; to get us started, let's take a look at creating one using feGaussianBlur – the technical name for a filter I'm sure you will have used before, although you probably know it under a different name...

Manipulating Content with Filters

Anyone remember the days when we might have had to edit an image to add a blur effect?

Yes, feGaussianBlur is the basis for that well-known, but equally oft-overused effect, blur; long gone are the days where we have to edit images and can simply apply this effect directly in code. This is one of the simpler effects to apply as a filter primitive – we only need to pass in a single value, which represents the amount of blur effect to apply to our image. To see what I mean, let's run a simple demo to see the effects of blur a SVG shape using this filter primitive; we'll apply to this to a filled-in circle, as shown in the next exercise.

CREATING A BLUR EFFECT

Let's make a start on creating our filter:

1. We'll begin with setting up our basic markup – for this, go ahead and drop the following code into a new document, saving it as `simple.html` at the root of our project folder:

```
<!DOCTYPE html>
<head>
  <meta charset="utf-8">
  <title>Beginning SVG: Creating a Simple SVG Filter</title>
  <link rel="stylesheet" href="css/simple.css">
</head>
<body>
  <h2>Beginning SVG: Creating a Simple SVG Filter</h2>
</body>
</html>
```

2. Next, we need to add in our SVG – for this, add the following code, immediately before the closing `</body>` tag:

```
<svg width="230" height="120" >

 <circle cx="60"  cy="60" r="50" fill="darkgrey" />
 <circle cx="170" cy="60" r="50" fill="darkgrey" />
</svg>
```

3. Go ahead and save the file - if we preview the result at this point, we will see two circles – both gray in color, and with perfectly defined radiuses.

4. We're going to add a blur filter to the circle on the right – for this, we first need to define our filter. Leave a blank line before the first of our `<circle>` elements, then drop in this code:

```
<filter id="demoBlur">
  <feGaussianBlur in="SourceGraphic" stdDeviation="5"/>
</filter>
```

5. This isn't enough for the filter to take effect – for this, we need to amend the targeted element. Go ahead and amend the code in the second `<circle>` element, as indicated:

```
fill="darkgray" filter="url(#demoBlur)" />
```

6. Save the file, then preview the results in a browser – if all is well, we should see something akin to the screenshot in Figure 5-3.

Beginning SVG: Creating a Simple SVG Filter

Figure 5-3. *Creating a simple blur filter*

See how easy it was to apply that filter? SVG filters work in a similar manner to standard SVG elements – we still have to set up `<svg>` tags for our SVG shape, but this time, add in a `<filter>` tag for our effect. There are a couple of key points we should get accustomed to when working with filters, so let's review our code in more detail.

Dissecting Our Code

Although implementing our `feGaussianBlur` primitive as a filter is very straightforward, one might be forgiven for asking what the benefit of using it is, in comparison to using the standard blur() property.

It's a valid point – after all, it does seem like a good chunk of extra code, when we can use a single property! The reason though for using the primitive is the level of customization afforded to us: not just within our filter primitive, but within the SVG itself. Our example is probably a little too simplistic to show off what we can do, but when we get to later demos, you will begin to see something of the level of customization we can achieve when using filter primitives.

Bringing it back to our demo though – how does it work? We start by defining our standard SVG, which contains two circles that are created using the `<circle>` element. Both have been filled in a dark gray color; one has the extra filter applied. Our filter is defined using `<filter>` tags – we've given it the ID of `demoBlur`, and set it against `SourceGraphic` (our image). We've only specified a single value of 5 for the amount of blur to apply (controlled by `stdDeviation`), but we could have specified values for both the x and y axes. In this instance, the value is applied equally to both the x-axis and y-axis. The filter we've created is then applied inline using a standard CSS filter attribute: notice that we specify a value using the `url()` property, which is required for the filter to operate correctly.

Okay – let's change tack and take things up a notch: we've created a simple filter to blur content, but what if we had wanted to change color? For this, we need a different filter primitive; color changes are usually handled by altering values specified for `feColorMatrix`. This is a really versatile filter: at the heart of this is a matrix of numbers, which control the colors and strengths to use in our filter. We can omit or mix color channels to achieve the desired result – let's dive in and take a look in more detail.

Creating and Applying Filters

A question – how many times have you applied a filter in CSS, using something akin to this example?

```
.saturate-filter {
  filter: grayscale(50%);
}
```

Hopefully the answer is more than once – it's a great way to apply an effect without the need to edit the original image. Yet, there is one drawback with this approach: we can't change what "grayscale" means as a color! To work around this, we can make use of primitives in our filter – such an example would look like this, assuming we were using `grayscale()`:

```
<svg>
  <filter id="gray-on-light">
    <feColorMatrix type="matrix" values="1 0 0 0 0 1 0 0 0 0 1 0 0 0 0
    0 1 0 "/>
  </filter>
</svg>
```

This filter makes use of the `feColorMatrix` property – this versatile primitive is great for replicating a whole variety of existing filters, and creating new ones. To prove this, we'll work through how the grayscale example operates.

Notice that long string of numbers we used in that example? It might look like binary, but in reality is a color matrix that defines the value of each color channel. We can better explain it using the diagram shown in Figure 5-4.

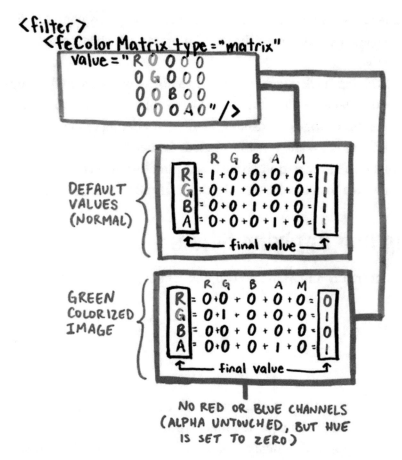

Figure 5-4. *The matrix explained – Source: AListApart.com*

So – what does it all mean? Each value can be anywhere from 0 to 1; zero turns off that color, whereas a value other than zero increases the level of a specified color. The fourth column represents the alpha value, which controls the level of transparency; set to 0 for completely transparent, or 1 to make a color fully opaque.

The fifth column, M, or matrix multiplier can be used to create a new color if we add it to the total of R, G, B, and A. However, in many cases it doesn't change, so it will be zero – for example, if we were to use the `feColorMatrix` equivalent for the standard CSS `sepia()` filter. We can safely ignore it for the purposes of this demo.

We can then add or multiply values together, to arrive at the final color in use. There is a little algebra involved to work out the specifics of our filter; before we dive into this in more detail, let's put together a simple demo to see what happens when we change a color in a filter.

Changing Color with Filters

As we've already seen from earlier in this chapter, we have a range of different filters we can use to apply effects – one of the most useful is feColorMatrix. This allows us to manipulate colors at a channel level; we can use this to achieve almost any change, from a simple color, through to changing light or darkness levels.

For our next exercise, we're going to keep things relatively simple – we'll use a basic image of a landscape, then apply a green tint to the whole image, using the feColorMatrix filter. It's a basic example but perfect for illustrating how we can manipulate each channel level to achieve the desired result.

USING FECOLORMATRIX

Let's make a start on creating that filter:

1. We'll start by setting up the markup for our demo – for this, go ahead and drop the following code into a new file, saving it as changecolor.html:

```
<!DOCTYPE html>
<head>
  <meta charset="utf-8">
  <title>Beginning SVG: Changing Colors with Filters</title>
  <link rel="stylesheet" href="css/changecolor.css">
</head>
<body>
  <h2>Beginning SVG: Changing Colors with Filters</h2>
</body>
</html>
```

2. Next up, let's add in our source image – for this, go ahead and add this code; this will use the SVG <image> element to store a picture wihtin it:

```
<svg width="1198" height="730">
  <image href="img/landscape.png" x="0" y="0"></image>
</svg>
```

3. If we preview the results now, we won't see any change to the image; to make this change, we now need to apply our filter – for this, go ahead and insert the following code after the opening `<svg>` tag:

```
<defs>
  <filter id="colorChange">
    <feColorMatrix type = "matrix" values="0 0 0 0 0 0 0.47 0 0 0 0
    0.15 0 0 0 0 0 1 0 "/>
  </filter>
</defs>
```

4. For our filter to work, we need to make one more change – go ahead and modify the code as indicated:

    y="0" **filter = "url(#colorChange)"**

5. Save the file – if we preview the results in a browser, we'll see the results shown in Figure 5-5.

Beginning SVG: Changing Colors with Filters

Figure 5-5. *The results of applying a feColorMatrix filter*

Ouch – I know that a landscape picture will have a certain amount of green in it, but even this image takes it a bit too far! This aside, it illustrates how we can manipulate colors, without altering the base image. It's an important technique to master, so let's dive in and take a look in more detail.

Understanding Our Code

A quick look at our image should confirm that we've used far too much green – it's clear to see that choosing colors must be done with care!

This aside, we've used similar principles in this demo, compared to the previous exercise; we specify our standard <svg> tags, into which we've defined our filter. We have a couple of differences though: the first is the introduction of the <defs> tag – this is to define a section where we set up properties (in this case, our new filter), ready for use.

The second comes in the form of our primitive – we've specified use of a feColorMatrix primitive, along with a string of numbers that form our color matrix. For space reasons, it's displayed as one long string in our code; we could easily display it as a grid of 4 by 5 (as shown back in Figure 5-4). We then finish it by applying our filter inline, to the image specified in the <image> element, where we specify the filter attribute inline, using url() to specify our inline filter.

Our demo added a green tint to the entire image; this does raise a question though: How do we specify which color to use? Or a more pertinent question might be: How do we turn that color into our filter? It's a good question: we could work it out manually, or a more sensible option might be to use the tool that forms part of our next exercise.

Calculating Colors to Use

When working with SVG filters, we have a few of options open to us – we can either change individual values using a certain amount of guesswork, use something created by others as a starting point, perform a few calculations, or use a generator.

I don't know about you, but I think the last option is likely to be the most popular! Entering a number and having it produce our matrix automatically is a real timesaver – we can then copy the code straight into our development (although it may need a little tidying up, as it is a little out of date!).

However, there is something to be said for working through the calculations needed – they are not as difficult as we might think. In each instance, we work on the premise that a color's channel value will be somewhere between 0 and 1. We take each RGB channel value in turn, then simply divide it by 255 to arrive at our feColorMatrix value.

The number will need to be rounded down to 2–3 decimal places; there is no benefit in having anything longer. To prove this works, let's put it to the test in a quick demo, and compare it against a RGBA to feColorMatrix application that is available online.

CONVERTING RGBA TO FECOLORMATRIX

Okay – let's make a start:

1. Pick a color – it doesn't matter which, but we need the RGBA value for it; for this, you can browse to a site such as ColorHexa (https://www.colorhexa.com). For my example, I will assume we're using rgba(103, 117, 138, 1) – this equates to a shade of largely desaturated dark blue.

2. Next, fire up a calculator – for the first value, divide 103 by 255 – the value you get back will 0.4039, which we round down to 0.40. Repeat step 3 for the other two values – you should get 0.46 and 0.54 respectively, rounded down to 2 decimal places.

3. Now try entering the original RGBA values into RGBA to feColorMatrix generator, created by Andres Galante, at http://andresgalante.com/RGBAtoFeColorMatrix/. You should see the result as indicated in Figure 5-6.

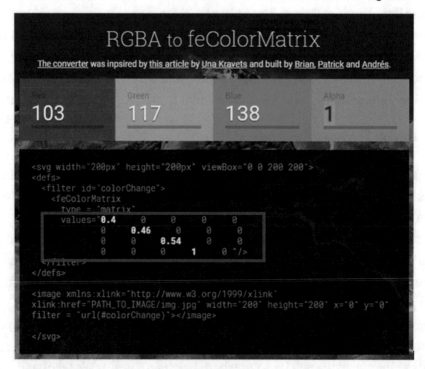

Figure 5-6. *Converting a color to feColorMatrix*

Notice anything? The values we generated in step 3 (and 4) are an identical match for the ones shown in the RGBA to feColorMatrix generator. Granted, there may be some instances where this approach won't work, but performing these calculations should result in a matrix that is somewhere in the region of where we want to be in our code. Of course we can always test the RGBA value in the generator to see how close we are, but then again – this would come as part of standard testing, right?

Okay – let's move on: it's time for a little fun! I'm sure you will have heard of Facebook's Instagram; in this day and age, it's hard not to see a site making reference to it in some form.

One of its unique selling points is the ability to apply a filter effect on any image we upload – a quick scout on the web will show dozens of examples where others have tried to replicate similar effects. This is a perfect opportunity to create something using SVG filters, so without further ado, let's dive in and take a look at this in more detail.

Re-creating filters à la Instagram

Instagram – it's hard to believe that a site now worth $1.5 billion dollars, came about through the simple principle of sharing and enhancing photos, and that its name makes reference to a technology invented back in 1832!

Anyone who has used Instagram will be familiar with some of the filters available for use – these include such exotic names as Mayfair, Sierra, or Ludwig. Even though each filter may sound exotic, they all serve a simple purpose: to adjust the color or appearance of a chosen image. To achieve this, we can apply filters; SVG filters lend themselves perfectly to this function!

To see what I mean, we're going to create our own version of one of the Instagram filters – the Amaro filter. I should point out that this won't be a direct copy of the original; it will be a close approximation. It will be enough to illustrate how we can apply a series of filters to achieve the final effect – we can of course use the shortcut names such as `contrast()`, but then we'd miss out on the fun of tweaking each filter to be...just perfect!

Anyway – let's dive in and take a look at what is involved in creating an Instagram-style filter:

CREATING INSTAGRAM EFFECT FILTERS

Let's make a start on creating our filter:

1. We'll begin by downloading a copy of the changecolor folder – rename it as instagram, and save it at the root of our project folder.

2. Within the folder, rename the CSS style sheet as instagram.css and the markup file as instagram.html.

3. Go ahead and open up instagram.html – look for the opening <defs> tag, then replace the code as shown:

```
<defs>
  <filter id="amaro">

    <!--- contrast -->
    <feComponentTransfer color-interpolation-filters="sRGB">
      <feFuncR type="linear" slope="0.9" intercept="0.049" />
      <feFuncG type="linear" slope="0.9" intercept="0.049" />
      <feFuncB type="linear" slope="0.9" intercept="0.049" />
    </feComponentTransfer>

    <!--- brightness -->
    <feComponentTransfer color-interpolation-filters="sRGB">
      <feFuncR type="linear" slope="1.1" />
      <feFuncG type="linear" slope="1.1" />
      <feFuncB type="linear" slope="1.1" />
    </feComponentTransfer>

    <!--- saturate -->
    <feColorMatrix type="matrix" color-interpolation-filters="sRGB"
values="1.394 -0.358 -0.036 0 0 -0.107 1.1575 -0.036 0 0 -0.107 -0.357
1.464 0 0 0 0 0 1 0" />
  </filter>
</defs>
```

4. Next, we need to apply our new filter to the image – for this, go ahead and amend the filter name, as shown:

```
filter = "url(#amaro)"></image>
```

5. As a final touch, we should change the title of our image – for this, change the text between the <h2> tags, as indicated:

    ```
    <h2>Beginning SVG: Applying Filters à la Instagram</h2>
    ```

6. Save the file and preview the results in a browser – if all is well, we should see the same landscape image from the *feColorMatrix* exercise, but this time with added light, as shown in Figure 5-7.

Beginning SVG: Applying Filters à la Instagram

Figure 5-7. *Applying filters à la Instagram*

Adding a filter such as Amaro opens up a wealth of opportunities – limited only by our imagination! If we were to compare the image from Figure 5-7, one might be forgiven for thinking this shot was taken in the summer, whereas in reality it was taken in early autumn!

That aside, this demo has illustrated a useful technique we should master when working with SVG filters – how to apply multiple filters as one filter. There is an important distinction to make though, which applies to *how* the filters are applied; to understand more, let's take a look at the code in more detail.

Understanding How It Works

Anyone who is a fan of using Instagram will be familiar with applying one of the many filters available within the application.

In reality, these filters are made up of composite elements – in the case of Amaro, we're using `contrast`, `brightness`, and `saturate` filters to create our final effect. The first two use the `<feComponentTransfer>` filter primitive – this one handles the remapping of data for each pixel, and is designed for instances where we have to adjust light or contrast levels. This uses a linear equation to modify the color of each pixel in our image: the rate of change is controlled by the `slope` and / or `intercept` values provided in our code.

In comparison, the saturate filter is applied using the `feColorMatrix` primitive – this takes a series of numbers in the form of a color matrix. Our code shows it as a single line of numbers, but it is better written as a grid of five by four numbers, as we saw back in Figure 5-4.

The key to making this demo work is *how* these filters are applied – in our example, the filters are applied sequentially instead of concurrently. In a sense, this means we're making three changes to our image, before we see the final result – it works well but isn't the most effective means!

To make it more effective, we can apply the filters concurrently – for this, we can make use of the `<feMerge>` attribute to store the results of each primitive, before applying it as one entity to our image. This requires a simple change to our code – let's dive in and take a look in more detail.

Blending and Merging SVG Filters

When creating filters, we can always start with a single primitive – this serves a purpose, but will soon become somewhat limiting! In the words of that famous Charles Dickens book, "I want more..."

And more we shall have – to achieve this, we need to venture into the world of blending and merging filters. This might at first seem complicated, but in reality it isn't as difficult as it looks – there are some key principles we should follow:

- When defining filters, it is sensible to create a `<defs>` section at the start, as a place to store definitions for each filter; this will allow you to reuse them anywhere in that project.

- Always specify a results attribute – this will store the results of applying the effect to your image or SVG graphic; we make use of this when merging the filters as the last step in our SVG.

- The last step should always be the `<feMerge>` block – we use this to combine the filters into the final solution. The order of each `<feMergeNode>` is not critical, but the in reference must tie back to the result name of defined primitive.

The great thing about merging and blending is that we've already covered most of the principles involved; we create a `<defs>` area to store our filter primitives, specify one or more said filter primitives, and tie them together with a `<feMerge>` block.

Taking It Further in Watercolors

Our next demo takes creating SVG filters in a different direction – for this, we're borrowing one of several effects created by the developer Bennett Feely, namely Watercolor. You can see the original at `http://bennettfeely.com/image-effects/#watercolor`; for our demo, we will translate the existing shortcut values into SVG filter primitive equivalents. This gives us the perfect base for tweaking the overall effect at a more granular level.

Bennett's original filter effect combines three shortcut filters – `brightness(1.3)`, `blur(2px)`, and `contrast(2)` – we can use this as a basis, but once the filter is in place, we can then tweak it to suit our needs.

APPLYING A WATERCOLOR EFFECT

Let's take a look at what's involved:

1. We'll begin by downloading a copy of the `watercolor` folder from the code download that accompanies this book – this contains the necessary CSS styles, image, and font used to style the demo. Store this folder at the root of our project area.

2. Next, go ahead and open `watercolor.html` – it doesn't contain a lot, but we will soon fix this! Start by adding these lines, immediately after the `<h2>` tags, to define our SVG element.

```
<svg width="0" height="0" xmlns="http://www.w3.org/2000/svg">
  <defs>
    <filter id="watercolor" width="200%" height="150%" x="0" y="0">
    </filter>
  </defs>
</svg>
```

3. Within the <filter> tags, we can now add our primitive declarations – we'll begin with the equivalent for brightness(1.3):

```
<feComponentTransfer result="bright">
  <feFuncR type="linear" slope="1.3"/>
  <feFuncG type="linear" slope="1.3"/>
  <feFuncB type="linear" slope="1.3"/>
</feComponentTransfer>
```

4. We have two more primitive declarations to add – go ahead and leave a blank line, then add this one in as our replacement for blur(2):

```
<feGaussianBlur stdDeviation="2"  edgeMode="none" result="blur"/>
```

5. The last one to add in is our replacement for contrast(2); for this drop in the following code, leaving a blank line after our blur primitive declaration first:

```
<feComponentTransfer result="contrast">
  <feFuncR type="linear" slope="2" intercept="-0.5"/>
  <feFuncG type="linear" slope="2" intercept="-0.5"/>
  <feFuncB type="linear" slope="2" intercept="-0.5"/>
</feComponentTransfer>
```

6. Last but by no means least – we need to merge it all together! For this, go ahead and leave a line, then add in the following <feMerge> block:

```
<feMerge>
  <feMergeNode in="bright"/>
  <feMergeNode in="blur" />
  <feMergeNode in="contrast" />
</feMerge>
```

7. With our filter declaration in place, we can now add in our image – for this, add the following code immediately after the closing </svg> tag:

```
<div class="preview watercolor-effect">
  <img src="img/orchids.jpg" alt="Image of orchids">
</div>
```

8. Save the file – if we preview the results, we should see an abstract watercolor style image of an orchid, as shown in Figure 5-8.

Beginning SVG: Applying a Watercolor Filter

Figure 5-8. *Our finished watercolor effect*

It's certainly an interesting effect, isn't it? Although some may say it bears no resemblance to a true watercolor effect, it doesn't matter – it's a perfect example of what we can achieve with relatively little difficulty when merging multiple filters together.

Creating Our Filter – an Epilogue

At this point, I would strongly recommend having a good read through the style sheet for this demo – we've not touched on it in detail in our demo (for reasons of space), but there are nevertheless two interesting concepts of note:

- Bennett has made good use of both `:before` and `:after` pseudo-selectors for this demo – it goes to show that we don't have to just rely on filters to achieve our effect! The image is overlaid several times using these selectors but are slightly displaced – this is needed to set the base for our watercolor effect.

- We've made use of `<feMerge>` within our SVG filter to create our filter effect, but we equally need to make use of background-blend-mode, `background-position`, and `mix-blend-mode` to create the final effect – simply creating and applying our filter isn't always sufficient to achieve the final result.

You will also notice that the demo isn't actually 100% complete – inasmuch as the `.watercolor` effect still uses three shortcut filter names! This is deliberate: it's a useful exercise to learn how to convert these filter shortcuts to SVG equivalents. It takes a little trial and error, but two useful tips are the following:

- If you search online, you will see a number of sites where the owners have created their own interpretation of well-known (or less well-known) filters such as Amaro. This is perfect for working out what the basic filter primitives of each filter should be, and which can act as a starting point for your own design.

- Have a look at `https://www.w3.org/TR/filter-effects-1/#ShorthandEquivalents` initially; it makes for some dry reading, but gives all of the SVG filter equivalents for the shorthand properties such as `blur()` or `grayscale()`.

- If we use the `brightness()` filter that we used in our example but wanted to change the level, then we simply replace the `[amount]` value with the original value from the shorthand version. For example, if we wanted a slightly darker version, we might have specified `brightness(0.9)`. Instead, we would translate this as indicated in the example below, where two out of the three `<feFunc..>` elements have been updated:

```
<filter id="brightness">
  <feComponentTransfer>
      <feFuncR type="linear" slope="0.9"/>
      <feFuncG type="linear" slope="0.9"/>
      <feFuncB type="linear" slope="[amount]"/>
  </feComponentTransfer>
</filter>
```

Have a go at making the change – the key to this is to not try to get an exact match, but use it as a basis for creating your own filter designs. Remember: there is no right or wrong answer – it's all down to what you want to see as your final solution!

Okay – let's move on: Many of our examples provide good visual interest, but they are somewhat...well...static? Fortunately it's easy to fix: we can use CSS animation to add a transition effect, right? Well, yes – and perhaps not...before you ask, I've not lost the plot; there is a real sting in this tale. Before we find out what, let's quickly knock up a demo that applies such a transition effect, so we can understand why this method isn't the most effective one to use.

Animating Filter Effects

Animating any form of content can be a double-edged sword – add with care, and it can really take a site to the next level; add it without some forethought, and people are likely to vote with their feet! Unfortunately, it's no different where SVG filters are concerned – for some, the temptation might be to use JavaScript in some form, while others may use CSS.

There are a whole host of options open to us to animate SVG content – we'll explore this in more depth in Chapter 6, "Animating Content." To give you a flavor of what is possible, we're going to knock up a quick demo that transitions a picture of an orchid from gray to its more usual color of pink.

ANIMATING FILTERS

Let's take a look at what is involved:

1. We'll start by extracting a copy of the `animate` folder from the code download that accompanies this book – go ahead and store it at the root of our project folder.

2. Next, open up `animate.html`, and add the following lines of code immediately after the `<h2>` tags – we'll start with defining our filter:

```
<svg>
  <filter id='grayscale'>
    <feColorMatrix type='matrix' values='0.3333 0.3333 0.3333 0 0
      0.3333 0.3333 0.3333 0 0 0.3333 0.3333 0.3333 0 0 0 0 0 1 0' />
  </filter>
</svg>
```

3. We now need to apply it to our image – leave a line blank, then go ahead and add the following code:

```
<div class="polaroid">
  <img class="grey" src="img/orchid.jpg" title="orchid" />
  <img class="color" src="img/orchid.jpg" title="orchid" />
  <span class="name">Phalaenopsis orchid</span>
</div>
```

4. Save the file – if we preview the results, then hover over the image, we will see it transition from gray to pink. Figure 5-9 shows this in action.

Figure 5-9. *Animating an SVG*

It's a great effect, right? We're not using any JavaScript, so the code is kept nice and light; our image fades from a gray to pink, which is perfect for browsing in a gallery. However, there is a sting in this tail – not everything is as rosy as it seems...

Is This the Right Solution?

We've just produced a great little simple demo of a close-up image of a Phalaenopsis (or "moth") orchid – as anyone who has read my books will know, I love orchids! At face value, everything looks perfectly acceptable. Take a closer look at the code though – you will see not one but **two** images in our code. This clearly isn't good, so what gives?

Well, the real issue lies in the fact that we can't animate an SVG filter using CSS animation directly on an SVG filter (this doesn't apply to CSS shorthand filters). It's a real pain, as it means we would be limited to using JavaScript-based methods to animate, or we can implement a workaround by adding a copy of the image. We can then set one to have the grayscale filter applied by default, with the other remaining as-is, and transition between the two using a standard CSS transition, as indicated in Figure 5-10.

```
18    img.grey {
19       filter: url(#grayscale);
20       transition: filter 2s;
21    }
22
23    img.color {
24       opacity: 0;
25       transition: opacity 2s;
26    }
27
28    img.color:hover {
29       opacity: 1;
30       transition: opacity 2s;
31    }
```

Figure 5-10. *Exploring our animation code*

Clearly not an ideal solution – it works, but is not the most efficient! Fortunately there is a better way to animate SVG; one option is to make use of the `<animate>` tag, or one of the several SVG animation libraries available on the Internet.

We will revisit this, and more around animation, in more detail in Chapter 6, "Animating Content."

For now, let's park this concept, and turn our attention to something more practical – SVG filters can produce some really creative effects, but there are occasions where we might have to think in more practical terms.

Fortunately this isn't an issue with SVG filters: What better than to use blur() as an example? We can use this to great effect as a background to a banner – to learn more, let's dive in to our next example to see what is involved in creating our filter effect.

Creating a Practical Example

So far, we've learned about applying filters in a variety of different instances – from changing a single color, through to mixing multiple primitives to create some interesting effects. There is one more effect we should take a look at – in this instance, it includes using another...*image*?

Yes, you hear correctly – we're going to apply an image! We'll use an image mask to help create a blur effect as part of a hero banner. This effect is perfect for creating original banners for use on websites or even content management systems such as WordPress. We'll use an image of a vintage camera (available from Flickr at https://flic.kr/p/pQ1wbF) as a basis for this exercise – let's dive in and take a look at what is involved.

APPLYING SVG FILTERS IN A PRACTICAL CONTEXT

Let's make a start:

1. First, go ahead and download a copy of the practical folder from the code download that accompanies this book – save it in our project folder.

2. Next, open up practical.html in a text editor – go ahead and add the following lines; they will form the basis of our SVG filter:

```
<svg xmlns="http://www.w3.org/2000/svg">
    <defs>
        <filter id="blurlayer" width="110%" height="100%">

        </filter>
    </defs>
</svg>
```

3. For this filter, we're not going to just use the equivalent of the standard
    blur() – we're going to mix in four primitives. The first makes use of
    feColorMatrix – add these lines immediately after the opening <filter
    id="blurlayer"...> statement:

```
<feColorMatrix type="matrix" values=".7 0 0 0 0 0 .7
0 0 0 0 0 .7 0 0 0 0 1 0" />
```

4. The next primitive is the SVG equivalent of blur() – for this, add the following
    code straight after the <feColorMatrix> statement (around line 13):

```
<feGaussianBlur stdDeviation="4" result="blur"/>
```

5. We need to make use of a mask, so that the blur effect is limited to the
    central band in our image – for now open up the mask.txt file from the
    code download, then copy the contents and paste in immediately after the
    <feGaussian> blur code line.

6. The last primitive we need to add in is <feComposite> - for this, go ahead
    and add the following line of code immediately after the mask from step 5.

```
<feComposite in2="mask" in="blur"  operator="in" result="banner" />
```

7. We now need to merge the filters together: it's time to revisit using
    <feMerge>! To achieve the right effect, go ahead and add in this code block
    before the closing </filter> tag:

```
<feMerge result="merge">
  <feMergeNode in="SourceGraphic" />
  <feMergeNode in="banner" />
</feMerge>
```

8. Last, but by no means least, we need to add in our banner – for this, go ahead
    and add the following code after the closing </svg> tag, on or around line 27:

```
<section class="banner">
  <img src="img/camera.png"/>

  <div class="sitetitle">
    <h1 class="">Classic Cameras</h1>
      <p class="byline">Timeless pieces from yesteryear</p>
  </div>
</section>
```

9. Save the file – if we preview the results, we will see a picture of an old camera, upon which is our "Classic Cameras" title on a suitably blurred background strip, as shown in Figure 5-11.

Beginning SVG: A Practical Use of SVG Filters

Figure 5-11.   *Applying filters*

A finished version of this code is available in the code download, as `practical -finished example.html`.

The combination of a classic camera, the soft black-and-white tones and blurred title has a real vintage appeal and is just one way of making use of SVG filters in a more practical context. This aside, this demo highlights some useful tips about merging filter primitives, so let's pause for a moment to examine them in more detail.

Understanding What Is Happening

Throughout the course of this chapter, we've applied filters to a variety of different uses, from adjusting a single color, through to what can only be described as a unique watercolor effect! Our latest demo applies filters in a more practical use case, to create a striking blur layer within a hero banner.

If we take a look at the code in more detail, we have a standard SVG tag defined, inside of which is a definition block for our filter. Our first primitive, `feColorMatrix`, is used to darken the blur effect slightly; without it, the banner won't have quite the same impact! The second primitive is self-explanatory – this one provides the blur effect; it is the equivalent of applying `blur(4)` in a rule within a style sheet.

The effect that starts to bring it all together is the mask – this is applied as a data URI. We've already talked about using data URIs (see back in Chapter 3, "Working with Images and Text") – you will notice that we have used a base-64 URI in this instance. Where possible, the recommendation is **not** to use them; in this instance, as we are only using a single black mask, and not a complicated image, then we can get away with using it.

The last two primitives, `<feComposite>` and `<feMerge>` have the effect of merging our content together – the former takes the black mask and blur and creates a composite image of both (similar to the flatten process when working with applications such as Adobe Photoshop). The feMerge process then merges everything together to produce the final result.

The mask image used in this demo was created with the online Method Draw application, available at `http://editor.method.ac/` – gone are the days when we have to download and install applications; Method Draw is perfect for creating all kinds of graphics with ease!

Summary

One of the key strengths of working with SVG as a format is the ability to customize images and graphics, without having to resort to image editors – working with filters is no exception! We've covered a lot of ideas around how we can change the appearance of any image using SVG filters, so let's take a few moments to review what we've learned in this chapter.

We kicked off with an introduction into the benefits of using SVG filters, before reviewing what is currently available as CSS shorthand filters, and introducing the primitives that make up SVG filters.

Next up came some examples of how we can apply filters – we started with the SVG equivalent of the classic blur option as an example, before moving on to learn how to change the color hue of an image. We then took a look at creating our own variations of classic Instagram filters, as a way of mixing and matching multiple filter primitives, before exploring how to merge and blend such filters together into one final version.

We then rounded out the chapter with a look at a practical use-case example of creating filters, in the form of a blur effect in a hero banner; this illustrates how filters can be used in all manners of different instances, and that we are only limited by the extent of our imagination!

Okay – it's time to move on. We briefly touched on one subject in this chapter: animation. The need to provide some form of animated content on any website (no matter how small or large an effect), is quickly becoming a must, if we want to give our projects an edge over other solutions. It's time therefore to get a little animated (oops – sorry!), and explore how we can start moving SVG content in the next chapter...

CHAPTER 6

Animating Content

I don't know about you, but I'm partial to a nice glass of wine – a nice rounded glass of red goes down a treat, after a long day of developing code. It's a good excuse to kick back, relax, and dream of making lots of money – or at least I hope so! But I digress. At this point, I suspect you're wondering what wine might have to animating content (and in particular, SVG graphics), but bear with me on this – let me reveal all.

Take a look at `https://fournier-pere-fils.com` – it's a website for a wine producer, based in the Sancerre region of France. The site may take a few minutes to complete loading, but it is worth the wait! When it has loaded, it shows some great effects: just imagine – sun shimmering through the leaves of the tree, early dawn mist, and not a soul in sight. In fact, the only things we can see are two birds flying – and there lies the source of my inspiration for my next demo...

Animating with CSS

A closer look at the code behind the website for Fournier Père et Fils shows that the birds are part of a 10-second video clip. Although I'm never quite sure about the virtues of using video as a background, this site pulls off the effect very well: it's kept deliberately short, so loading times are not excessive.

But – what if we could use SVG to animate part of that image, such as the birds? Well, one kind soul has already tried this out for us; take a look at `https://codepen.io/matchboxhero/pen/RLebOY`. This design by Steven Roberts, a developer based in the United Kingdom, shows it is possible – he's used a suitably sourced background image, and animates the birds over the top, using standard CSS animation.

© Alex Libby 2018
A. Libby, *Beginning SVG*, https://doi.org/10.1007/978-1-4842-3760-1_6

I've created my own version of his example, using a different image (taken from https://unsplash.com/photos/lVDnLUACI18) – the CSS has been cleaned up and simplified (two birds, instead of his four), but otherwise shows a great effect that we can use in future projects. Let's take a look at it in more detail:

ANIMATING WITH CSS

For this next exercise, we'll break with tradition and perform a review of the code – for this, go ahead and extract a copy of the `animatecss` folder from the code download that accompanies this book. Save the folder to our project area; let's take a look at that code in more detail:

1. The markup in `animatecss.html` is a simple affair: we have a `<div>` that acts as our container, inside which we have two individual bird containers `<div>`s. Inside each bird-container `<div>`, we have an individual bird `<div>` – these are for the birds; this arrangement allows us to animate them across the screen and move their wings as they are flying.

2. Next, let's take a look at the style sheet – we have a whole bunch of style classes, but the ones of interest to us are the ones beginning with `bird-*` or `bc-*`, along with the three `fly-*` keyframe animations.

3. We place our bird onto the background – if you take a look at the SVG, you will see that we have 10 frames within it. Once we've worked out what size we want our frame to be, we use this to calculate the position of the next frame in our demo.

4. The animations are managed in two different places – we control the flapping wings with the `fly-cycle` keyframe animation; we use the `animation-timing-function` to step through each frame, much like flicking through the pages of a notebook.

5. On its own the fly-cycle animation isn't enough – to move the birds across the screen, we implement the `fly-right-one` and `fly-right-two` keyframe animations. The timings and delays are such that it gives the effect of the birds meandering across the screen, as shown in Figure 6-1.

Beginning SVG: Animating Birds

Figure 6-1. *Our finished version of flying birds demo*

Although our demo appears to require a fair amount of code, much of it follows standard CSS animation principles – if you've spent any time animating content with CSS, then many of these principles should not be totally unfamiliar – we've applied two animations using named keyframes and set appropriate duration, delay, and timing counts.

Looking at the bigger picture though, CSS animation has indeed improved immensely over the last few years; it is fast reaching a stage where it will start to really challenge JavaScript for animation. That said, it still has some weaknesses – for example, it can't animate attributes such as `<span>`; this requires JavaScript. This clearly will have an impact on how we animate content, so with this in mind, let's take a look to see what this means in practice.

Understanding the Different Methods

Where possible, I always prefer to work with CSS when animating content – there are some clear benefits to using this approach, particularly when working with SVG:

- If you like the syntax of CSS, and most of your design work uses it, then it makes sense to use it for animation;

- Your project uses inline SVG, and you only need it to animate basic properties, such as fills or strokes;

- You want to make use of browser optimizations when working with CSS animation.

Sometimes though we might have to resort to using a JavaScript-based solution – this is particularly true if our project is fairly complex, we need to use more heavyweight tools, and we don't want to have to worry about matching timings for multiple elements.

If we must resort to using JavaScript, then what does this mean for us? Well, we have a few routes we can take (although it's likely we may use a mix of all three in reality):

- `<animate>` - SVG has its own built-in animate tag; this means we can keep our animation within the SVG and do not have to rely on third-party libraries to manage animation;

- Plain JavaScript – most properties can be referenced using standard JavaScript syntax;

- jQuery or third-party library – this route opens up a host of opportunities for us, such as using the likes of jQuery or the popular Snap.svg library. This places an additional overhead in terms of importing the library but will often remove some of the manual grunt required in creating the animation.

So – we have a few options available to us; which should we use? Clearly this will depend on the nature of our requirements (I feel "how long is a piece of string?" or "what are you trying to achieve?" questions coming at this point!). To get a flavor of what is available, we'll run through using examples of each route throughout the course of this chapter – we'll begin with a look at transforming content using the CSS `transform` method.

Transforming SVG Elements Using CSS

Cast your mind back to Chapter 4 – remember the `preserveAspectRatio` demo we built, which featured an image of an apple? I only ask, as it's going for an en-core (oops, sorry!) in our next demo.

If we were to keep to a pure SVG solution, then we would look to use a tag such as <animateTransform>; this will work perfectly well, but it is overkill for our needs. Instead, we can simply make use of the standard CSS transform attribute – this is just as good, and would look something like this within code:

```
.406-87.378z" transform="translate(-181.4 -224.71)"/><path
```

This is a perfect example of a transformation within SVG – this is one of four options available for use. Each of them works in a similar fashion to CSS but use different arguments, which must be separated by whitespace or a comma. We can see all four summarized in Table 6-1.

Table 6-1. *Transformation Options for SVG*

Type of transform	Purpose of function
translate(<tx> [<ty>])	Move a shape to a specified set of coordinates – the tx value is along the x-axis; the (optional) ty value is for the y-axis.
rotate(<rotate-angle> [<cx> <cy>])	Rotate a shape x degrees, around point 0,0, or the cx and cy values (if they have been specified).
scale(<sx>, [<sy>])	Scale a shape up or down in size – the values specified represent the scaling values along the x- or y-axes respectively.
skewX(<skew-angle>) skewY(<skew-angle>)	Skew an image on either the x- or y-axes, as appropriate.
matrix(a,b,c,d,dx,dy)	Define a custom transform using mathematical functions such as cos() or sin() – preference is to use transforms already listed in this table, if they can achieve the desired result.

For a detailed explanation of the math behind how transforms work, it's worth having a look at the article on CSS-Tricks.com, by Ana Tudor, at https://css-tricks.com/transforms-on-svg-elements/.

We are by no means limited to just applying a single effect though – we can chain multiple transforms to achieve more complex results. All we need to do is simply leave a space between each effect; each will be executed in turn, so it's important to get the order right!

To see what this means in practice, let's pause for a moment and work through a little demo. For this, we'll reuse that apple from Chapter 4, as a basis for combining a couple of transforms to rotate and move it on screen.

TRANSFORMING CONTENT

Let's make a start:

1. Go ahead and extract a copy of the `transform` folder – save it (and the files within) to the root of our project area.

2. Next, open a copy of `transform.html` in your text editor, then look for this code, on or around line 10:

    ```
    preserveAspectRatio="xMidYMid meet">
    ```

3. We're going to add a transform to the main SVG element – in our example, we'll rotate it by 15 degrees. Add the highlighted code to our markup, then save the file:

    ```
    <svg width="200" height="200" xmlns="http://www.w3.org/2000/
    svg" viewBox="0 0 300 550" preserveAspectRatio="xMidYMid meet"
    transform="rotate(15)  translate(20, 30)">
    ```

4. Go ahead and preview the results – if all is well, we should see something akin to the screenshot shown in Figure 6-2.

Beginning SVG: Transforming Images

Figure 6-2. *Transforming our apple SVG image*

This was admittedly a simple change to make, but we're only scratching the surface of what is possible – why not try using one of the other transformation commands to see what happens or chaining multiple ones together? Try skewX(30) for example, – the result will put a whole new slant on things, so to speak!

As an aside – If we had to keep to a pure SVG solution, then take a look at transform-alternative.html in the code download; this is our apple demo reworked to use SVG for the main rotation effect. Note though, that you may see differences in behavior (such as here); it's worth bearing this in mind when developing your solution.

Okay – let's move on: if our demo had been more complex, then a CSS transform statement might not have been sufficient; instead, we need something that would cope with more complex animations. Fortunately, SVG has several options available, such as <animate>, <animateMotion>, and <animateTransform>. I feel it's time for another demo (and yes, sorry, pun intended) – let's dive in and take a look at this in more detail.

Moving Content with <animate>

In the previous demo, we touched on the use of transform to manipulate the position of our apple – for a simple demo, this CSS attribute works very well. However, what if our demo had been more complex, and that a simple CSS attribute would not be sufficiently powerful to handle the animation...?

Well, don't worry – SVG can be animated using animation elements; these were defined originally in the SMIL Animation specification, but to which SVG has added some extensions that are compatible with the original specification.

Put simply, there are three SVG elements we can use when animating content: <animate>, <animateMotion> (for animating content on a motion path), and <animateTransform>. For now, we'll focus on using simpler <animate>, which takes a number of parameters – these define the element to animate, where it should be animated, and for how long this animation should last. A full list of the properties is summarized in Table 6-2.

Table 6-2. *Properties for <animate>*

Property	Function
attributeName	**Required** – Must be a valid attribute on the element the animation is being applied to.
From	**Optional** – If left out, the animation will start at the current values of the selected attribute.
to	**Required** – The value the attribute should be animated to.
dur	**Required** – The duration of the animation; we can use time values such as 2s or 1300ms.
href	**Required** – If our animation is outside of the element being animated, we can specify the ID of the element.
begin / end	**Optional** – Specifies when the animation should begin or end, such as on a click.
fill	**Optional** – Specifies what should happen when the animation is completed, such as freeze (remain as the animation ends), or remove (remove any effect the animation had on our element).

Now – anyone spot that I dropped a pun toward the end of the previous section, but that I didn't allude to what that pun was? Well, it's time to reveal all – it seems somewhat apt that our next demo will feature a working clock, and that it's time (sorry!) to take a look at how the properties of <animate> work, in more detail.

Creating a Clock Using <animate>

When working with SVG animation, there are a whole host of use-case scenarios where animation could be applied – take, for example, the Fourier Père et Fils site we visited at the beginning of this chapter, which adds little extra touches that give the site some added sex appeal.

Sometimes though we may have a more practical need to animate SVG – for our next demo, we're going to put our spin on a demo created by Mohamad Mohebifar, which you can see at https://codepen.io/mohebifar/pen/KwdeMz. This is a basic clock, but I'm going to tweak the styling, and use JavaScript to insert longer lines at the 3, 6, 9, and

12 o'clock positions. It's worth taking a closer look at this demo, as it makes good use of JavaScript to help animate the hands – we'll explore this in more detail at the end of the exercise.

USING <ANIMATE> AND JAVASCRIPT

Okay – let's crack on with our demo:

1. We'll start by extracting a copy of the `animatetag` folder that is available in the code download that accompanies this book – save it in our project folder.

2. Next, we need to start adding our markup – the first is add a background shadow effect; add the following code immediately after the opening `<svg>` tag:

```
<filter id="innerShadow" x="-20%" y="-20%" width="140%" height="140%">
  <feGaussianBlur in="SourceGraphic" stdDeviation="3" result="blur"/>
  <feOffset in="blur" dx="2.5" dy="2.5"/>
</filter>
```

3. Next, we're going to add the two circles that form our clock – drop these two lines in immediately after the closing `</filter>` tag:

```
<g>
  <circle id="shadow" style="fill:rgba(0,0,0,0.1)" cx="97" cy="100"
  r="87" filter="url(#innerShadow)"></circle>
  <circle id="circle" style="stroke: #FFF; stroke-width: 5px;
  fill:#c0c0c0" cx="100" cy="100" r="80"></circle>
</g>
```

4. The third block contains the code that displays (and animates) the hour, minute, and second hands – go ahead and add this code in, immediately before the closing `</svg>` tag:

```
<g>
  <line x1="100" y1="100" x2="100" y2="55" transform="rotate(80 100
  100)" style="stroke-width: 3px; stroke: #fffbf9;" id="hourhand">
    <animatetransform attributeName="transform" attributeType="XML"
    type="rotate" dur="43200s" repeatCount="indefinite"/>
  </line>
```

```
<line x1="100" y1="100" x2="100" y2="40" style="stroke-width: 4px;
stroke: #fdfdfd;" id="minutehand">
  <animatetransform attributeName="transform" attributeType="XML"
  type="rotate" dur="3600s" repeatCount="indefinite"/>
</line>

<line x1="100" y1="100" x2="100" y2="30" style="stroke-width: 2px;
stroke: #C1EFED;" id="secondhand">
  <animatetransform attributeName="transform" attributeType="XML"
  type="rotate" dur="60s" repeatCount="indefinite"/>
</line>
</g>
```

5.   Save the file – if all is well, we should see a clock ticking, when previewing the
     results in a browser, as indicated in Figure 6-3.

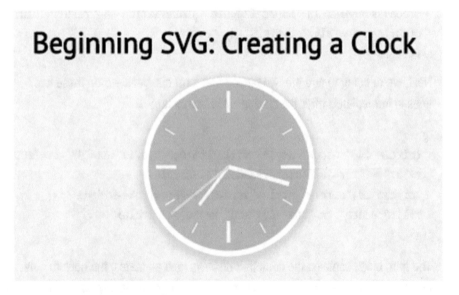

Figure 6-3. *Creating an SVG clock using <animate>*

Although we now have a working clock, some of you may have noticed the presence
of this line in our code:

```
<script src="js/animatetag.js"></script>
```

The sharp-eyed will have noticed we've not made reference to this in our demo – it is with good reason: our demo is about using `<animate>` so we should, of course, focus on this first! Nevertheless, we can't achieve the effect without some JavaScript, so let's pause for a moment and take a closer look at our code.

Dissecting Our Code

If you cast your mind back to *Understanding the different methods*, from earlier in this chapter, you will remember that we touched on several different ways to animate SVG content. In our clock demo, we've used two methods – not only did we use the SVG `<animate>` tag, but also plain JavaScript.

If we delve into the code, we can see there isn't anything out of the ordinary; we kick off with creating an array, into which we cache the selectors for the hour, minute, and second hands.

We then work out the current time, based on using `Date()` – this is then used to set where the hour, minute,, and second hands should be displayed on the clock face; we pass each value into the `hands[]` array. We then set the position of each hour on the clock – this is done in two stages: the first for statement takes care of any number that is **not** 3, 6, 9, or 12. The second function fills in the gaps with the remaining numbers, to make up our clock face.

Now – creating a clock is great, but it's still something of a theoretical example: how about creating something a little more down-to-earth and practical? Well, one example that comes to mind is a loader – you know, the little spinner we get when waiting for content to be displayed on anything less than a superfast connection! The `<animate>` tag is perfect for this, so let's dive in and take a look at an example in more detail.

Creating Animated SVG Loaders

If you spend any time surfing the web, then you will no doubt come across a spinning icon of some description; a search using Google will show dozens of examples created using the likes of CSS or a graphics package such as Photoshop.

As a format, SVG is perfect for creating animated spinners, if for one reason only – their responsive nature means we can create and adjust their size without any loss of quality. To illustrate this in action, we're going to build a quick demo that shows off three different types of spinning icons, as a Codepen demo.

CREATING A LOADER

Let's make a start on creating that demo:

1. First, browse to Codepen at `https://www.codepen.io`, then click on Create.

2. From the `loader` folder in the code download that accompanies this book – copy and paste the contents of `html.txt` into the HTML pane.

3. From the code download – copy and paste the contents of `css.txt` into the CSS pane.

You might want to click on Change View | Editor Layout, then right-click to change the page layout if it makes it easier to view the demo.

---

4. Go ahead and save the pen as Anonymous (this is perfectly fine for the purposes of this demo).

5. If we preview the results in a browser, we should see three random loaders running, as indicated in Figure 6-4.

Creating Loaders using SVG

Figure 6-4. *Creating loaders using SVG*

Understanding How the Code Works

Although this appears to be a simple demo, with little CSS in use, much of the magic takes place within the SVG elements we've added to the HTML pane. Let's take a moment to explore this code in more detail, as it contains some useful tips for us:

- All three spinners are made up of nothing more than standard SVG elements, with an `<animate>` tag embedded within – in this case, we have <circle> (in the first spinner), <path> (used in the middle spinner), and <rect> (used in the right spinner).

- You will notice that in comparison to other demos, the initial <svg> tags may appear stripped back, and to be missing some of their attributes. This is intentional – not all of the tags are required for an SVG to be rendered, and that what we have here is sufficient for our needs. Indeed, specifying size attributes within the SVG would be pointless, as they would be overridden by our CSS style rules!

- If we take a closer look at each animate statement, notice though how we're using two different tags to animate the SVG elements? In the first spinner we make use of the <animate> tag; the remaining two make use of `<animateTransform>`. There is a subtle but important difference between the two – the first will animate any property or attribute of an element (including to a new location on screen). Unfortunately IE9-11 don't support CSS transforms on SVG elements, so we must use `<animateTransform>` instead, if our project requirements dictate these browsers should be supported.

- A closer look at these statements will show that we have some common attributes in use: we, of course, have `attributeName` (for the attribute being animated), the `dur` property to control the length of the animation, and the `values` property to determine how the animation should run. All three demos make use of the <begin> property, to introduce a slight delay – this is particularly important for the third demo; otherwise the animation will look rubbish!

There is one very important tip that we have yet to cover – all of the animations we've created thus far have been single animations. What if we needed to create something that required multiple animations, such as moving and scaling a box at the same time?

Much of this will depend on how we propose to animate our SVG element – can we use CSS, or do we need to use native SVG or a JavaScript solution instead? Each will offer its own benefits – there is one crucial point though, which must be considered over and above any solution: Question is, any ideas as to what that might be...?

Managing Multiple Animations

Well – what is the answer to that question, I hear you ask? It's simple – it's all about timing.

Okay, at the risk of stating the obvious, timing is indeed key to running multiple animations; it's where we not only need to understand our code, but also the impact that code has *as part of the bigger picture.*

It's important to understand that SVG animations (and for that matter, CSS-based ones), are always processed in a single pass. This means we need to be mindful of what happens, and when – to control the flow, we can introduce delays using properties such as animation-delay (CSS), or delay (SVG).

I'm a great believer in the KISS principle (Keep it Simple...you get the idea!) – for me, a more effective animation is one that provides a nice touch rather than one that takes over everything else. Remember that example of the flying birds we talked about at the beginning of this chapter? This (for me) is a great example of how simple animation works well – not only is the overall design kept simple, but the SVG animations do not overtake the overall design.

So – how could we translate this into real code? Well, assuming we decide to use native SVG as our solution, one approach we can use is this:

- We first encompass our SVG element within a set of <g> or group tags – this is to prevent cross-contamination with other SVG elements.

- We then add our second animation in immediately after our closing shape tag, but before the closing </g> tag.

Seems simple enough, right? This is ideal for instances where we might only want a couple of animations per SVG element, but what if we needed more? Take, for example, this Codepen demo I've put together, at `https://codepen.io/alexlibby/pen/OvjEOR`, and a version of which is reproduced below:

```
<svg width="275" height="275">
  <rect x="10" y="10" width="20" height="20"
    style="stroke: black; fill: slategrey; style: fill-opacity: 0.25;">
    <animate attributeName="width" attributeType="XML" from="20" to="200"
    begin="0s" dur="8s" fill="freeze"/>
    <animate attributeName="height" attributeType="XML" from="20" to="150"
    begin="0s" dur="8s" fill="freeze"/>
    <animate attributeName="fill-opacity" attributeType="CSS" from="0.25"
    to="1" begin="0s" dur="3s" fill="freeze"/>
    <animate attributeName="fill-opacity" attributeType="CSS" from="1"
    to="0.25" begin="3s" dur="3s" fill="freeze"/>
  </rect>
</svg>
```

At first glance, you might be forgiven for thinking this would collapse into a heap, with four animations clashing! But it doesn't – if you look carefully at the code, you will see that delays have been introduced, to help manage the effect. We are also using two types of animation – it's the same `<animate>` tag in use, but we're animating both XML and CSS properties (hence the use of `animateType`). This shows that, with some careful planning, we can produce effects that work well, and achieve the desired result.

At this point let's change tack – we've used the native SVG `<animate>` and `<animateTransform>` elements to add motion to our SVG elements. This works very well, but there will come a point where we may want to animate something more complex, which will take us beyond the limits of what these two elements can handle.

Fortunately, we are not short of alternatives – these range from the popular Snap.svg library through to heavyweight alternatives such as D3 or GSAP. We're spoiled for choice, so without further ado, let's take a look at a selection of the possible contenders in more detail.

Working with Third-Party Libraries

If we're working on a complex animation that needs the power of a heavyweight tool, then JavaScript is a good contender. There is a downside to using it though – it was never designed with animating SVG in mind, and it was developed as something more of a generic tool for manipulating content within the browser.

Don't get me wrong – JavaScript is perfectly capable of animating SVG content, but it is not the only heavyweight option available: there are others we can use, which make the effort required easier. Let's take a look at the list, which includes the following:

- Two, available from `https://two.js.org/` – a 2D library that requires the use of Underscore.js and Backbone.js events;

- SVG.js, hosted at `http://svgjs.com/` – a lightweight SVG animation package, which can achieve the same effects as some of its bigger brothers, but which has been optimized for speed.

- Snap.svg, downloadable from `http://snapsvg.io/` – arguably the most well-known and popular library available for animation (we'll use it in a demo later in this chapter).

- SnapFoo (`http://yuschick.github.io/SnapFoo/`) – a relatively new library that extends the power of Snap.svg animation, to make it easier to develop using the library.

- D3 (`htp://d3js.org/`) – this veteran library has been around since 2011; it's used for producing dynamic data visualizations using SVG, HTML5, and CSS3.

- GreenSock Animation Platform (or GSAP – `https://greensock.com/`) – describes itself as a high performance, professional grade animation library, which can be used to animate SVG content.

- Velocity (available at `http://velocityjs.org/`) – created by Julian Shapiro, this animation engine has the same API as jQuery's animate and can be used as a drop-in replacement for jQuery.

- Vivus (from `https://maxwellito.github.io/vivus/`) – this library provides a different take on SVGs; it allows you to animate them as if they were being drawn.

- Anime.js (`http://animejs.com/`) – this lightweight animation library includes support for SVG and works in all of the more recent browsers.

Note   You may hear of Raphael – this was the predecessor to Snap.SVG, and caters for very old browsers, such as Firefox 3. It has not been updated for several years.

There are dozens of other libraries available for SVG, so it is definitely worth a look online to see what is available – as with any option, it's recommended you try out a few possibilities to see how they perform, before settling with your favored choice(s) of library.

To set you off on that path of discovery, we're going to dive into a quick demo that introduces of the more popular options – Snap.svg. Although it looks and works in the same way as jQuery, it doesn't require that library to operate; it does make it much easier to manipulate graphics! Let's take a look at the library in more detail, to see why it is so easy to use.

Introducing Snap.svg

If you spend any time animating SVG content, then you will eventually come across Snap.svg. Originally created by Dmitry Baranovskiy, this library can trace its background to the days of Raphäel.js, which was originally released back in 2008 and soon became very popular.

It offered great support for browsers as far back as IE5.5, but this ultimately proved to be too limiting – it couldn't keep up with what users were demanding, while still providing that backward compatibility; a complete rewrite to take advantage of what SVG can offer, resulted in what we now know as the Snap.svg library.

With the introductions out of the way, now is a good time to take a look at how it works – if you look closely at the code in the next demo, you will soon see some similarities to jQuery! We don't need to make use jQuery though, which makes it easier to use: to see what I mean, let's dive in and take a closer look.

INTRODUCING SNAP.SVG

Let's make a start:

1. We'll begin by extracting a copy of the `snap` folder that is in the code download that accompanies this book — save it in our project area.

2. Next, open up the snap.html file, then add the following line of code immediately after the <h2> tags:

```
<div id="iconDiv"></div>
```

3. We have our SVG content in place, but need to animate it – for this, go ahead and add the following code to a new file, saving it as snapsvg.js in the js subfolder with our snap folder:

```
window.onload = function () {

  var s = Snap("#iconDiv");

  Snap.load("./img/icon.svg", function(f) {
    whiteRect = f.select("#whiteRect");
    icon = f.select("#icon");

    icon.hover(function() {
      whiteRect.animate({y:960}, 500, mina.elastic);
    }, function() {
      whiteRect.animate({y:977.36218}, 500, mina.elastic);
    }
  );

  s.append(f);
  });
};
```

4. Remember to save both files – if we now preview the results in a browser, we should see the screenshot shown in Figure 6-5.

Beginning SVG: Animating with Snap.svg

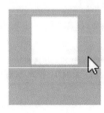

Figure 6-5. *Our finished Snap.svg demo*

Try hovering over the white square in the middle – you will see it move up and down; this movement will feel very elastic, thanks to the `mina.elastic` easing that has been applied in our code.

This is one of several easings that come built-in to the Snap.svg library; we could use one of these, but with a little help, we can create our own custom easing with little difficulty. Let's take a look at how we might achieve this – there are several options available, which are all worthy of consideration.

Applying Easing Effects to Elements

When animating an element, we might be content with simply letting it move from position X to position Y. In many cases, this will suffice – there are occasions when we might want to add a little extra effect to that movement.

We can of course achieve this with an easing effect – Snap.svg comes with some built-in options such as `easeIn`, `elastic`, or `bounce`. These are similar to easings you might use elsewhere, such as jQuery – trouble is, things will get a little stale if we limit ourselves to just these attributes.

To see the built-in easing functions in action, head over to this Codepen by Mike Tempest: `https://codepen.io/mike-tempest/pen/myvbrw`

We can easily change this – with a little extra work, it's possible to add in a custom easing effect using a cubic-bezier curve; don't worry, this is easier than it sounds! Let's dive in and take a look – to start with, we need to get our cubic-bezier values first.

Getting Prepared

The core part of our next demo centers on the use of a cubic-bezier curve – for the uninitiated, and assuming we had to plot it on a graph, our curve action would look something like that shown in Figure 6-6.

Figure 6-6. *Our cubic-bezier curve – Source: easings.net*

Unfortunately, a chart on paper won't mean a great deal – to see how it works in action, we need to head over to `http://easings.net/#easeInBack`, which shows an example of this easing effect. If we wanted to refine its appearance, we can also do this – browse to `http://cubic-bezier.com/#.6,-.28,.735,.045`, and slide around the circles within the main chart to fine-tune the values.

Assuming we now have our cubic-bezier values, we now need to implement it in our code – for this, we can make use of a simple plug-in created by Arian Stolwijk, and which is available at `https://github.com/arian/cubic-bezier`. I've included a refined version of this plug-in in the code download – the original code is a few years old, and contained a function that has been found to be buggy and can be safely removed.

Okay – let's crack on: we now have our values, so time for us to get stuck into some code!

EASING CONTENT

For this next exercise, we're going to add a custom easing, based on a cubic-bezier curve – let's make a start:

1. First, take a copy of the `snap` folder from the code download that accompanies this book – save it as `snapeasing` in our project folder.

2. Our cubic-bezier plug-in is in the `js` subfolder – we now need to tie this into our demo. For this, go ahead and add the following lines of code, immediately before the closing `</body>` tag in our demo:

```
<script>
  var timing = bezier(0.6, -0.28, 0.735, 0.045);
  var paper = Snap(800, 800);
  var r =  paper.rect(0,0,200, 200).attr({fill: "darkslategrey" });
  r.animate({ x: 600 }, 1000, timing);
</script>
```

3. Save the file – if all is well, we will see a dark gray square from the race across the screen (Figure 6-7), using the new cubic-bezier easing effect we've just added to our code.

Beginning SVG: Adding a Custom Easing Effect

Figure 6-7. *Applying a custom easing effect*

This is a somewhat more complex yet useful way of adding a custom easing effect to any shape we animate using Snap.svg – it means we are not forced to have to use one of the built-in methods and can begin to use something a little more original. Although the code isn't extensive (at least within the main markup file), it highlights a couple of useful tips – let's dive in and take a look at our code in more detail.

Exploring the Code in Detail

Take a look at the code in the main markup file – our main markup now contains the code to initiate a rectangular SVG shape, using Snap.svg. This uses similar principles to the previous demo, except this time, we've added an extra function to translate our cubic-bezier value into something that can be understood by Snap.svg.

The key to making this work lies in the function created by Arian – we're using a simplified version to allow for changes to browser support since the original function was created. The only way to see how this works is to dive into your browser's Developer Console – it's outside of the scope of this book, but if you want to get stuck into the depths of the code, you can see evidence of it in the Sources tab if using a browser such as Google Chrome. In short, we use the bezier plug-in to convert the values into something that can be rendered by Snap.svg, and apply this as an additional parameter to the animate statement in our code.

Thinking further afield, we may prefer to dial things back a bit, and use something a little simpler; fortunately, there is a plug-in available that reworks the well-known easing equations originally created by Robert Penner. The plug-in can be downloaded from `https://github.com/overjase/snap-easing/`, and it is as simple as adding a link to it in the markup, then specifying the name in place of our existing easing code.

If you really fancy getting down and dirty with the source code for Snap.svg easings, then the functions for the built-in easings are available at `https://github.com/adobe-webplatform/Snap.svg/blob/master/src/mina.js` – head to the bottom of the file for the code.

Okay – we've come to the end of our journey through animating SVG content: there is one small area we should cover off before moving onto the next chapter in our adventure. We've explored some of the options around how we animate content, but it's worth taking a few moments to understand the impact of using each option, and how we can go about selecting the most appropriate solution for our needs.

Choosing Our Route – an Epilogue

Over the course of this chapter, we've explored a variety of different options to animate our content – each has its own benefits, with some being more suited than others to particular circumstances.

The question is – how do you choose which route to take? Is there a right or wrong answer, or does it depend on our requirements? These are valid questions – only you can answer, but here's hoping the following pointers might help guide you to that answer:

- The first question is – how simple is your animation? Is it just one layer of animation – if so, then CSS is probably a good bet.

- Does your project require multiple instances of the same animation, or a host of different animations? Should these animations be chained, or run individually? Again, CSS is likely to be a good candidate here – timings may be an issue, but if you're not chaining too many, then you should be OK.

- Should your animations be fired at the point of your user interacting with an element, such as a hover or click? At this point, we'll almost certainly need JavaScript to handle the event, but can get away with CSS for the animation effect, rather than having to use JavaScript to provide it.

- Is your animation very complex, with multiple animations being chained, and where timing is super critical? If this is the case, then we will likely have to resort to using either JavaScript/jQuery, or one of the third-party libraries such as Snap.svg. The former is possible, but given that the libraries we've talked about are dedicated to animation, it makes sense to use these instead.

- Consider whether your SVG element is one you could reuse at a later date, or in multiple places in your project. If either are true, or you have a particular preference to using native SVG, then the `<animate>` tag (or one of its sister tags, such as `<animateTransform>`) could be a better option at this point.

The old adage "there is never a right or wrong answer" frequently rings true in cases like this; there may be occasions where the right solution to animating your content is obvious, but more often than not, there will be different ways to crack that nut!

Using an SVG animation tool – something to consider:

Throughout the course of this chapter, we've explored how to animate SVG content manually, using CSS, the `<animate>` tag, and through the use of CSS and JavaScript. As an alternative, it's worth keeping an eye out for an upcoming project – SVGator (`https://www.svgator.com`). The website is still in beta at the time of writing but claims to make SVG animation easy as drag and drop; early indications are promising!

Summary

Mention the word animating, and there would have been a time when the only answer might have been JavaScript – a perfectly valid option, but not always the right one today! Over the course of this chapter, we've discovered the ups and downs of how to animate SVG content, and we've seen there are other options available, such as native SVG tags or using CSS. Let's take a moment or two to review what we've covered in this chapter.

We kicked off with a quick look at an example to understand how SVG could replace options such as video, before summarizing each of the available options for animating SVG content. We explored the first option, animating using pure CSS, in more detail, before moving onto covering the native SVG `<animate>` element. We created a couple of examples to understand how this works in more detail, before quickly exploring how we might manage multiple animations.

We then moved onto looking at the use of third-party libraries, such as Snap.svg, before learning how to apply them in a practical use-case scenario. We then dived into learning how to add that extra touch using custom easings, before rounding out the chapter with a section on determining how to choose the best option to use when it comes to animating SVG content.

Phew – we've certainly covered a lot: our journey doesn't stop here though! Throughout the course of the book, we will cover a lot of code in various demos – the one key thing we should always to is to ensure it is optimized to be as efficient as possible. There are a few tricks we can use when it comes to SVG, which we will explore in the next chapter.

CHAPTER 7

Optimizing SVG

So far, we've learned how to create basic shapes, manipulated website content, and applied effects to imagery – this is great, but there is one thing we should also consider: some SVG content can be a little bloated, so there is always room for optimizing our content. Over the course of the next few pages, we'll look at some of the pain points where content might be less than optimal, and cover some of the tips and tricks we can use to ensure our content is working at optimal efficiency.

Exporting SVG Images for Use

When working with SVG, it's all too easy to simply hit the export button to save content as an SVG file – most packages such as Illustrator, Sketch, or even the online tool Vectr make it a real cinch to save our work.

The trouble is, we will frequently end up with bloated content – take, for example, this extract of code from an SVG image:

```
<?xml version="1.0" encoding="utf-8"?>
<!-- Generator: Adobe Illustrator 16.0.0, SVG Export Plug-In . SVG Version:
6.00 Build 0)  -->
<!DOCTYPE svg PUBLIC "-//W3C//DTD SVG 1.1//EN" "http://www.w3.org/Graphics/
SVG/1.1/DTD/svg11.dtd">
<svg version="1.1" id="Layer_1" xmlns="http://www.w3.org/2000/svg"
xmlns:xlink="http://www.w3.org/1999/xlink" x="0px" y="0px"
        width="612px" height="792px" viewBox="0 0 612 792" enable-
        background="new 0 0 612 792" xml:space="preserve">
```

It is perfectly valid code, but most of it is unnecessary and can be safely discarded. In many cases, we can reduce this through more judicious use of features in our SVG; as an example, Sarah Soueidan has a great article on how making some simple changes in an application such as Illustrator can already begin to reduce our code.

© Alex Libby 2018
A. Libby, *Beginning SVG*, https://doi.org/10.1007/978-1-4842-3760-1_7

You can see the full article at `https://www.sarasoueidan.com/blog/svg-tips-for-designers/` – it is a couple of years old, but the principles within are still relevant.

Getting to the point where we have an exported image will, of course, vary from package to package; the exact processes required are outside of the scope of this book. We will going forward assume we have something that has already been optimized and is ripe for optimization. There will be plenty we can do, but before we do so, there is one thing we should cover off first – that is answering the question: Why is it important to optimize our SVG content?

Understanding the Importance of Optimization

At this point, we now have a set of exported images – we can drop these into a page, add some content, and away we go, right...? Wrong. Sure, our page will display – people will see our content...eventually. But I will lay very good odds that it will be slow, cumbersome, and in many cases, people will vote with their feet. As the developer Brad Frost once said:

The road towards better performance doesn't start with developers or technology stacks (though I'm certainly not suggesting those things are unimportant). It begins with a shared interest on everyone's part in making a product that's lightning fast.

I recommend reading the original article by Brad Frost at `http://bradfrost.com/blog/post/performance-as-design/` – it may be a few years old, but many of the principles still hold true!

To prove how important it is, imagine you have a small site, with only 50 pages. Navigating this won't be an issue, but imagine this has been scaled up by a factor of 60. It's going to start getting slower to navigate – and that may only be static pages! Just imagine what it would be like for a dynamic site serving in the region of 500,000-plus products...

In an age where mobile is rapidly overtaking desktop as a platform of choice, performance is king – pages that have not been optimized will directly affect the user experience and have an impact on page metrics. This may be less apparent on desktops, but the impact will be exacerbated by the lower connection speeds on mobile devices, which is now the platform of choice for many individuals around the world.

Now – this isn't to say that SVGs are the only items that need to be optimized; everything being referenced on the page must be fine-tuned for optimal performance. However, SVGs can contain a lot of extra content such as meta tags, values that run to several decimal places or extra nodes that are not always necessary.

In many cases, designers who create SVGs will optimize images as part of the design process. However, this may not always happen – it's up to us as developers to ensure that images have been optimized, so that this extra cruft is removed, while maintaining the desired look and feel as created by the designer. It may only be a few bytes here and there that we remove, but these will all add up over time!

The great thing about SVGs, though, is that they are easy to optimize – there are a few tricks we can use to remove redundant content and bloat from our images and still keep the look and feel that we need for our site. To see what a difference we can make, let's begin first with a look at where we can make changes to improve the performance of our SVG images.

Assessing Performance

Once our images have been exported, the next stage in development should be to optimize them – many of the principles we use for HTML, CSS, and JavaScript can also be used to remove cruft from our SVG images.

The process comes in two parts – we should run each image through an optimization process, but then spend time tweaking images to fine-tune each to optimal efficiency. It's worth noting that for some images this isn't sensible (if they are really small or simple), but for larger images there may be additional changes we can make that have not already been implemented by optimization tools.

Most of the process can be done automatically for us (as we will see shortly, in the section "Shrinking Images with SVGO"), but it is worth understanding some of the key areas where we can make changes to help improve the performance of our SVG images:

- Check the size of your canvas – this may be larger than necessary, which will increase the file size of your SVG graphic.

- How many decimal places do the values in your SVG have? If they have lots, then consider dropping them down to whole integers, or at least removing some of the precision, making your files smaller and faster.

- Does your source graphic contain lots of gradients, and store these in the `<defs>` block at the start of the SVG? If so, it's worth checking them: if there are lots present, then try running the code through the gradient optimizer tool available on Codepen at `https://codepen.io/jakealbaugh/full/OVrQXY`. This will collapse any unused gradients into those that are needed for your SVG graphic, which will reduce the file size and increase performance.

- If we have multiple shapes within our SVG that are very similar, we can consider making use of the use statement; thus:

```
<svg height="300" width="400" viewBox="0 0 300 400">
  <defs>
    <rect id="sourceRec" x="0" y="0" height="300" width="400"/>
  </defs>
  <use href="#sourceRec" fill="#57A0C3" x="0" y="0" />
</svg>
```

  This will reuse a predefined shape that is already in the `<defs>` block, reducing the need to create new shapes.

- Make use of CSS sprites to store multiple SVG images; this works really well for this format.

- If you are only making use of a handful of SVG images, then consider putting them inline to your code – this will reduce the number of HTTP requests made, but this is at the cost of losing caching (so not suitable for lots of SVG images!)

Now – I should point out that these changes are not the only ones we should consider making; many of the changes include smaller tweaks, such as removing redundant XML instructions. We'll take care of many of these smaller changes through using the optimization tool, but as we will see later in this chapter in "Learning How to Micro-optimize Content," we can fine-tune our SVG content further, for optimal efficiency.

Talking of micro-optimizing though, we have an obligation to ensure our content remains accessible to all who visit our pages; depending on your analytic metrics, we may have a need to adjust our images to allow for users of assistive technology (such as screen readers).

The downside is that there aren't any tools available to automatically make images accessible – sorry to disappoint: this is one area where we might have to get dirty with code! However, before we get stuck in with code, there are a few things to consider; let's dive in and take a look at the practicalities involved.

Taking Care of Accessibility

Anyone who uses your website may have a disability – this might be visual, cognitive, hearing, or motor-based; it might even be a case of that individual suffering from nothing more than a broken arm or be forced to use older equipment when surfing the web.

Although the need to comply with accessibility legislation may differ from country to country, accessibility should be considered as part of the development process; there is always a risk that we might be sued if our content isn't made accessible. A good starting point for any existing site is to check metrics – what do they tell us?

If the metrics show little use then we should work out the reasons for this – is it that our offer is such that it will not appeal to users of assistive technologies? Or – is it more likely that our site needs work to make it more accessible? This might range from something simple as adding ARIA tags, through to developing content for a completely new platform; in many cases customer feedback will help determine priorities for implementing these changes.

Assuming we establish a need to make our content more accessible (and in this instance, SVG in particular), there are a few steps we can take to facilitate this process. This will depend a little on whether our SVGs are held inline or externally; let's take a look first at what we might need to change or add for externally hosted images:

- If we're including SVG images externally, then alt tags should always be used for important images.

- External images should include an ARIA `role='image'` attribute, as some browsers may ignore images that do not have an alt tag present.

ARIA, or WAI-ARIA to give its full name, is a specification created by the W3C, to provide a set of attributes that can be applied to elements to help improve accessibility, such as those who use screen readers.

- If our external SVG image is purely decorative, then include an empty
  `alt="` tag; otherwise a screen reader may read the source tag, which
  will sound awful!

Adapting images that are hosted inline is a little more involved, but nothing
complex – we should make the following changes to any SVG that is important for the
site, and **not** those that are there for decorative purposes only:

- Each SVG we create should have a <title> tag within the definition,
  directly below the opening <svg> tag. It should be brief – treat it in the
  same way as we might for an `<alt>` attribute tagged against an image.

- In the SVG tag, add an aria-labelledby attribute that points to the
  <title> tag.

- As an optional (but recommended) extra, consider including a
  longer <desc> tag (description) in addition to the title tag – this is
  very helpful for users of assistive technology. The <desc> tag should
  communicate the purpose or design of the SVG.

- If we want to include text within our SVG, then use the <text> tag;
  standard text can't be detected by screen readers, search engines
  and makes for a poor UX experience when resizing or being read by
  people with low vision.

- If there is more than one shape, you may want to consider including
  separate title tags for each shape group.

Allowing for these changes, let's take a look at an example block of code, to see they
would look (changes are highlighted in bold):

```
<svg aria-labelledby="title">
  <title id="title" lang="en">Red Rectangle</title>
  <desc id="details">A red rectangular shape</desc>
  <rect x="0" y="0" width="100" height="50" fill="red" />
</svg>
```

As we've seen from this code block, making an image more accessible isn't difficult –
it will require time and effort to plan and implement the changes, which should be
prioritized according to demand and the scale of work required. The best way to see
what is involved is to implement the changes to a real image, so without further ado, let's
dive into our next exercise to see what is required in practice.

Making Content Accessible

For our next exercise, we'll use one of the Open Iconic icons, hosted at
https://useiconic.com/open. It's a great source of SVG icons for all manner of
uses and is also perfect for testing the code changes we'll make in our demo. We'll apply
the same accessibility principles that we've just discussed to this image, so you can get a
feel for how easy it is to amend the markup in any SVG image.

MAKING AN IMAGE ACCESSIBLE

Let's make a start on that demo – this time around, we will use Codepen to host it:

1. We'll start by extracting a copy of the accessible folder from the
   code download that accompanies this book – save it to the root of our
   project folder.

2. Next, browse to http://www.codepen.io, then go ahead and paste the code
   from within accessible.txt file into the HTML frame.

3. There a single style rule we should apply, for our demo to work correctly, so
   go ahead and paste in the contents of the accessible.css file into the CSS
   frame.

4. We can now alter our code to make it more accessible – for this, go ahead and
   add in the aria-labelledby tag, as indicated:

   ```
   <div class="icon-container" aria-labelledby="title">
   ```

5. Next, add in the following two lines of code immediately below the opening
   <svg> tag – these are the title and description tags that we talked about
   earlier:

   ```
   <title id="title" lang="en">Shopping Basket</title>
   <desc id="details">A typical shopping basket for an e-commerce
    site</desc>
   ```

6. If all is well, we should have something akin to the code shown in Figure 7-1 –
   you can see the finished article at https://codepen.io/alexlibby/pen/
   BrqQRj.

Figure 7-1. *Making our SVG image accessible*

Shrinking Images with SVGO

When working with SVG images, there should always be one task that we complete for any image – we should optimize it, no matter what the size or its complexity. Granted, a smaller image won't show a great deal of improvement in size, but larger ones certainly will; there should be no excuse for not optimizing our content, and putting bloated SVGs onto a diet, so to speak!

Thankfully there are several tools available that help make this process a breeze – one of the most popular solutions is the Node.js-based tool, SVGO. This tool comes in three flavors: the original Node.js version, versions that can be used with task runners such as Grunt, or through an online version available at `https://jakearchibald.github.io/svgomg/`.

This last version will be the subject of our next demo – this uses the same settings as the original tool but makes the changes in real time; we can easily see the impact of how something will look, before committing it to disk through the Node.js version.

Optimizing Manually

The first option for optimizing our SVG images comes in the form of the online SVGOMG tool (or SVGO's Missing GUI). Created by Jake Archibald, this tool makes it very easy to see what happens when optimizing an image. It's perfect for single-use instances, or to help get accustomed to what we might expect to see when optimizing images.

We will cover how to automate this process using Node.js, but for now, let's get stuck in and see how the process works in more detail.

```
┌─────────────────────────────────────────────────────────────┐
│                     USING SVGO ONLINE                         │
└─────────────────────────────────────────────────────────────┘
```

Let's make a start with optimizing our image:

1. We'll begin by extracting a copy of our source image – it's in the code download that accompanies this book, within the `svgonline` folder.

2. Next, let's browse to the online version of SVGO, which is at `https://jakearchibald.github.iosvgomg/`.

3. Once on the site, click on Open SVG, then browse to our project folder and select the source image.

You can equally drag and drop the image onto the page if preferred – drag it over the gray area to activate the optimization process.

---

4. The image will load and be optimized automatically, using the default settings, as shown in Figure 7-2.

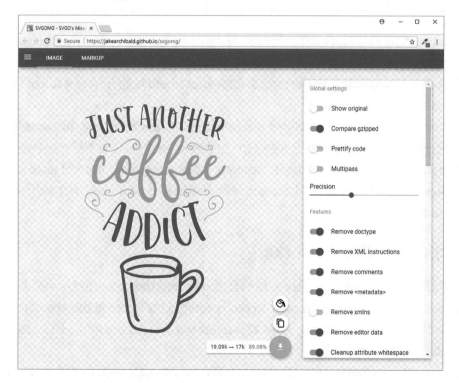

Figure 7-2. Optimizing our image using SVGO

5. Go ahead and click on the white arrow pointing downward to download our image, as indicated in Figure 7-3.

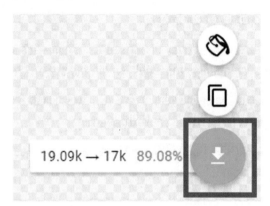

Figure 7-3. *Downloading our SVG image*

6. We should at this point run one final check – go ahead and open the image that we've just optimized; it's in the optimized image folder within the code download that accompanies this book. Check to make sure it still shows as the original image – if all is well, you shouldn't see any noticeable difference!

A drop of 6KB in size for our optimized image may not see a great deal in itself. However, this should always be seen as part of the bigger picture – anything we can reduce while not impacting on the overall appearance will help improve the overall speed of our site.

In many cases, the default settings will be sufficient, but there may be occasions where changing the settings might result in additional savings. The beauty about using this route is that the changes are instantaneous – they are not committed until we hit the download button. To see what I mean, let's dive in and take a look at how this demo works in more detail.

Understanding How It Works

The online SVGOMG process hides a lot of the work required to optimize SVG images – it makes it a breeze to run the process on our content. This is one of those tools that follow the 80:20 rule; we may only have 20% of the work to do, but 80% of it is done for us through the tool automatically.

The tool exposes most (if not all) of the optimization options of SVGO, so it is perfect for learning how the tool works, and what settings we should use to get the best result from the process. For us, it's a matter of dragging and dropping an image on the page, then moving the sliders left or right to enable or disable a specific optimization feature.

For example – if we move the Precision slider to the far left, this activates the `cleanupNumericValues` plug-in option within SVGO. Moving it to the left reduces the precision down to whole integer values only (and reduces the size), but moving it to the right will increase precision and increase the file size.

To help understand what each setting does, I have included a PDF ("SVGO Properties") in the code download that lists the full set of attributes that can be enabled or disabled – in many cases, simply leaving them as they are by default will be a good starting point. However, it's worth trying them out over a period of time – not every SVG graphic will have the same attributes specified, so a bit of trial and error will be required to achieve the best optimization!

A word of note – you will see that the file sizes shown in Figure 7-3 don't appear to correspond with what is stored on your PC. This is deliberate – the smaller sizes mean that the "Compare gzipped" option is enabled; slide this to the left to show the real file sizes.

Okay – let's move on: running the process manually works well, but it will soon become limiting; there is no way we have time to optimize lots of images by hand, when we have better things to do! Question is: Can we automate our process?

Automating the Optimization Process

Absolutely we can! The option I have in mind uses the same SVGO tool we've just used in the previous demo, but this time we'll use it through a task runner, with Grunt as our example. This demo will come in two parts – we first have to install Node.js and test that it works, before adding in our plug-in to use SVGO with Grunt.

Don't worry if Grunt is not your task runner of choice: there are plug-ins available for dozens of other systems, such as PostCSS, Gulp, and Broccoli.

We will use our original coffee addict image from the previous demo – you can download a fresh copy if needed, from https://www.freesvgimages.com/just-another-coffee-addict/. Let's take a look at what is involved in more detail:

OPTIMIZING USING TASK RUNNER – PART 1

For the purposes of this demo, we will assume we're starting with a new installation of Node.js and Grunt – if you already have it installed from the previous chapter, then please skip straight to step 2.

1. Install Node.js according to instructions from site for your chosen platform – accept all of the default settings, which will be sufficient for this demo.

2. Next, go ahead and extract a copy of the svgopt folder to your project folder.

3. We now need our coffee addict image – go ahead and save a copy from the code download that accompanies this book, into the svgopt folder we created in step 2, as addict.svg.

4. Now run Node.js command prompt (or terminal session, for Mac users) as local administrator, then change the working folder to the svgopt folder stored in our project folder.

5. At the prompt, enter npm install –g svgo then hit Enter – it will go ahead and install SVGO.

6. Once the install has completed, type svgo in/addict.svg out/addict. svg at the prompt, then press Enter – Figure 7-4 shows the image has been successfully optimized, with a 15.2% (or just over 6KB) saving.

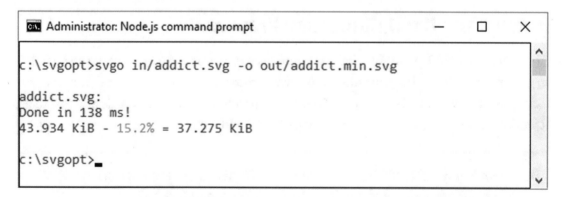

Figure 7-4. *Results of optimizing our image*

7. We can now preview the results – if all is well, we should see something akin to the image shown in Figure 7-5; we should not see any visual change but can rest happy in the knowledge that it has been optimized.

Figure 7-5. *Previewing our optimized image*

At this point, we now have SVGO installed and working, using Node.js – this means we can optimize images locally, without having to rely on using the online version of the SVGO tool. It's a great way to test changes, but there is something to be said for being independent!

That said, running a command-line operation is still a manual process – let's correct that, by adding in Grunt to run the SVGO tool over multiple files in one pass.

OPTIMIZING USING TASK RUNNER – PART 2

Let's make a start with updating our installation:

1. We'll begin by firing up a Node.js command prompt session (or terminal session, for Mac users); at the prompt, go ahead and type this command, then press Enter: `npm install -g grunt-cli`

2. Next, we need to create a `package.json` file, which contains details of the packages we will use for our optimization process. For this, enter the following command at the prompt, then press Enter: `npm init --yes`

3. Node will run through the process of creating the file automatically using default values from within the folder and save it to our folder. Once completed, we will see something akin to the screenshot shown in Figure 7-6: Enter after each question, or to accept the default shown in brackets.

```
Node.js command prompt                              —    □    ×

c:\svgopt>npm init --yes
Wrote to c:\svgopt\package.json:

{
  "name": "optimize",
  "version": "1.0.0",
  "description": "Optimize SVG images",
  "main": "index.js",
  "scripts": {
    "test": "echo \"Error: no test specified\" && exit 1"
  },
  "author": "Alex Libby",
  "license": "ISC",
  "devDependencies": {
    "grunt": "^1.0.3",
    "grunt-svgmin": "^5.0.0",
    "grunt-watcher": "^1.0.0"
  },
  "dependencies": {},
  "keywords": []
}


c:\svgopt>
```

Figure 7-6. *Details for the package.json file*

4. After the last entry (the license), it will display your values, then prompt you to confirm it is OK – press Y or Enter to accept the values.

5. With our package.json file created, we can now install Grunt, using this command: `npm install grunt --save-dev`.

6. Next up comes the core of our optimization process – we need to install the Grunt plug-in for SVGO: `npm install grunt-svgmin --save-dev` (as shown in Figure 7-7).

```
Administrator: Node.js command prompt                    —   □   ✕

c:\svgopt>npm install --save-dev grunt-svgmin
npm WARN optimize@1.0.0 No repository field.

+ grunt-svgmin@5.0.0
updated 1 package in 3.453s

c:\svgopt>▂
```

Figure 7-7. *Installing grunt-svgmin*

7.   We have one last tool to install – grunt-watcher, which looks out for changes to our folder, and runs the optimization process: `npm install grunt-watcher --save-dev`

8.   The next task is to set up our Gruntfile – this has already been created for us and should be present at the root of our `svgopt` folder.

9.   We now have everything installed and configured – time to try it out! Go ahead and fire up a Node.js command prompt session (or terminal session, for Mac users), then change the working folder to the `svgopt` folder and entering `grunt svgmin`, as shown in Figure 7-8.

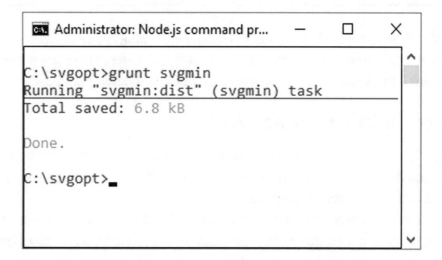

```
Administrator: Node.js command pr...    —   □   ✕

C:\svgopt>grunt svgmin
Running "svgmin:dist" (svgmin) task
Total saved: 6.8 kB

Done.

C:\svgopt>▂
```

Figure 7-8. *Testing our setup*

10.   Assuming we get a positive result, we can now test the process – for this, enter the command `grunt` at the command prompt, then press Enter (Figure 7-9).

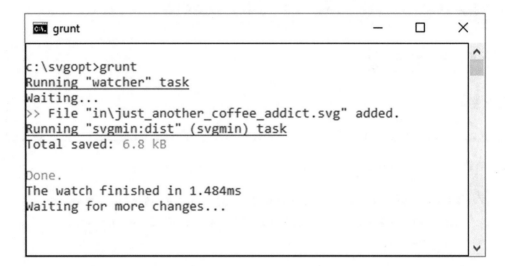

Figure 7-9. *Testing our Grunt setup*

11.   Go ahead and drop a copy of the coffee addict SVG into the in subfolder within the `svgopt` project folder.

12.   If all is well, we should see a new image show in the out folder within the `svgopt` folder – this one will be around 6KB smaller in size.

Phew – we've covered a few steps but now have a working optimization process in place! We've only touched the surface of what is possible, so let's take a few minutes to review what we've created, to learn how we can tweak it for better performance.

Exploring the Demo in More Detail

Although it may feel like our demo required a lot of installation work, in reality much of this may already exist in your environment, particularly if you already use Node.js (or something that serves a similar purpose).

The real magic happens in the Gruntfile.js file – if we take a look at it, we can break it down into three sections: the initial configuration, loading the relevant tasks, and initiating the watcher task when we start Grunt at the command line.

The first section configures the svgmin plug-in – in this example we've configured it to keep the `viewBox` but remove redundant strokes and fills, and empty attributes. We've set it to pick up any SVG dropped into the in folder and drop it into the out folder with the `.min.svg` extension.

To facilitate the automation, we're using the grunt-watcher plug-in in the watcher task – we've set some options to record the time and show a prompt when waiting for new images. The task is set to only run when adding new images or changing existing ones; this is to stop it running when images are deleted. As soon as it detects a valid change, the task fires off the `svgmin` task to complete the optimization process.

It's worth noting that the configuration we've used is just an example – I would recommend adapting it to match the settings you find most effective, from the "Optimizing Manually" demo earlier in this chapter. A list of settings (and what they do) is available as a PDF in the code download; look for "SVGO Properties" within the Chapter 7 folder.

Okay – let's change tack: we've learned how to optimize our content both manually and through the use of a task runner; there are still changes we may be able to make to improve our content. A key part of the process is to run a final check to see if we can make any final changes – let's take a look at micro-optimizing our content in more detail.

Learning How to Micro-optimize Content

Although we've put our SVGs through an optimizer (you did do that, I hope?), there are always occasions where optimizers may not be able to fine-tune an SVG as much as we would like. It might be down to design, or that an optimizer simply doesn't have that capability built in – we might not be able to change that, but we can at least perform a final check to see if there are any more changes that can be made to our code.

Unfortunately, this does mean getting down and dirty with our code – to help with this, there are a few candidates that can be checked:

- If your image contains elements that are hidden (or perhaps too small to be viewed easily), then consider simply removing them – this will help reduce file sizes, remove unnecessary code and make it easier to manage the SVG.

- If your SVG has some inline styles (such as `fill`), then consider moving them to a style sheet: this will help keep our code cleaner and be more intuitive. It may not suit all circumstances, such as designing a corporate logo that must retain the right colors and dimensions.

- There is an argument for removing width and height values, if you are already using CSS; the latter will by default override the former.

- Check the viewBox values – is yours set with a high level of decimal precision? We touched on this back in *Assessing performance* – the higher the precision, the larger the file size. The trick is to strike a balance between precision and visual fidelity, so that we don't break our image by specifying too low a level of precision. Consider this extract:

```
viewBox="-351.7474061, 2051.85204372, 2520.3925946,
2520.13473217"
```

It's very possible that we can reduce it by using a couple of simple tricks: repositioning our SVG and viewBox to use 0,0 as starting coordinates, setting whole integers rather than decimal places, and scaling down the original image. The resulting file size will be smaller, but without any loss of fidelity to the image – we can end up with a viewBox nearer this size:

```
viewBox="0, 0, 252, 252"
```

At the same time, we should check through our SVGs to see what has been removed by our optimizer tool – at least for the first few images. If it hasn't been configured to its optimal best, then we may miss opportunities for improvement:

- Unnecessary attributes on the SVG element – many of the properties shown in Table 7-1 are frequently ignored or surplus to requirements; they can be removed if our optimizer tool has not already removed them.

Table 7-1. *Redundant SVG Properties*

Redundant Property	Explanation
X,Y attributes	These are coordinates for the top left position of the image – in many cases, they can be set to 0,0 or be removed from an individual SVG.
version="1.1"	Although it may be needed to comply with standards, just about every browser will ignore this value, so it can be removed.
xmlns="http://www.w3.org/2000/svg"	This is only needed for external files; if your SVG is inline, it can be safely removed.
id="layer"	ID values represent the layer of the image – if you are not making use of it when styling, it can be removed; note though that the layer will disappear if you subsequently edit it in an application such as Illustrator or Vectr.
xmlns:xlink="https://www.w3.org/1999/xlink"	If this isn't being used, then it is safe to remove. If you are unsure, try removing it, and monitoring for any adverse effects.
style="enable-background"	This property is meant to help make the background available to child elements; it's useful for filter effects. It was deprecated in 2014, so can be safely removed from those SVGs that may still have it.
Width / Height	These attributes control the dimensions of the image – these can be removed if you are using CSS-based styling.
xml:space="preserve"	This has officially been removed from Web standards, so it can be removed from code if it is still present.

- The XML doctype and comments aren't needed: as the image will inherit the doctype from the parent, so both can be removed.

- Remove groups where possible – they are useful when creating SVGs, but if you don't have multiple images in the same SVG (particularly when animating content), then they can be removed. Bear in mind though, that if an image has a lot of elements, then I would consider using groups for ease of readability.

- Remove any whitespace from new lines, tabs, and indents.

It's important to stress that many of the settings shown in Table 7-1 should already be removed automatically by an optimizer tool. I would recommend getting to know what these values are, so that you can either remove them manually when needed or alter them in the event your tool is not available.

There is one further place where we can optimize our content, which we've not covered in detail thus far: data URIs. At face value, you might not expect to be able to make any improvements, but remember us talking about them back in Chapter 3? Well, there is always room for improvement, so time we revisited these, to see how optimizing them can reduce the page weight and subsequent file sizes.

Paying Attention to Data URIs

Cast your mind back to Chapter 3 if you will – in particular to the section marked "Working with Images and Typography." Yes, I know it may seem like a long time ago, but there is a reason for this, so let me explain.

We touched on several different formats of data URIs and created a simple demo that showed how we can display an image using four different data-URI formats, to learn which is the most efficient. Clearly the base-64 format came out worst (which you may or may not expect); the most effective solution was to use the native SVG format, with only a moderate increase in size when fully optimized.

Why is this important? Well, the simple answer is that it's another area where we can optimize our code. Many of the standard SVG optimizers are not likely to include this level of fine-tuning, so we need to allow for it in the overall optimization process if we don't want to miss out on an opportunity. It may not seem like we save many bytes with each image, but over time this will all add up – it's important to focus on the bigger picture, and not just the individual savings we get from each image.

The developer Chris Coyier has a great article on the finer points of optimizing dat-uris, which is available at `https://css-tricks.com/probably-dont-base64-svg/`

Okay – enough chit-chat: let's get active! For our next exercise we're going to set up a simple demo to automate the optimization of an SVG image. For the purposes of this demo we'll use the same coffee addict image we've already used before; if you want to use a different image, then please adjust the steps accordingly.

Optimizing Data URIs

For our next exercise, we'll make use of the mini-svg-data-uri plug-in, available from https://github.com/tigt/mini-svg-data-uri. Created by the Ohio-based developer, Taylor Hunt, this plug-in encodes standard SVG files for use as data-URIs; they can then be specified as images within a project's style sheet. For the purposes of this demo, we will assume that Node.js is already installed and ready for use, and that we will use an (optimized and renamed) copy of the coffee addict image from earlier demos.

OPTIMIZING DATA URIS

Let's make a start with setting up our script:

1. We'll start by extracting a copy of the `datauri` folder from the code download that accompanies this book – save it at the root of our project folder. This contains our script and example image, all ready for use.

2. Next, go ahead and fire up Node.js command prompt (or terminal session, for Mac users) as administrator, then change the working folder to `datauri`, and run this command at the prompt: `npm install mini-svg-data-uri --save-dev`

3. We now need to set up the script that will convert our SVG image into something that can be used as a background image. Go ahead and paste the following code into a file, saving it as `datauri.js` in the `datauri` folder:

```
var fs = require('fs');
var svgToMiniDataURI = require('mini-svg-data-uri');

fs.readFile('in/coffee.svg', 'utf8', function(err, data) {
  if (err) throw err;
  var optimizedSVGDataURI = svgToMiniDataURI(data.toString());
  console.log(optimizedSVGDataURI);

  fs.writeFile("out/coffee.min.svg", optimizedSVGDataURI,
  function(err) {
    if(err) { return console.log(err); }

    console.log("\r\nThe file was saved!");
  });
});
```

4. Switch back to the command prompt (or terminal session), then run node `datauri.js` and press Enter. We should see something akin to the image shown in Figure 7-10.

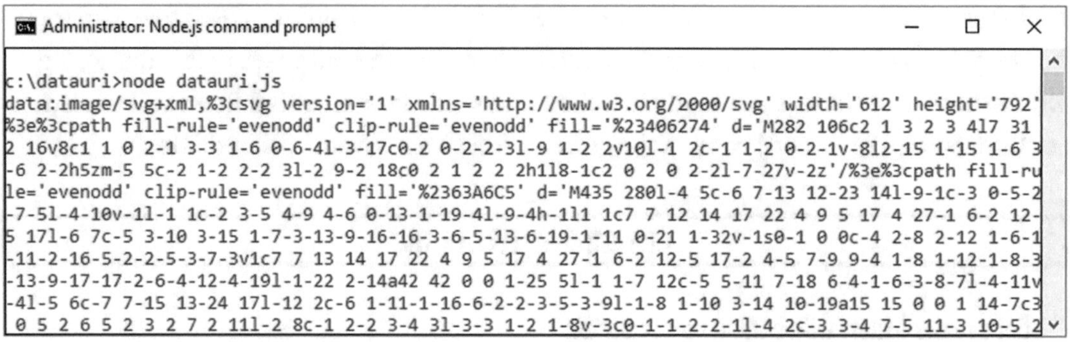

```
Administrator: Node.js command prompt                                    —    □    ×

c:\datauri>node datauri.js
data:image/svg+xml,%3csvg version='1' xmlns='http://www.w3.org/2000/svg' width='612' height='792'
%3e%3cpath fill-rule='evenodd' clip-rule='evenodd' fill='%23406274' d='M282 106c2 1 3 2 3 4l7 31
2 16v8c1 1 0 2-1 3-3 1-6 0-6-4l-3-17c0-2 0-2-2-3l-9 1-2 2v10l-1 2c-1 1-2 0-2-1v-8l2-15 1-15 1-6 3
-6 2-2h5zm-5 5c-2 1-2 2-2 3l-2 9-2 18c0 2 1 2 2 2h1l8-1c2 0 2 0 2-2l-7-27v-2z'/%3e%3cpath fill-ru
le='evenodd' clip-rule='evenodd' fill='%2363A6C5' d='M435 280l-4 5c-6 7-13 12-23 14l-9-1c-3 0-5-2
-7-5l-4-10v-1l-1 1c-2 3-5 4-9 4-6 0-13-1-19-4l-9-4h-1l1 1c7 7 12 14 17 22 4 9 5 17 4 27-1 6-2 12-
5 17l-6 7c-5 3-10 3-15 1-7-3-13-9-16-16-3-6-5-13-6-19-1-11 0-21 1-32v-1s0-1 0 0c-4 2-8 2-12 1-6-1
-11-2-16-5-2-2-5-3-7-3v1c7 7 13 14 17 22 4 9 5 17 4 27-1 6-2 12-5 17-2 4-5 7-9 9-4 1-8 1-12-1-8-3
-13-9-17-17-2-6-4-12-4-19l-1-22 2-14a42 42 0 0 1-25 5l-1 1-7 12c-5 5-11 7-18 6-4-1-6-3-8-7l-4-11v
-4l-5 6c-7 7-15 13-24 17l-12 2c-6 1-11-1-16-6-2-2-3-5-3-9l-1-8 1-10 3-14 10-19a15 15 0 0 1 14-7c3
0 5 2 6 5 2 3 2 7 2 11l-2 8c-1 2-2 3-4 3l-3-3 1-2 1-8v-3c0-1-1-2-2-1l-4 2c-3 3-4 7-5 11-3 10-5 2
```

Figure 7-10. *Our converted SVG as a data-uri*

It's worth noting that the contents of console log will have been saved to disk – in this case, as `coffee.min.svg`. The file itself will not be viewable by itself (if you try to open in a browser, for example), but it is designed to save a copy of the data URI, so it can be incorporated into our CSS style sheet at a later date.

Although we've kept our script short and simple, there are a number of improvements we could make – let's first take a look at the code in more detail.

Exploring the Code in Detail

We begin by linking to Node.js' File System module, before reading in the contents of the `coffee.svg` file and assigning to a storage value named `data`. We then run it through the `svgToMiniDataURI` module, which converts it to a data URI, before rendering it onscreen (`console`). The contents of `data` are then saved to disk as `coffee.min.svg`, so that we can then use the data URI in our code at a later date.

At this point, let's step back for a moment: going to all of this effort to add what seems to be just a few extra characters might not feel right; after all, why not just use a standard base-64 conversion as the source for our background-image statement?

It's a valid question – to really understand the benefit we get from this process, let's strip it back to a simpler example and run some comparisons with a smaller SVG. For the purposes of this demo, I'll use an icon from the Open Iconic project that we made use of earlier, hosted at `https://useiconic.com/open`:

COMPARING DATA-URI VALUES

For this exercise we'll use the SVG code for the align-center icon – you can of course use any icon for this, as long as it the SVG code is simple:

1. We'll begin by browsing to `https://npm.runkit.com/mini-svg-data-uri` – this allows us to run the mini-svg-data-uri plug-in, in an online environment that is already set up to run this plug-in.

2. Go ahead and add the following code into the code box on the left side of the page, replacing what is already there – the code box is immediately below the words "…Try it out":

   ```
   var svgToMiniDataURI = require('mini-svg-data-uri');

   var svg = '<svg xmlns="http://www.w3.org/2000/svg" width="8"
   height="8" viewBox="0 0 8 8"><path d="M3 0v1h4v5h-4v1h5v-7h-5zm1
   2v1h-4v1h4v1l2-1.5-2-1.5z" /></svg>';

   var optimizedSVGDataURI = svgToMiniDataURI(svg);
   ```

3. Click on the Run button to the bottom right of this code box, then select Full Text from the drop-down, a little to the left; if all is well, you will see the code shown in Figure 7-11:

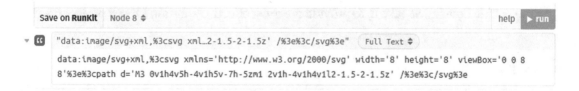

Figure 7-11. *The results of running our data-uri plug-in*

This seems straightforward enough, right? Let's compare the results of our change, against other data-URI formats. First up is the original, unaltered SVG code:

```
<svg xmlns="http://www.w3.org/2000/svg" width="8" height="8" viewBox="0 0 8
8"><path d="M3 0v1h4v5h-4v1h5v-7h-5zm1 2v1h-4v1h4v1l2-1.5-2-1.5z" /></svg>
```

This weighs in at 150 characters, including spaces. In comparison, here's the resulting code after we've run it through the optimization process:

```
data:image/svg+xml,%3csvg xmlns='http://www.w3.org/2000/svg' width='8'
height='8' viewBox='0 0 8 8'%3e%3cpath d='M3 0v1h4v5h-4v1h5v-7h-5zm1 2v1h-
4v1h4v1l2-1.5-2-1.5z' /%3e%3c/svg%3e
```

This weighs in at 181 characters, which is an increase of 31 characters, or just under 21% of the original value. Now compare that with a standard base-64 conversion – we can already see a bigger increase in code:

```
PHN2ZyB4bWxucz0iaHR0cDovL3d3dy53My5vcmcvMjAwMC9zdmciIHdpZHRoPSI4IiBoZWlna
HQ9IjgiIHZpZXdCb3g9IjAgMCA4IDgiPjxwYXRoIGQ9Ik0zIDB2MWg0djVoLTR2MWg1di03a
C01em0xIDJ2MWgtNHYxaDR2MWwyLTEuNS0yLTEuNXoiIC8+PC9zdmc+
```

This weighs in at 200 characters, which is a 33% increase on the original code – clearly not so good! Granted, there will always need to be an increase in code to allow for any conversion, but it's clear to see that base-64 conversions aren't as efficient as simply encoding our SVG using the plug-in.

Leaving conversion theory aside for a moment, and thinking further afield, how could we improve on our code? Well, as a starter for 10 – how about making it dynamic, then integrating it with a watch task, so it performs this change for any image dropped into an inbox folder automatically? We've created the background-image URL code, so how about creating the CSS rule to suit? These are just two of the ideas that come to mind – it's really up to us to decide how far we take it, to provide the most effective solution for our project needs.

Summary

When working with SVGs, optimizing our code is just as important a process as creating content. If done with care, it can make a real impact on the size of our files, help reduce bandwidth usage, and ultimately lead to a faster experience for our customers. We've covered a number of useful tips to help with this process, so let's take a moment to review what we've learned.

We kicked off with a brief overview of the best way to export images, before moving swiftly on to explore why optimization is important and taking a look at some of the areas we should target for improvement.

Next up came a quick look at how we can maintain accessibility as part of this process, before learning how to shrink our images using the SVGO tools. We then moved onto covering how we can micro-optimize our content further, to alter or remove code those other optimizers can't reach, before finally working on how we can improve data-URIs that frequently need more special attention.

Phew – another monster chapter bites the dust, to (mis-) quote the words from that famous song! Still, our journey continues apace; over the course of the next three chapters we will take a look at some example uses of SVG, kicking off with a dive-in to creating interactive charts.

PART III

Putting SVG to Use

CHAPTER 8

Creating SVG Charts

It goes without saying that SVG is, of course, a very visual technology – it lends itself to a multitude of different uses. One great use though is through the creation of charts; yes, it's hard to believe, but it is a perfect tool for this purpose! We can take it even further though, by animating said chart content – with a little care, we can produce some really powerful content that is visually engaging for our visitors.

Throughout these pages, we'll take a look at some of the techniques we can use to produce anything from simple pie charts through to more complex infographic solutions. To kick off our journey though, we should take a few moments to explore the answer to this question: What makes SVG such a great format for charting?

Understanding the Benefits of SVG for Charts

If we're tasked with creating a chart, then there are several ways of skinning this problem – one might decide to use the HTML `<canvas>` element, or simply create it as an image and embed it into the page. Sure, these will work *technically*, but are they the best solution?

For one – if we create an image that then needs to be resized, we can't simply change the dimensions in code; chances are the image will lose its sharpness. Making use of the canvas element isn't much better either; we might be able to resize the element in code, but we lose the ability to interact and have to create extra code, to manage fallback and accessibility (canvas elements are not part of the DOM). Ouch... yes, there may be plug-ins available to help ease the process, but do we really need to introduce yet another plug-in?

As a format, SVG is perfect for charting – we've already seen how well it works for images or icons, where it offers us several benefits:

- Small file sizes that compress well;

- Scales to any size without losing clarity (except very tiny sizes);

© Alex Libby 2018
A. Libby, *Beginning SVG*, https://doi.org/10.1007/978-1-4842-3760-1_8

- Looks great on retina displays;

- Design control like interactivity and filters.

We can add a couple of extra benefits to this list, if we use SVG to create our charts:

- SVGs are accessible to screen readers (with a little bit of work);

- There are plenty of SVG-based chart frameworks out there to help with creating charts;

- There are a number of online sites available that can help with creating prototypes online, such as the online editor of AMCharts (`https://live.amcharts.com/`) or Method Draw (`http://editor.method.ac/`)

We could just work with the simplest option for adding charts to our pages – create it in Illustrator, then embed it as an SVG using `<img>` tags in our code.

It's a valid option, but one where we miss out on so many benefits – not only will it be inaccessible to screen readers, we also lose the ability to interact with the chart, using a mouse or keyboard. This is clearly not great as a customer experience – there is something to be said for being able to select a segment in a pie chart to show data, or even just be able to hover over that segment and have it change color!

To really make the most of SVG, we need to bring the code inline – we can style it using CSS, make it fully interactive using JavaScript, and retain all the benefits of accessibility at the same time.

There are two routes we can use to creating SVG-based charts, without having to resort to applications such as Illustrator; we can craft them by hand or use an online service such as AMCharts to experiment before exporting the code for use in our project. We'll take a look at the latter option a little later in this chapter, but for now, let's crack on with creating some charts by hand, so we can get a feel for what is involved.

Designing Individual Charts Using SVG

I don't know about you, but I'm one of those people where the phrase "spoilt for choice" can be a double-edged sword! We may only have a select few different types of chart available to us, but each allows a variety of different designs, depending on how we configure each chart.

Over the course of this chapter, we will examine examples of some of the more popular chart types. Each of the charts use elements we've already seen from earlier in the book, so it should not come as too much of a surprise in the demos. Let's start that journey, with a look at creating donuts.

Creating Donuts

If someone were to ask me how I would create a donut, you might be forgiven for thinking they were referring to food – in this case, we're clearly thinking of something else!

Leaving aside any analogy to foodstuffs, donut charts are very easy to create – the key is the <circle> element; one might be used to create a background ring, with another displaying the visual representation of our statistic. We've already been introduced to this element, so much of the code in the upcoming demo should come as no surprise to us. To see what I mean, let's dive in and take a look at what is involved to set up our example donut chart.

CREATING A DONUT CHART

We'll start by setting up the basic code files:

1. We'll begin with extracting a copy of the donut folder from the code download that accompanies this book; save this to the root of our project folder.

2. Next, go ahead and open donut.html – we will add in the markup to create our chart. This will come in three parts, beginning with adding the SVG container immediately after the <h2> tag in our code:

    ```
    <svg x="0px" y="0px" width="340px" height="333px" viewBox="0 0 340 333">
    </svg>
    ```

3. Next, add in the following definition code immediately below the opening <svg> tag – this is what we will use to style our donut gauge:

    ```
    <defs>
      <linearGradient id="gradient">
        <stop stop-color="#2f4f4f" offset="0%"></stop>
        <stop stop-color="#bbd6d6" offset="100%"></stop>
      </linearGradient>
    </defs>
    ```

4. We now need to add in the all-important markup for our donut – go ahead and add in the following below the closing `</defs>` tag, leaving a blank line in between:

```
<g transform="translate(115, 115)">
  <circle r="70" class="circle-back" />
  <circle r="70" class="circle-front" transform="rotate(270.1)" />
  <text x="-30" y="10">25%</text>
</g>
```

A finished version of this demo is available in the code download as donut – finished version.html, in case you need a reference!

5. Go ahead and save the code – if all is well, we should see something akin to the screenshot shown in Figure 8-1.

Beginning SVG: Creating a Donut Chart

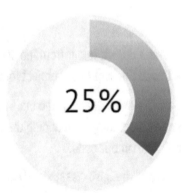

Figure 8-1. *Creating our donut chart*

Ah – the sweet smell of success...granted, I can't help but think of that typical sweet delicacy, but I must refrain for now; our demo has created a great way to illustrate results in a more interesting format than a simple bar or line chart. There are several good use cases for this chart type, so without further ado, let's dive in and see how our code works in more detail.

Understanding How Our Chart Works

This is a relatively simple chart to create – the crux of it relies on using two `<circle>` elements to create the back and front circles seen in Figure 8-1. Our code starts with creating a typical SVG container of 340px by 333px, limited by a viewBox of the same size.

We then create a definition for our linear gradient, which is called (unsurprisingly!) `gradient`. This is set to a very dark cyan color and ends with a grayish tone of the same color. This gradient is then use in our front circle – both elements are set to a radius of 70, with the gradient effect applied using the `.circle-front` class. The demo is then topped off with a single `<text>` element that provides the 25% displayed within the two circles.

Now – there is a key point we should be aware of: the presence of the two transform statements. The first one, applied to the `<g>` tag, merely slides the circles into view – without it, the chart would appear off center, with most of it hidden. The second one is more critical: SVG charts of this type usually start at the three o'clock position, which isn't so intuitive for the user. To correct this, we simply rotate the front circle anti-clockwise by 90 degrees, so it becomes more recognizable as a chart.

However, this isn't where the real magic happens – that is in how we calculate how much of the gauge should be displayed. There is a little formula we can use for this purpose; let's take a moment to explore this in detail.

Working Through the Formula

Unfortunately, with this type of chart (and others too), we have a little calculating to do – we've displayed both circles on screen, but how do we calculate how much of the front circle should show?

Well – rest assured, the math required is a relatively straightforward two-step process. The first step is to work out the circumference of our circle – we can calculate that with a simple formula:

```
2 x π x radius
```

So – to translate that into figures we have this:

```
2 x 3.14 x 100, or 628.
```

Now – question is: Where did the 100 come from? Well in this case, we will use 100% as our circumference; the calculation is unit agnostic, hence just using the value 100, and giving us a value of 628, or 628px (or 39.25rem, as shown in the demo).

The next part gets a little more complicated – we now need to work out how much of the darker-colored ring to display. To get the value, we can use this formula: C x (1 – 0.25), where 0.25 represents 25% or the one-quarter-filled value of our ring chart. When calculated, we get 471px (or 29.4375rem, as shown in the demo); this part is offset, leaving us with 157px (9.875rem) or 25% of our circumference.

As an aside, you may ask why we're not using 70 as value for radius – after all, this is what is specified in the original markup, right? Well, there is a good reason for this – it simplifies the math involved, both for working out the circumference (which will always be 628px), and the values for stroke-dasharray and stroke-dashoffset: anything to make our lives easier! If you want to dive into the detail, Mark Caron has an extensive article on Medium, which explains the calculations; it's available at https://medium.com/@heyoka/scratch-made-svg-donut-pie-charts-in-html5-2c587e935d72.

Putting It into Practice

Armed with our newfound knowledge – let's put this into practice: take a look at the CSS style sheet for the donut demo, starting with the style rule for .circle-back.

We have two values present – one is stroke-fill, which is self-explanatory (it fills our circle with a light gray color). The second, stroke-width, needs more explaining: this is the width of the *border of our circle*. Normally we would set this fairly thinly, but here's the rub: when making the border thicker, it actually has the effect of drawing fully filled-in circles! Try adjusting the value using a browser's console, and you'll soon see what I mean…

Moving on, we have the .circle-front rule; this uses a slightly narrower stroke-width value, to give the effect of a border inside and outside of our grayish-color gradient effect. But – and here comes the tricky part: the use of stroke-dasharray. This property controls the pattern of dashes and gaps used on stroke paths; setting this at 629px effectively fills up our stroke completely. (If the value had been set low, to say 50px, then you will start to see the effects of this property.)

Now – remember the 471px value from earlier in this demo? Here, we use it to set the `stroke-dashoffset` value; this simply specifies how far in to start the dash pattern specified by `stroke-dasharray`.

But – there is a sting in this tale: the `stroke-dashoffset` value works anti-clockwise, whereas `stroke-dasharray` works clockwise, but starts on the right, at the 3 o'clock position. This can mean that if you were to produce a circle that had a dotted/dashed border effect, you might not get the effect you were expecting; to fix it, we can specify a value of 25 (or 25%) to reset the starting point of this effect to the top dead center of our circle. Note though – this 25% is **not** a negative number, as `stroke-dashoffset` works counter-clockwise, not clockwise.

To really understand how these properties work, I would recommend taking a look online; Mozilla Developer Network (MDN) provides some useful resources:

- For `stroke-width`, take a look at `https://developer.mozilla.org/en-US/docs/Web/SVG/Attribute/stroke-width`;

- The MDN article for `stroke-dasharray` is hosted at `https://developer.mozilla.org/en-US/docs/Web/SVG/Attribute/stroke-dasharray`

- The details for `stroke-dashoffset` on MDN can be found at `https://developer.mozilla.org/en-US/docs/Web/SVG/Attribute/stroke-dashoffset`.

Now that we've covered how to create our segment effect, let's take a look at a similar type of chart – the typical pie chart. No, I'm not thinking of visiting the local bakery (although it's a tempting prospect!), but a more in-depth chart with multiple segments. It uses similar properties to our completed donut chart, so let's dive in and take a look in more detail.

Eating Pie

I don't know about you, but for some bizarre reason, the title of this chapter reminds me of that sci-fi flick, *Men in Black,* with Will Smith's character who has something of a real penchant for eating pie! Our next example takes the form of a pie chart, such as the one shown in Figure 8-2, with varying segments representing our data:

213

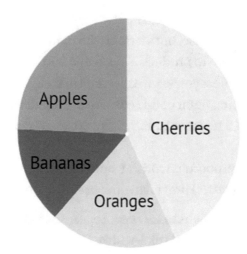

Beginning SVG: Creating a Pie Chart

Figure 8-2. *Our finished pie chart*

Thankfully SVG lends itself well to creating pie charts, as it does for other chart types; there is some math involved, but it isn't difficult. We'll work through it shortly, but for now, let's get on with creating our demo.

CREATING A PIE CHART

Okay – we'll start with setting up our markup:

1. We'll begin by extracting a copy of the pie folder and saving it to our project area.

2. Inside this folder, you will find a copy of pie.html, with a preconfigured `<svg>` container – go ahead and open it in your text editor.

3. We need to start adding our segments in – go ahead and add the first immediately after the opening `<svg>` tag:

```
<g>
  <circle class="first" r="16" cx="31" cy="31" stroke-dasharray="43
  100"></circle>
  <text x="75" y="-62" transform="rotate(90) scale(0.5)">
  Cherries</text>
</g>
```

4. For the second segment, add this in a similar manner:

```
<g>
  <circle class="second" r="16" cx="31" cy="31" stroke-dasharray="19
  100" stroke-dashoffset="-43"></circle>
  <text x="43" y="-22" transform="rotate(90) scale(0.5)">Oranges</text>
</g>
```

5. Segment number three is up next – go ahead and add this code in as before:

```
<g>
  <circle class="third" r="16" cx="31" cy="31" stroke-dasharray="14
  100" stroke-dashoffset="-62"></circle>
  <text x="7" y="-43" transform="rotate(90) scale(0.5)">Bananas</text>
</g>
```

6. We're almost done: the last segment needs to go in before the closing </svg> tag:

```
<g>
  <circle class="fourth" r="16" cx="31" cy="31" stroke-dasharray="25
  100" stroke-dashoffset="-76"></circle>
  <text x="12" y="-78" transform="rotate(90) scale(0.5)">Apples</text>
</g>
```

7. Go ahead and save the file – if we preview it in a browser, we will see the chart indicated at the start of this exercise.

This chart uses many of the same properties that we saw back in the donut demo, but we take a different route to calculating the width of each segment. This one requires the use of the viewBox values, so without further ado, let's dig in and find out how we arrived at the values used in this demo.

Exploring the Code in Detail

So – how does our pie chart work? And what's the connection to the viewBox values in our demo...?

Well, there are several key parts to making this demo work - we begin with setting our radius value at 16px, before multiplying twice to arrive at each of the cx and cy values, then multiplying that figure twice to arrive at our viewBox size:

```
<svg viewBox="0 0 64 64" preserveAspectRatio="xMidYMid meet">
```

So, let's take one of the four segments as an example:

```
<g>
    <g>
      <circle class="fourth" r="16" cx="31" cy="31" stroke-dasharray=
      "25 100" stroke-dashoffset="-76"></circle>
      <text x="12" y="-78" transform="rotate(90) scale(0.5)">Apples
      </text>
    </g>   </g>
```

Here, we set an initial radius (or r) value of 16 – this, along with the cx and cy values will remain constant throughout. Hold on a minute: doesn't that mean we will have equal segments for our pie chart? Well, no – because we make use of a little trick at this point: let me introduce you to the stroke-dasharray property.

Put simply, the stroke-dasharray property is like a mask; it tells our SVG how much of our chart to show, and what proportion should be (effectively) hidden. Let's work through a quick example, using the code we've just created in our previous demo.

In the code, the first item we're counting is Cherries – let's for argument's sake say our total is 43. The stroke-dasharray property works on the basis that 43% of our chart will be visible. The 100 value is to ensure that we complete a full turn of the circle, even though it will be hidden, as shown in Figure 8-3.

Figure 8-3. *The first of our segments...*

Seems straightforward, right? Well, it might – if only for one thing: stroke-dasharray works anti-clockwise, but starts *from the 3 o'clock position, not 12*. So how come our chart looks like it's doing the opposite? Easy – our SVG has a transform() statement in the style sheet, to rotate it anti-clockwise by 90 degrees.

Okay – hopefully you're still with me, as things are about to get interesting! Our chart has three more segments to add, so how are these added in, without each segment ending up being misplaced and clashing with each other?

The segments are set in a similar fashion to the first one, inasmuch as we have radius, cx, cy, and stroke-dasharray values. However, we have the presence of an additional property: stroke-dashoffset. This merely leaves a gap before we start applying stroke-dasharray; this has the effect here of bumping the segment round to the first available space after the previous segment. Let me explain with a quick walk-through:

We don't need stroke-dashoffset on the first segment, as it is assumed this will be zero by default. Clearly though, we need something to position segments two, three, and four, so we set values for each of these. Assuming we have set our stroke-dasharray values in the same way as before (they are 19, 14, and 25), we simply subtract the stroke-dasharray value from the previous stroke-dashoffset value. Take a look at segment two for example – we set the stroke-dashoffset value to -43; subtracting 19 from this value will give the stroke-dashoffset value for our third segment.

Now – some of you at this point may ask why we are specifying negative values: it's a perfectly reasonable question. The answer is simple: because stroke-dashoffset works *anti-clockwise* by default, we want our segments to run clockwise. Turning the number negative simply reverses the direction of travel!

It's worth pointing out that you may well see lots of other people try to specify complex formulae to create pie charts; in reality, this isn't necessary, as long as you can keep some of your initial sizes such as radius and viewBox as whole integers, and that you use percentage values where possible. It's not obligatory, but I'm a great believer in the KISS principle: after all, why make life complicated when you don't need to?

Okay – let's move on: our next example chart puts us on the straight and narrow (so to speak). It's time to take a look at the typical bar chart and see how we might implement it using SVG in more detail.

Raising the Bar

So far, we've created a couple of example charts that are circular – it's time to put a different spin on things and go straight. Our third example is a more typical bar chart; it's the kind you might see displayed within a poll.

For the purposes of our demo, we'll keep it simple with listing some values that you might see in a poll that has just been launched – in this case, ours would be based around finding out what people use as their main technology of choice. Before we get stuck into our code, Figure 8-4 shows a screenshot of the finished article:

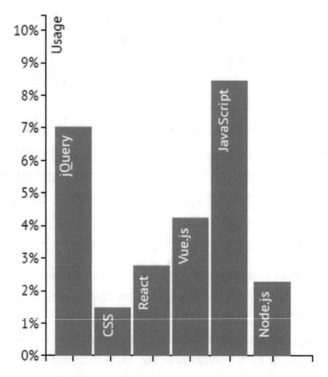

Figure 8-4. *An example bar chart*

CREATING A BAR CHART

Let's make a start on our code – all of the code text files mentioned in the steps are stored within the `code` subfolder:

1. We'll start by extracting a copy of the `bar` folder from the code download that accompanies this book – go ahead and save it at the root of our project folder.

2. Next, go ahead and open a copy of `bar.html` – this contains the base markup, into which we will add the code for our chart.

3. The first block of code to add is in the `x-axis.txt` file – copy and paste this on or around line 10, immediately after the opening `<g>` tag on or around line 10.

4. The second block takes care of the y-axis of our chart – for this, go ahead and copy the code from `y-axis.txt` in to or around line 36 of our code, immediately after the closing `</g>` statement of the `Create x-axis` block.

5. We have one more block to add – this looks after the bars, labels and styling for our chart. For this, copy the contents of `labels.txt` into our markup – this should be on or around line 42, after the closing `</g>` tag from the points block in the previous step.

6. Save the file, then preview it in a browser – if all is well, we should see the chart displayed at the start of this exercise.

If we examine the results of the last exercise, we will see a fairly simple chart – it wouldn't look out of place on a report, although it could use tweaks to add an x-axis label, for example!

That aside, if we take a look at the code – it looks scary, but in reality it is straightforward, and nothing that we've not already seen from earlier in the book. To understand what is involved, let's dive into that code in more detail, and see what makes our bar chart tick.

Understanding Our Code

Take a look at that code – we can see it comes in three parts: the first takes care of the x-axis, the second the y-axis, and the third covers the bars in our chart.

You will notice that we use the <g> or group element to separate each block, or in some cases, sub-block – our first block takes care of drawing the x-axis, using the command <path d="M0,6V0H300V6"></path>, toward the bottom of this first block.

The real magic for this block though comes in the form of multiple sub-blocks, which take care of each of the drop ticks that populate this axis:

```
<g class="tick" transform="translate(255.5,0)">
  <line y2="6" x2="0"></line>
</g>
```

Here, we simply draw a single line from point 6 up to point zero – this is repeated multiple times in this first block, using the transform() command to leave a gap between each tick line.

Notice something about each tick line? We only have one set of coordinates, so what gives? The reason for this is that the starting x1 and y1 are assumed to be 0,0 by default, so there is no need to include them explicitly.

There is a simple trick we've used here to ensure the ticks are evenly spaced – the first one is positioned at (30.5,0), using the translate command. To arrive at this, we simply take half of the width of each bar (20.5), and add 10, to allow for the space between the y-axis and the edge of the bar. The subsequent ticks are spaced at 44-pixel gaps – this is the width of the bar, plus 3 to allow for a little gap between each bar.

Moving on, the second block performs a similar task – we use the <path> element at the bottom of this block to draw the y-axis. Each of the tick lines are drawn using the same principle as we did for the x-axis (not forgetting the default 0,0 value for each starting point). We use a <text> element this time to add in the percentage values – each text element is positioned using the dy, x, and y properties.

We then round out our demo with the third and final block – this takes care of each bar shown in our demo. There is nothing complicated here; we set the x and y values to locate each bar, then set height and width properties to control the size of each bar. In each case, the width is set to 41px wide; the height is merely the sample value that would have come from our poll. Each bar is complemented by a <text> element to display the name of each technology in question; each is rotated 90 degrees anti-clockwise to align them with the top left point of each bar.

Okay – let's move on: there is one more chart type we should cover: line charts! This uses the same principles to create our axes that we used back when we created our bar chart example; this time though, we make use of the <path> statement to join the points of our line chart. Let's take a look in more detail at how this works in practice.

Connecting the Dots

Charts come in all shapes and sizes, with some more suited than others to displaying certain types of information. For example, if you wanted to track the history of a share price, pie charts clearly wouldn't work – this would be more suited to line charts.

As with other chart types, line charts use many of the same principles that we've already seen – we'd use <line> elements to draw our axes, with a <path> element to connect the reference points in our chart. Let's take a look at one such example to see how this would work – in our next demo, we're going to use example data that might indicate popularity of a certain browser over the course of five months – no prizes for guessing which heavyweight browser we're using as the basis for our demo: it is Chrome!

CREATING A LINE CHART

Let's make a start on our demo – all of the code text files mentioned in the steps are stored within the code subfolder, which you will find in the line folder in the code download:

1. We'll start by extracting a copy of the line folder from the code download that accompanies this book – go ahead and save it at the root of our project folder.

2. Next, go ahead and open a copy of line.html – this contains the base markup, into which we will add the code for our chart.

3. The first block of code to add is in the grid.txt file – copy and paste this on or around line 10, immediately after the opening <svg> tag.

4. The second block takes care of the data points that are on the chart – for this, go ahead and copy the code from points.txt in to or around line 34 of our code, immediately after the two <use...> statements.

5. We have one more block to add – this looks after the labels for our chart. For this, copy the contents of labels.txt into our markup – this should be on or around line 42, after the closing </g> tag from the points block in the previous step.

6. Save the file, then preview it in a browser – if all is well, we should see the chart displayed in Figure 8-5.

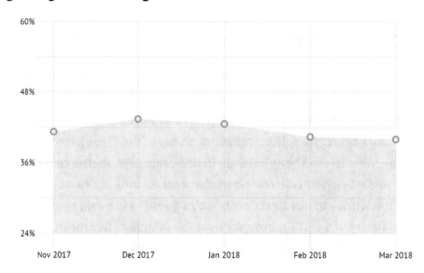

Beginning SVG: Creating a Line Chart

Figure 8-5. Creating a line chart

In our demo, we've produced a simple chart that illustrates the level of browser usage over the period of five months; in reality we would want to include mobile usage too, given how much it has exploded over the last few years! The simple design of our chart reveals a number of key techniques for creating this type of chart, so let's dive in and take a look at our code in more detail.

Dissecting Our Code

In our demo, we've created a typical line chart – we've specified a number of points, which we connect using a filled-in block to simulate a line that we might otherwise have used. A look at the code might give the impression that it is a complex setup – in reality, it's not difficult, as long as we break it down block by block.

The first block takes care of the x- and y-axes of our chart – here, we've created a number of vertical and horizontal lines using <line> elements in two separate groups, which have been evenly spaced out in our chart. These are then inserted onto the page using <use> elements – this would allow us to reuse these elements elsewhere on the page, although we're only using them once in our demo.

Next up we added a `<path>` element – this looks after the block that represents our values on the page; we could have used a line, but turning it into a block gives it a little more interest. Over the top of this block, and at specified points, we then add miniature circles – these represent the data values we are using in our chart. To finish off our demo, we then added x- and y- labels using `<text>` elements; the last element is then rotated anti-clockwise to position it nearer the y-axis of our chart.

Okay – let's change tack: we've covered the popular bar, line and pie charts; what's left? Well, there is one: if you want something to help spark some dynamism to an online report, then it's time to take a look at sparklines...and yes, pun most definitely intended!

Sparking Lines to Life

So far, our charts have all been larger stand-alone versions, designed to convey information visually from any web page. However, there may be instances where space might be at a premium – what do we do?

Well, how about using a mini chart? Officially created in 2006 (although some charts were seen as far back as 1988), sparklines are an effective way to display chart information inline within a text, particularly where space may be at a premium.

You might be forgiven for thinking that they require special techniques to construct; in reality, they can be built in the same way as standard SVG charts, albeit on a much reduced scale! To prove this, let's crank up a little demo that shows off a mini line chart; we can use this as a basis for animating in a larger version at a later date.

CREATING SPARKLINE CHARTS

Okay – let's make a start on our code:

1. We'll begin by extracting a copy of the `sparkline` folder from the code download that accompanies this book – save it to our project area.

2. Next, go ahead and open `sparkline.html` in your usual text editor. Now copy the contents of inline.txt from the code download, in between the `<p>...</p>` tags, to create our SVG.

3. Save the file – if all is well, we should see a new mini chart appear, as indicated in Figure 8-6.

Beginning SVG: Creating a Pie Chart

Here's an example of an inline 〜 sparkline chart.

Figure 8-6. *Showing off our sparkline chart*

See how easy that was? There really is nothing complicated about creating these mini charts – the best part though is that they can easily be made responsive, with little or no loss in quality.

If you would like to see additional examples of sparklines, code for two more examples is available in the download that accompanies this book. Go ahead and open additional code.html, then copy in the contents below the closing </p> tag of the first example. (The CSS is already stored in the demo for this extra code). Tip – I would recommend zooming in to see the effect close up!

The proof though is in the pudding – to see how they stack up against their larger cousins, let's dive in and take a look at our code in more detail.

Breaking Apart Our Code

If you're tasked with creating a sparkline chart (and let's assume for the purpose of this book that it is a line chart), then we can use exactly the same principles as if you were creating one of its larger cousins.

The majority of the code for this example is just the container markup for our page, and some text; the real key to this demo is on line 14, where we have our <path> statement:

```
<path class="sp-line" d="M0 10.5c.403-.35 1.613-1.283....>
```

At first glance, it may not be easy to spot, but we're actually using a series of *Bezier curves*, instead of straight lines. This gives a better effect for a sparkline – its normal size (i.e., really small), means that displaying numbers would be impossible, so we can go for the effect of a line graph instead.

But, the question I hear you all ask – how can I tell it's a set of Bezier curves? Well, there are two ways to do it:

- Use your browser to zoom in – notice how the ends of each line are not defined, but that we have a more curved effect?

- Take a look at the `<path>` statement – if you look closely, there are only two commands in it; an `M` to move to absolute point 0, 10.5, and a little `c` to initiate a curve using a given set of points. We don't use any other commands in the `<path>` element, which we would otherwise have if we were using normal lines.

The beauty though is that if we are using sparklines, then we can animate them to a larger size when hovering over them, using nothing more than standard CSS.

For an example of how you might animate a bar chart sparkline, head over to the pen created by the CSS Tricks website, at `https://codepen.io/team/css-tricks/pen/1f82250d67c9f9d15b7339543c28cb20`. It's a larger version, but the same principles still apply!

Okay – we've covered all of the common chart types; let's move on and explore something completely different. Charts are a great way to convey information, but no matter how we skin them, they can still be somewhat static.

Thankfully there are ways to take our charts to the next level – making them interactive has almost become an essential part of designing any chart for display online! For example, we could just animate a segment from a pie chart – it might fly out a little, or scale up and show more information, as if viewed under a magnifying glass. Over the course of the next few pages, we're going to explore a couple of simple techniques to get us started – there is so much more we can do, but we must begin somewhere!

Making Charts Interactive

A question, if I may - what do we *mean* by interactive?

Okay – at this point you're probably asking yourselves what I mean by that question, but there is a good reason for asking it: think of it as a case of "How long is a piece of string?" Let me explain what I mean.

There are lots of ways to make a chart interactive; this might be as simple as hovering over a segment, providing a tooltip, or even making content appear in an overlay when clicking on a point on a chart. The key though is to treat it as if we're adding animation: only add that which is necessary, and don't go overboard.

To see what I mean, let's put some of this into practice – our next demo will create a simple pie chart using a jQuery plug-in called drawPieChart. Available from `https://github.com/githiro/drawPieChart`, this simple chart is all that is needed to create an SVG-based pie chart. We'll use this to create one based around popularity of browsers in April 2018 (using information from TechAdvisor.co.uk), with tooltips to show which is which – no prizes for guessing the most popular!

Before we get stuck into our code, let's take a look at a screenshot of the chart we will create; the final version is shown in Figure 8-7.

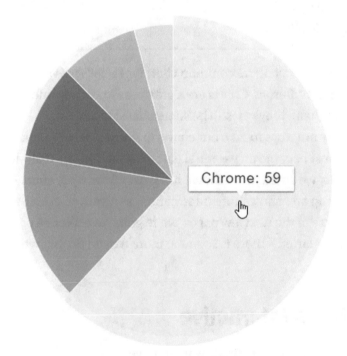

Beginning SVG: Creating an Interactive Chart

A chart to display the most popular browsers in use, as at April 2018:

Chrome: 59

Figure 8-7. *An interactive chart created with SVG*

INTERACTING WITH A CHART

For this exercise, we need to avail ourselves of a copy of the interactive folder that comes in the code download that accompanies this book – you do not need to extract it, as we will copy the contents of each file as needed.

With this folder open and ready, let's create that chart:

1. We'll start by browsing to `https://codepen.io`, then click on Create.

2. We need to add in jQuery, which is a dependency for this charting library, so go ahead and click on Settings | Javascript | Quick-add (at the bottom), and select jQuery.

3. Next, go ahead and add the following HTML markup in the HTML pane:

   ```
   <h2>Beginning SVG: Creating an Interactive Chart</h2>
   <p>A chart to display the most popular browsers in use, as at
   April 2018:</p>
   <div id="pieChart" class="chart"></div>
   ```

4. We need to add a number of CSS styles, so for this, open the `styles.txt` file from the `interactive` folder in the code download that accompanies this book, and then copy the contents into the CSS pane.

5. Our chart won't look up too much though, without the magic that makes it happen. For this we need to add our JavaScript – go ahead and copy the contents of `script.txt` from the same `interactive` folder into the JS pane.

6. With the code in place, go ahead and click on Save; you can save it as Anonymous if prompted, or use your own credentials if you already happen to have an account on Codepen.

With the chart now saved, we can preview the results of our work – we should see a chart appear as shown at the start of this exercise. It shows a tooltip where we've hovered over one of the segments, to see just how popular the browser is (figures given are in percentages).

There are a couple of points of note though for this demo – notice some of the color names we've used? These are specifically designed for use in SVG; you can see a full list of names at `http://www.december.com/html/spec/colorsvg.html`. I would also point out something we touched on back in Chapter 7, "Optimizing SVG."

The original demo hasn't been updated for some time – it contains a number of floating point numbers (as shown in Figure 8-8), which makes for bloated code in SVG. If we were building from scratch, the number should be optimized with as few decimal places as possible!

```
▼<div id="pieChart" class="chart">
  ▼<svg width="450" height="450" viewBox="0 0 450 450" xmlns="http://
  www.w3.org/2000/svg" xmlns:xlink="http://www.w3.org/1999/xlink"> == $0
      <circle cx="225" cy="225" r="218" fill="#fff"></circle>
    ▼<g opacity="0.9999998780673678">
      ▼<g data-order="0" class="pieSegmentGroup">
          <path stroke-width="1" stroke="#fff" stroke-miterlimit="2" fill=
          "antiquewhite" class="pieSegment" d="M 225 20 A 205 205 0 1 1
          82.46484378705858 372.33882463000845 L 225 225 Z"></path>
```

Figure 8-8. *An extract of our code from Codepen*

You can see a completed version of this chart at `https://codepen.io/alexlibby/full/JvYpNb` – hit the Change View button and select Editor View to see the code.

Animating Chart Content

If someone asked me to move after a large dinner on a Sunday afternoon, then chances are the only place I would have in mind is the sofa, so I can relax and let the meal digest!

This aside, making things move – and in particular when referring to charts – has almost become an essential part of creating charts that are displayed online. Sure, static charts can and will display our information, but to really engage users, we need to add something that provides a little extra sparkle and encourages a visitor to interact with our content.

There are several ways we can do this: two that come to mind are to animate segments (such as in radial charts) or provide a tooltip that conveys additional information. We've already touched on how to add in the latter in the previous demo, using nothing more than a simple jQuery-based plug-in. This time, let's switch focus, and start with adding animation using nothing more than pure CSS.

Animating Charts Using CSS

Cast your mind back to the donut demo we created earlier in this chapter – it's a nice design, but somewhat static, wouldn't you agree? Sure, it conveys the right information, but we're not designing for print! To give it a little sparkle, we can use standard CSS animation to animate one of the elements within our chart. This is just one of many ways we could take our charts up a level; the same principles might also apply to line or bar charts too.

To see how easy it is, we're going to animate the `stroke-dashoffset` effect on the donut example we built earlier in this chapter. It's a simple effect, but it is a great way to illustrate the type of changes we can make to existing charts.

ANIMATING CONTENT

Let's make a start on updating our code:

1. We'll begin by extracting copy of the `animatechart` folder that comes in the code download that accompanies this book – save this to the root of our project folder.

2. Now go ahead and change the opening `<svg>` tag as indicated:

    ```
    <svg viewbox="-10 -3 53.83098862 53.83098862" width="300"
    height="300">
    ```

3. We have to replace our SVG markup, so it fits in the viewBox – go ahead and replace lines 18–20 with this:

    ```
    <circle class="circle-back" cx="16.91549431" cy="16.91549431"
    r="15.91549431" />
            <circle class="circle-front" cx="36.91549431" cy="16.91549431"
        r="15.91549431" />
            <text x="17" y="36">25%</text>
    ```

4. Save `animatechart.html`, then go ahead and open a copy of `animate.css`, and remove the styles from the `circle` style rule, at line 18, to the end of the file.

5. Leave a blank line, then copy and paste the following code after the `svg` style rule:

```
.circle-back { stroke: #efefef; stroke-width: 0.3rem; fill: none; }
```

```
.circle-front { stroke: url(#gradient); stroke-width: 0.2rem;  stroke-
dasharray: 25,100; stroke-linecap: round; animation: circle-chart-fill
2s reverse; transform: rotate(-90deg); transform-origin: center; fill:
none; }
```

```
text { font-family: inherit; font-size: 1.2rem; transform: scale(0.5); }
```

```
@keyframes circle-chart-fill { to { stroke-dasharray: 0 100; } }
```

6. Save the file – if we preview the results, we should see the bar start to animate in a clockwise direction, as indicated in Figure 8-9.

Figure 8-9. *Animating a donut chart*

Our animation demo should by now look very familiar – we've used the same styling as in the donut demo from earlier, but this time around adding our animation to make the dark ring start to slide round from position 0 to 25%. We could have easily added more though – what about animating the percentage figure, so it increases as the bar slides round, for example?

230

That said, there are a couple of important changes to our code that are of interest to us – they can be found in the `.circle-front` and @keyframes rules:

```css
.circle-front {
  ...
  stroke-linecap: round;
  animation: circle-chart-fill 2s reverse;
  transform: rotate(-90deg);
  transform-origin: center;
}
```

...and the new circle-chart-fill keyframe animation:

```css
@keyframes circle-chart-fill {
  to { stroke-dasharray: 0 100; }
}
```

Notice how we've not included a `stroke-dashoffset` value this time – changes to animate the `stroke-dasharray` from 0 to 25%, make the `stroke-dashoffset` value redundant. Indeed, if we were to add it in, you will see the animation start from further round, which destroys the aim of animating the first quarter of our circle! It would also make the `transform` and `transform-origin` rules redundant; these were added in to counteract the fact that `stroke-dasharray` starts from the 3 o'clock position, and not top dead center.

Notice the use of 0 100 in the stroke-dasharray keyframe? This is to ensure that the gap between each segment of stroke-dasharray is evenly spaced; the values used mean that the start point for each dash will be top dead center, which is why you only see one, not multiple dashes. Think of it as dashes drawn on paper – spacing is key!

Okay – let's take things up a notch: we've created a simple animation using pure CSS, but there is more we can do when working with charts and SVG. We've already been introduced to some of the key techniques back in Chapter 6, "Animating Content" and will see more in the next chapter. As a taster though, let's take a look at how we might use a library to animate charts – there's no better alternative than revisiting Snap.svg, to see how it can take things up a level when working with SVG charts.

Animating Charts with Snap.svg

If you as a developer are ever tasked with animating content, then a natural step would be to consider using CSS; it has come up to such a level that it is beginning to snap at the heels of heavyweight animation! It still has some way to go, but current standards allow so much more than would have been capable 5 to 10 years ago.

This said, there are indeed still occasions where using JavaScript (or a third-party library) are a necessity; there are several options available to us, but the one considered most popular is Snap.svg. It's easy to see why – the syntax is very similar to jQuery, which makes it easy to learn and use in our projects, if you already use it. For our next project, we're going to create a simple demo of a bar chart – this time around, it's time for it to become a little animated (if you pardon the terrible pun!).

ANIMATING USING SNAP

For our next exercise, we'll focus on creating the Snap JavaScript to run our demo – the rest of the code is available in the snap folder within the code download that accompanies this book:

1. We'll begin by extracting a copy of the animatesnap folder from the code download that accompanies this book – save it to our project folder.

2. Go ahead and open animatesnap.js – we need to add our JavaScript, which we will do block by block, starting with the initiator for our bar chart:

```
var s = Snap("#barchart");
var button1 = Snap("#button1");
var button2 = Snap("#button2");
```

3. Next come the buttons and add text – add this after the initiating block, leaving a blank line first:

```
//create buttons
button1.rect(30, 0, 150, 30, 0).attr({ fill:"#fff" });
button2.rect(30, 0, 150, 30, 0).attr({ fill:"#fff" });

//add text to buttons
var label_1 = button1.text(50, 20,"Show chart 1");
var label_2 = button2.text(50, 20,"Show chart 2");
```

4. We can now add the code to create the bars, which will group into one element, and apply attributes:

```
//create bars
// rect(xCoords, yCoords, width, height, border-radius)
var bar1 = s.rect(100, 10, 0, 5, 0).attr({fill: "darkgrey"});
var bar2 = s.rect(100, 20, 0, 5, 0).attr({fill: "navajowhite"});
var bar3 = s.rect(100, 30, 0, 5, 0).attr({ fill: "silver" });
var bar4 = s.rect(100, 40, 0, 5, 0).attr({ fill: "black" });
var bar5 = s.rect(100, 50, 0, 5, 0).attr({ fill: "slategrey" });

//put the 5 bars into one group
var bars = s.group(bar1, bar2, bar3, bar4, bar5);

//apply attributes to all bars at once via the group
bars.attr({
  stroke: "rgba(0,0,0,0.2)",
  strokeWidth: 0.2
});
```

5. Last but by no means least, come the event handlers, which use the .animate() method to animate our graph:

```
//add click event listeners
button1.click(function () {
  bar1.animate({ height: 5, x: 20, y: 10, width: 60 }, 1100, mina.bounce);
  bar2.animate({ height: 5, x: 20, y: 20, width: 100 }, 1150, mina.bounce);
  bar3.animate({ height: 5, x: 20, y: 30, width: 220 }, 1200, mina.bounce);
  bar4.animate({ height: 5, x: 20, y: 40, width: 10 }, 1250, mina.bounce);
  bar5.animate({ height: 5, x: 20, y: 50, width: 40 }, 1300, mina.bounce);
});

button2.click(function () {
  bar1.animate({ height: 5, x: 20, y: 10, width: 150 }, 1100, mina.bounce);
  bar2.animate({ height: 5, x: 20, y: 20, width: 10 }, 1150, mina.bounce);
  bar3.animate({ height: 5, x: 20, y: 30, width: 20 }, 1200, mina.bounce);
  bar4.animate({ height: 5, x: 20, y: 40, width: 100 }, 1250, mina.bounce);
  bar5.animate({ height: 5, x: 20, y: 50, width: 70 }, 1300, mina.bounce);
});
```

6. At this point, go ahead and save your work – if all is well, when previewing the results, we will see the chart shown in Figure 8-10, once "Show chart 2" has been clicked.

Beginning SVG: Animating a Bar Chart

Show chart 1

Show chart 2

Figure 8-10. *Creating a chart with Snap.svg*

We now have a working demo that uses Snap.svg – although the markup may look minimal, this is because the magic happens in the script. This is just a taster of how we can easily make use of Snap.svg to animate content, particularly when we have more complex requirements – there are a few key points in this code, so let's pause for a moment to explore it in more detail.

Breaking Down Our Code

If we take a look at the code in more detail, we could easily be forgiven for thinking that it might not work – after all, it looks very much like standard jQuery, yet there is not a single reference to that library in sight!

This is one of the key benefits of using Snap.svg – it has been designed to make it easy to learn, particularly for those familiar with jQuery. We kick off our demo by initializing three objects – our SVG container, plus two buttons; the code uses a syntax similar to initializing objects in jQuery, albeit with Snap, instead of a $.

Next up, we create two buttons and apply text to both, using the button.text() property; to this we assign appropriate values to determine their size and labels. We then create five bars using s.rect(), before grouping them together (to allow us to apply the same values to each, in one go). These form the basis for our chart. You will notice that the color scheme used here (and throughout this book) is based on various shades of black, gray, or white; this is purely for printing purposes. We can of course use any colors at this point; Hex codes, color names or RGB values work fine.

234

Last but by no means least, is where the real magic happens – we set up animate commands for each of the bars in turn, using the `buttonX.click()` event handler (where X is either 1 or 2). The syntax here is identical to basic jQuery – we first specify the properties to animate (here, it is `height`, `x`, `y`, and `width`), before specifying the duration in milliseconds and closing with an optional easing effect.

Okay – let's move on: over the course of these pages, we've covered a lot of content around creating simple charts and providing some form of animation. Before we switch topics, I want to give you a little inspiration – as a starter for ten: have you ever created an infographic before?

Making Charts Interactive – a Postscript

When researching for this book, I spent time exploring infographic charts – for the uninitiated, these is a way of presenting information in a visually appealing manner, which is more than just a simple chart. In many cases, these infographics can be interactive; they can be somewhat large and complex to create though!

Infographics have been in use for many years – the original principles date back from 1857, although people have been known to use very early versions from as far back as the early 17th century. Today, it's a tool that is suited for use on the web, and it is ideal for incorporating SVG graphics. Part of this is, of course, the ability to retain a sharp image, no matter what it's size; it can be made responsive without too much additional markup.

To see what I mean, and the inspiration for this little postscript, take a look at "The Evolution of the Web," hosted at `http://www.evolutionoftheweb.com/`. It's a really visual site that makes use of SVG. If you browse to it now, then use your browser's DOM Inspector and search for the term "svg," you will soon see proof (such as the example shown in Figure 8-11).

Figure 8-11. *The art of possible with SVG infographics...*

Unfortunately, for reasons of space, we can't explore the site in any great depth – the code base is enormous! However, I would recommend taking a look at the compiled markup in a DOM inspector; the markup on its own isn't enough, as most of the functionality is provided through using JavaScript (and jQuery). It does go to show that SVG really is versatile – you are only limited by your imagination!

Exploring Other Library Options

Up until now, several of the demos that we've created, and which contain animated elements, use the Snap.svg library. There is a reason for this – a check online will soon tell you that it is one of the most popular libraries for animating SVG elements!

However, this does not mean that we are limited in choice – far from it. There are dozens of libraries available online; we are spoilt for choice! There are a few questions we can ask to help select a library suitable for our needs, such as:

- Is the library paid for, or a free one? If you have the budget available, then a paid-for option might be suitable, otherwise a free library will be your only option.

- Is Open Source a possibility? This will depend on licensing compatibility – are you redistributing your solution, or will it remain internal?

- Does your project have any dependencies? You may find you need something such as the SVG library, D3, or jQuery, or that there are no dependencies to consider.

- What kind of features or support do you need? Does a library offer the feature set or support you need for your project? Is help available from the developer (or others), either on a community basis, or paid-for as an extra (or in the license)?

To help get you started, there are a few examples you can take a look at:

- D3.js – available from `https://d3js.org/`; this is perfect for visualizing data-driven documents and is sometimes a dependency for other charting libraries such as C3 (`http://c3js.org/`).

- Chartist – weighing in at only 10KB and downloadable from `https://gionkunz.github.io/chartist-js/`; this is designed for simple chart construction, where the feature set doesn't need to be extensive.

- `https://stanko.github.io/sektor/` – I've picked this out as an example of one of the smaller libraries that serves a single purpose: to create and animate SVG circle sectors. It is still fairly new, and only works with more modern browsers (sorry IE9 or below!).

- AmCharts – Hosted at `https://www.amcharts.com/`, this is a very detailed option that allows both online and offline creation of charts. There is a bit of a learning curve involved but worth spending time on to really understand how we can create visually appealing charts, before committing to an offline solution.

On that note – I've just talked about creating charts online; is there a good reason for doing so? Well, creating SVG charts can be a double-edged sword – we can make it as simple or as complex as we need!

Creating charts online is a good way to focus on how our chart looks, while the hosting site takes care of writing the code – in the case of our next demo, we can even export it for offline use, so that the same code can be used in both online and offline projects. Interested? Let's take a look and see what this means for us in practice.

Creating Charts Online Using amcharts.js

Throughout the course of this chapter, we've created several different types of charts using SVG – the format lends itself particularly well to creating charts, as we can resize without loss of quality, and retain a high level of accessibility for those who need assistance.

There may be occasions when creating a chart from scratch is overkill, or if a project throws up uncertainty around how a chart might look. Instead of spending time creating something from scratch (as such), we can use an online service to mock up our chart relatively quickly. One such service is AMCharts, available at `https://www.amcharts.com`; this has the added benefit of allowing us to export code for direct offline use, once we've completed our design.

To see what I mean, let's take a brief look at using it – it's a highly configurable tool, so it's fair to say that the learning curve is somewhat heavy; it is definitely worth spending time getting familiar with it! With that in mind, we should make a start on our next exercise:

USING AMCHARTS

For the purposes of this exercise, I've created a sample chart using figures from `http://gs.statcounter.com/browser-market-share` – you can view it at `https://live.amcharts.com/Y4NzI/edit/`; we'll use this to have a play with the service.

1. First – go ahead and browse to the above link; we'll see the chart shown in Figure 8-12.

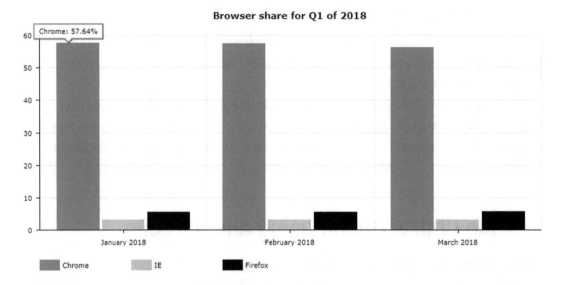

Figure 8-12. *Our graph, made using AMCharts online*

2. You will see a Code tab just below the chart; click on it.

   Try changing the value in the Font Size spinner box – you will see the chart automatically update with the new size. If you take a look at the HTML code, you will see the value you select against the fontSize property (shown here, increased to 17 from 11): "backgroundAlpha": 0.8,

   "fontSize": 17,
   "theme": "default",

3. On the right side of the screen, are a series of small buttons – these control the theme. Click on one to change the current theme; you will see the HTML code update automatically.

   "startDuration": 1,
   "backgroundAlpha": 0.8,

```
"theme": "patterns",
"categoryAxis": {
```

4. Scroll down the HTML code further, until you see a fillColors entry. This controls the fill color for one of the bar types; try changing the one under "Firefox" to "#8123FC". It should turn a medium purple color in the chart.

5. Click on Legend in the left menu list – you will see a number of options show in a submenu. These correspond to the "legend" entry in the HTML, where we have entries such as "labelWidth." Try changing Label width in the menu – notice any difference in the chart?

In this demo, we've only tweaked a couple of settings, but there is so much more available to us; it is definitely worth spending time with changing the settings, so you can see how tweaking one affects the exported code. There are a few pointers that might help speed up the process:

- Don't worry about how the code is created – AMCharts will allow you to export the code for reuse offline, so focus on what the chart looks like, not the code behind.

- Consider installing and using a color picker plug-in for your browser – it makes it much easier to track which color is being used and where, so you can update the code.

- Take a look at the demos – there are plenty of good examples, which come with code. You can easily copy over the configuration code for a setting, as long as you match where it needs to be inserted in your code.

- Some of the settings don't take effect unless you hit the Save button; if you make a mistake, simply refresh the page to reset it back to the last known working state.

At this point it's over to you – AMCharts is infinitely configurable, so I would recommend spending time working your way through settings, to see how they influence your chart (and your code). AM Charts can also be used offline, so any settings you change online can be used as-is in your own projects.

If you would like to see AMCharts in action offline, try out this demo on Codepen:
`https://codepen.io/amcharts/pen/ogwNob`

Summary

Creating charts affords us a great opportunity to create something visually appealing – after all, the saying "a picture is worth a thousand words" is especially apt when communicating data using charts! It's no different if we add SVG into the mix – over the course of this chapter we've covered a number of useful techniques for this, so let's review what we have learned

We kicked off with a quick foray into the benefits of using SVG, but particularly for charting – we then swiftly moved on to creating examples of some of the more common types of charts, such as bar, pie, or line. Next up came a look at how we can make our charts interactive – we created a simple example with tooltips, as a taster of what is possible. We then took a look at how we can animate chart elements – with the medium of online, we can do more than we might otherwise be able to in print, so clearly an opportunity not to be missed! We then rounded out the chapter with a quick look at an alternative to creating offline charts, which we can use to develop our solution before committing it to code.

Phew – it may not look much, but we've certainly covered a lot! Our journey continues on apace; we've already touched on using SVG libraries throughout the book, so why not spend a little more time to explore what we can achieve, in greater detail? There are several good libraries available online, so as someone once said, there's no time like the present, to take a look...

CHAPTER 9

Incorporating SVG Libraries

Throughout the course of this book, we've explored many of the techniques we can use to create and manipulate SVG content – much of this will have been through manual effort using a text editor.

In some cases though, there may be instances where the effort required would outweigh the benefits gained; to avoid that, we may need to resort to using third-party libraries to help facilitate development. Fortunately, there are some good libraries we can use – in this chapter, we'll explore some of the plug-ins available, and discover how we can make use of them within our own projects.

Why Use a Library?

This is indeed a good question – with the emphasis on speed and increasing usage of non-desktop environments (such as tablets or games consoles), we clearly need to be careful about which dependencies we introduce!

There is a very good reason why many of these libraries exist – although they each have their own take, or serve their own purpose, many exist to help abstract the grunt work required to modify SVG documents. This is a tedious process when using vanilla JavaScript, such as in this example:

```
var paragraphs = document.getElementsByTagName("p");
for (var i = 0; i < paragraphs.length; i++) {
  var paragraph = paragraphs.item(i);
  paragraph.style.setProperty("color", "white", null);
}
```

© Alex Libby 2018
A. Libby, *Beginning SVG*, https://doi.org/10.1007/978-1-4842-3760-1_9

Take a library such as D3, for example – it does away with much of the code required for that last example, and simplifies it to this:

```
d3.selectAll("p").style("color", "white");
```

This code selects every instance of a p (or new paragraph) element, and styles the text white. D3's ability to write this as a one-liner compared to the five lines used in the pure JavaScript solution is clearly a better, more efficient solution! The challenge though for us is to ensure we pick the right library; as is the case with many, each offers different facilities, or which may conflict with other libraries already in use within your project. To help narrow the choices, there are a few questions we can ask ourselves – we may not arrive at a final solution, but we can at least reduce the choices!

Choosing the Right Library

Choices, choices! Where does one start, I hear you ask…?

It is true that thanks to the power and flexibility of SVG, we are not short on libraries that can work with the format! We have options such as Snap.svg (which we cover elsewhere in this book); a library such as Paper.js (http://paperjs.org/), designed to manipulate SVG elements on HTML5 Canvas; or Two.js (https://two.js.org/), for drawing 2D shapes using SVG. It goes without saying that not every library will be a perfect fit; some may fit better than others, and that we may even have to use multiple offerings to satisfy our needs. That said, we can ask ourselves a number of questions to help reduce the variety of choice to a short list of contenders, before making the final decision.

The questions we ask should be common sense – in summary, they are about assessing what we have, any limitations or constraints we face, and whether a potential candidate will work with existing technologies in use in our project. The questions we can ask include (but are not limited to) the following:

- Are you using SVGs in a specific context? For example, if your need is to display charts, then it might be preferable to use a library such as D3, rather than Snap.svg.

- Are you making use of a library such as jQuery, and need to remove this dependency in favor of say plain JavaScript? If your ultimate need is to animate an SVG element, then Velocity.js may be worth considering.

- Is support an issue? Some libraries offer commercial support, while others rely on a community effort; it can mean that bugs would be fixed, but this is reliant on people providing fixes that take time.

- Does your project use an existing framework such as React, where an SVG library might have support for it as a plug-in?

Asking the right questions is not rocket science; the key is to be objective, and not be swayed by what we might like the sound of, or be tempted by a new feature in a library, if the rest of the library is not suitable for our needs. It's important to realize that there is more than one way to crack a nut – if a library turns out not to be suited to our needs, then we can change to use a new one. However, this will take time – the more questions we can ask now, the less painful it will be later!

An Overview of Available Libraries

So – now we've set our hearts on using a library: where next, I hear you ask?

The power and flexibility of SVG means we could just use jQuery, which is a perfectly valid choice. However, there are a fair few libraries that are dedicated to SVG, or can easily be used with the format; these include the following:

- Vivus – available from `https://maxwellito.github.io/vivus/`, this library is great for producing line-drawn effects, as if we might sketch out a shape in 2D or 3D.

- Paper.js – this library, described as being the Swiss Army Knife of vector graphics scripting, offers a large range of options. It's available from `http://paperjs.org/` and takes a different approach: it is a framework that runs on top of the HTML5 Canvas, using its own DOM and API to manipulate vector graphics.

- Snap.svg - `http://snapsvg.io/`; this is arguably one of the more well-known libraries; its syntax is similar to jQuery, which makes it very easy to learn for those who already use this library.

- SVG.js – downloadable from `http://svgjs.com/`, this library doesn't offer quite the same range and functionality as some of its bigger cousins; it makes up for this by staying as close to the SVG specification as possible, while being fast and lightweight.

- D3.js – spend any time working with SVG and data manipulation, and you will soon come across this library (or one of the many that work on it, such as Raw.js). Available from `https://d3js.org`, this library is ideally suited to the visual display of data, such as line charts, stacked bars, or bubble charts.

- Two – available from `https://two.js.org/`, this library offers a 2D API, offering render-agnostic capabilities that allow the same API to operate in different contexts, such as SVG, WebGL, and Canvas.

- Velocity JS – mention animation without using jQuery, and chances are you will hear of this library. Available from `http://velocityjs.org/`, this offers a drop-in replacement for jQuery's animation, using the best of jQuery and standard CSS animation code, and can easily be used with SVG.

There are a couple of other options that we've not included in this list but which nevertheless may be worth a look:

- Raphaël has been available for some years and works well for much older browsers, such as IE5 or above. It's available to download from `http://dmitrybaranovskiy.github.io/raphael/`. Although still in use, its low barrier to entry (supporting browsers such as Chrome 5.0) made it difficult to support newer features so has been largely superseded by its replacement, Snap.svg.

- Bonsai (available from `https://bonsaijs.org`) is a lightweight SVG library that is still available for download. However a lack of updates since August 2014 and high level of unresolved issues makes it less attractive if you require any form of support – I would suggest looking at more recent alternatives that will provide better levels of support.

This list represents just a handful of some of the options available when using SVG. I would recommend spending time researching options online when it comes to choosing a library; the first one that comes up should not be the final solution, unless it turns out to be the closest fit for a project.

There are plenty of options available – to tempt you as a starter, we're going to create some examples over the next few pages, to show you what is available, and how they operate when working with SVG. Our first example is a simple but intriguing library – how often have you seen images being drawn onscreen in real time, as if someone were drawing them in front of you?

Using Vivus to Draw SVG Images

Yes – I thought that last question might intrigue you: there is indeed such a library that can produce this effect!

Let me introduce you to Vivus – this simple library allows us to create this effect where elements appear to be hand-drawn on screen. Vivus comes in two flavors: a downloadable library (available from `https://maxwellito.github.io/vivus/`) or an online tool to create quick demos. We can apply this to all kinds of examples; for instance, we might use it to create button animations, such as the ones shown at `https://codepen.io/iamryanyu/pen/XdQxmb`.

A neat effect to replicate is hand-drawn text, in much the same way as we might sign a document – we're going to use this as a basis for our next demo. To make it easier, we will avail ourselves of the Vivus Instant online tool – it's a good starting point to create something we can later update using the library.

DRAWING WITH VIVUS

For our next demo, we're going to use the Vivus Instant online tool, available at `https://maxwellito.github.io/vivus-instant/`. This demo has a couple of prerequisites that we need to take care of first, so make sure you've done the following:

- Installed Node.js (and NPM), if you haven't already done so from previous exercises; this is required for the font conversion step.

- We're using the Dancing Script font available from Google Fonts at `https://fonts.google.com/specimen/Dancing+Script`. Feel free to substitute it for something else if you have it already installed. (We will go into this in more detail after the exercise.)

With these in place, let's make a start:

1. We'll start by extracting a copy of the `Vivus` folder from the code download that accompanies this book – go ahead and save it to our project folder.

2. Next, we need to install our conversion tool – for this, fire up a Node.js command prompt (or terminal session, for Mac users), then change to the working folder you downloaded in step 1.

3. At the prompt, enter this command, and press Enter:

    ```
    npm install --save text-to-svg
    ```

    NPM will install the text-to-svg tool; it will show a flashing prompt when this is completed.

4. With the tool now installed, we can go ahead with converting our font; for this, enter the following at the prompt and press Enter:

    ```
    node js/convert.js
    ```

5. Node.js will go away and convert the font into an SVG equivalent set of commands; when completed, copy and paste the text from the console window into a plain text file, and save as `helloreader.svg` in the `img` folder.

There is a copy of this in the code download; if you get stuck copying the file – it is labeled `helloreader - example.svg`.

---

6. At this stage, we can now animate it – for this, browse to `https://maxwellito.github.io/vivus-instant/`, then drag and drop the image into the window.

7. You will see it appear onscreen – try changing the settings to see how it affects the image. For example, try changing the `Duration` value to 6000, and the `Path timing function` to `Erase in out`. Make sure you hit Update after any changes, to save them to the image!

8. When you are happy with your design, click on Download, and save the resulting image to the `img` subfolder under the `Vivus` folder as helloreader.svg.

9. We need to make one small change to it though, otherwise the SVG may appear clipped – go ahead and open the SVG in a text editor.

10. Look for the width="343.8" value in the first line of the code – increase it to 350.8, and save the file.

At this point, we can now preview the results – if all is well, you should see something similar to the screenshot shown in Figure 9-1.

Beginning SVG: Animating text with Vivus

Figure 9-1. *Animating text with Vivus.js*

This is a great effect to add to any page, although it's important not to go overboard in using it – this will end up destroying the effect you're trying achieve! With this in mind, there are a few important points we should explore, so let's take a moment to review the code in more detail.

Understanding How It Works

At first glance, you might be forgiven for thinking that this effect requires special magic; after all, we didn't add any code when dropping our SVG image on the Vivus Instant site, so how does it all work?

Well, it relies on one simple principle – our shape must have a stroke (which can be dashed or solid) or border that we can animate. We've already met (and used) this attribute in earlier demos, but the trick here is not what we use, but *how* we use it. Let me explain:

If we take a close look at the screenshot shown in Figure 9-2, we can see the presence of stroke and fill attributes.

```
▼<body>
    <h2>Beginning SVG: Animating text with Vivus</h2>
  ▼<svg width="356.8" height="86.4">
      <path fill="#faebd7" stroke="#000" d="M6.55 61.06(
      72.5c.91 0 1.85-.38 2.81-1.15.96-.77 1.68-1.92 2.1
      7.7-24.7 2.02-.19 4.36-.32 7.02-.4 2.67-.07 5.92-.
```

Figure 9-2. *An extract of the source code for our demo*

247

These will, of course, not be present in standard text, so we added them in the conversion script; Vivus makes use of the stroke attribute to draw the required shape. The animation that creates this drawing effect is automatically added by Vivus Instant, as indicated in Figure 9-3.

```
1.36 2.06 0 .62.21 1.1.64 1.44z" style="animation:WGQzfuSG_draw_0 10200ms linear
10200ms linear 0ms infinite" stroke-dasharray="2416 2418" stroke-dashoffset="2417
▼<style data-made-with="vivus-instant">
    @keyframes WGQzfuSG_draw{to{stroke-dashoffset:0}}@keyframes WGQzfuSG_fade{0%,96
    opacity:1}to{stroke-opacity:0}}@keyframes WGQzfuSG_draw_0{7.8431372549019605%{s
    dashoffset:2417}66.66666666666666%,to{stroke-dashoffset:0}}
</style>
```

Figure 9-3. *Example code produced by Vivus.js*

The beauty about this is that we can easily extract this code and store it in a separate style sheet – although it may look a little odd, this is just how Vivus adds it; it is a standard keyframe-based animation. It's up to us to decide whether we want to keep it inline (for instances such as creating company logos), or export it to a separate style sheet.

If you look carefully at the code in convert.js, you will see that we've used an .otf format font. We can use standard TTF fonts, but these produce a **lot** more SVG code; it's worth converting it to OTF format! We can do it very quickly online, using the conversion facility at https://everythingfonts.com/ttf-to-otf.

Okay – let's change tack: it's time to revisit creating chart types. Remember how we looked at building standard pie or bar charts back in Chapter 8, "Creating Charts"? Well, they were just a few types of charts that we can building using SVG; there are plenty more that we can create – how about creating something different, using bubbles?

Creating Bubble Charts with D3

Okay – I'd better explain that little joke: hopefully it will become clear when I say we're about to create bubble charts!

We've already explored several different ways to express data in chart form – this might be using a standard bar or pie chart, for example. However, we are not limited in our choice; there are dozens more available, which we can create by hand, but using a library will certainly make it easier for us.

The library I'm thinking of is D3.js – this has been designed for manipulating data that needs to be displayed visually on screen. It can handle bar or pie charts with ease, along with more exotic-sounding charts such as Voronoi tessellations, scatterplot matrices, and azimuthal projections, to name but a few. Fortunately we're not going to do something as complicated as this; instead, let's take a look at creating a straightforward bubble chart, using some imaginary data based on car manufacturers.

CREATING FORMS WITH D3

Let's get cracking on our demo:

1. We'll start by extracting a copy of the `bubble` folder from the code download that accompanies this book; go ahead and save this to our project folder. This sets up our basic style sheet, font, and various D3 libraries ready for use.

2. Next, open a new blank document, saving it as `bubble.js` in the `html` folder.

3. We can now add in our D3 code. There is a fair bit to go through, so we'll break it down section by section, starting with our raw data:

```
var json = {
  'children': [
    {'name': 'Ford', 'value': 60},
    {'name': 'Skoda', 'value': 34},
    {'name': 'Jaguar', 'value': 55},
    {'name': 'Seat', 'value': 29},
    {'name': 'Citroen', 'value': 20},
    {'name': 'Peugeot', 'value': 5},
    {'name': 'Volvo', 'value': 40}
  ]
}
```

4. Leave a line, then add in these three variables – we'll make use of these throughout our demo:

```
var diameter = 1000, color = d3.scaleOrdinal(d3.schemeCategory10);
var bubble = d3.pack().size([diameter, diameter]).padding(5);
var margin = { left: 0, right: 100, top: 0, bottom: 0 }
```

5. We now get onto the important part: the SVG container. Go ahead and add the following lines in, to set it up:

```
var svg = d3.select('#chart').append('svg')
  .attr('viewBox','0 0 ' + (diameter + margin.right) + ' ' +
diameter).attr('width', (diameter + margin.right))
  .attr('height', diameter).attr('class', 'chart-svg');
```

6. Next up comes a little visualization: we're using the D3 Hierarchy plug-in to convert our data into nodes before appending them to the chart:

```
var root = d3.hierarchy(json).sum(function(d) { return d.value; });

bubble(root);
```

7. With our nodes defined, let's turn them into filled circles – for this, add the following lines:

```
var node = svg.selectAll('.node')
  .data(root.children).enter()
  .append('g').attr('class', 'node')
  .attr('transform', function(d) { return 'translate(' + d.x + ' ' +
  d.y + ')'; }).append('g').attr('class', 'graph');
```

8. Our circles won't mean a great deal, without at least some form of indication as to which bubble relates to which piece of data. We can do this (at least in part) by adding text labels:

```
node.append("text")
  .attr("dy", "0.3rem").style("text-anchor", "middle")
  .style("font-size", "3rem").text(function(d) { return d.data.value;
}).style("fill", "#ffffff");
```

9. Last, but by no means least, we need to add a legend so we know which color corresponds to which make of car:

```
svg.append("g").attr("class", "legend").attr("transform",
"translate(950,20)");

var legend = d3.legendColor()
  .shape("path", d3.symbol().type(d3.symbolSquare).size(150)())
  .shapePadding(13).scale(color);

svg.select(".legend").call(legend);
```

10.   Save the file then open it in a browser to preview the results – if all is well, we will see the chart shown in Figure 9-4.

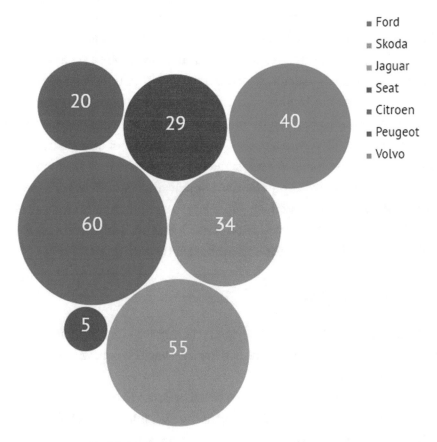

Beginning SVG: Creating Bubble Charts

■ Ford

■ Skoda

■ Jaguar

■ Seat

■ Citroen

■ Peugeot

■ Volvo

Figure 9-4. *Creating a Bubble chart*

Hopefully you'll agree that this is a little more interesting than a standard bar or pie chart! Although our demo is somewhat simplistic and limited in size, this will really come into its own with a much larger data set, such as comparing competitor size in a particular industry. No matter what the source of the data is though, the same principles apply – let's take a look in more detail at what makes our demo tick.

Note   Much of the code has had to be compressed for reasons of space; if you need help, then please refer to bubble – finished version.js in the code download, for a view on how it should look.

Exploring Our Demo in Detail

For a simple demo, it sure looks like we've produced a lot of code! So how does it all work, to give us our bubble chart?

Well, we start with creating a JSON object that stores details of our data – this contains values for the car make and the number. We then assign a handful of variables, before using D3 to define our SVG container and apply it to the #chart element.

Next up, we use the D3 hierarchy to turn the values defined under json into nodes that we can insert into our bubble chart. As part of this, we use a transform method to move each circle into the right position. These circles are then appended using node. append, before being filled with a color from the D3 color scheme defined at line 13.

We then added text labels to each circle to identify which circle equates to which value. For each of these, we apply standard font attributes such as text-anchor, font-size and dy, to center each label in white to its appropriate circle. The last stage is to use the D3 legend plug-in to create our chart's legend, and affix this to the page, with appropriate text labels as a key for our bubble chart.

Improving Our Design

Thinking further afield though, our design lacks impact – its simplicity actually makes it look like it punches with the weight of a featherweight boxer, whereas we want it to deliver more of a knockout blow!

There are several ways to do this, but two that come to mind are: add a little animation on displaying each bubble, and apply SVG filters to each of the bubbles in our chart. Yes, it seems ironic, but we can use SVG to enhance SVG!

For the former, we can simply add in some standard CSS animations – we need to specify one for each bubble, giving us seven in total. The first one would look like this:

```
.node:nth-child(1) .bubble {
  animation-delay: 0.075s;
}
```

...and the remaining six can be added in a similar fashion, increasing the delay value by 0.075s for each animation. We can then tie this into our demo using these rules:

```
.bubble {
  opacity: 0;
```

```
animation: 1s forward animateIn
}

@keyframes animateIn {
  0% { opacity: 0; transform: scale(0.6) rotate(-15deg); }
  100% { opacity: 1; transform: scale(1) rotate(0); }
}
```

To really give our bubble chart some color, we can add in a filter effect for each bubble – there are a few considerations, such as type of filter, suitability, and so on. However the basic principle would require us to add in SVG code to define our filter, before adding a call to use it when appending each circle to our chart:

```
node.append("circle")
  .attr("r", function(d) { return d.r; })
  .style("filter", "url(#drop-shadow")
  .style("fill", function(d) {
    return color(d.data.name);
  });
```

To get a flavor for how we would add in the SVG filter, look for the bubble – with dropshadow.js file in the code. If you update the bubble.js link in the original demo to point to this file, you can see the effect in action.

Time for a change methinks – and to chart a new direction (oops, sorry!) We've only scratched the surface with regard to charting; for me, it's all about trying different things, to see what works best for your needs.

Talking of trying things out – I love trying different effects; after all, one doesn't learn if one doesn't try, right? A great effect that I've discovered is Anime.js – this library provides a hand-drawn animation, which works beautifully with SVG images. To see what I mean, let's dive in and take a look.

Getting Creative with Anime.js

When developing code, I frequently like to try different things out – it doesn't matter what it is; I've played with all manner of different libraries and frameworks over the years!

One library that did pique my interest is the subject of our next demo – Anime.js. Available from `http://animejs.com/`, it's a fairly lightweight library, but it allows us to create a great effect: drawing an SVG image in real time, as if we were drawing it ourselves. We can use this for all kinds of situations though: How about adapting a range input to give the slider a little elasticity, for example? (Take a look at `https://scotch. io/tutorials/build-an-elastic-range-input-with-svg-and-animejs`, if you want to see just how anime.js is used…)

We're going to do something that is a little simpler though – we will take an existing SVG and adapt it so that the borders appear as if we are drawing them in real time. I should warn you though: this exercise is a little fiddly, so patience is key – it will be worth it!

DRAWING SHAPES WITH ANIME: PART 1

For the purpose of this demo, we will use an SVG image from Free SVG Images (FSI), at `https://lovesvg.com/2018/04/theres-a-chance-this-is-wine-6275/`.

This exercise runs over a good few steps, so will come in two parts; the first part will set up the base markup and styles. We will cover the animation in the second part; don't worry – there will be time to catch your breath before we move onto to start the second part.

Unfortunately, due to licensing restrictions, the SVG file is not available in the code download that accompanies this book; you will need to download it from the LoveSVG website.

Assuming we have our image downloaded, let's make a start on updating our SVG image:

1. We'll begin by extracting a copy of the `anime` folder from the code download that accompanies this book – go ahead and save it in our project folder.

2. Next, we need to download a copy of the image from the Love SVG site, – go ahead and save this in the `anime` folder.

3. We need to optimize the file, so browse to the online SVG optimizer at `https://jakearchibald.github.io/svgomg/`, and drag and drop the file over the window (as we have done in previous exercises).

4. SVGO will automatically optimize the file; click on the Download arrow to save the file to the `img` folder in your project folder. Leave the file open but minimized for now – we will revert back to it shortly.

You may prefer to save it under a different name – if you do, then please adjust the next steps accordingly.

---

5. Next, revert back to the SVG file we created back in step 4, then copy and paste the contents of the SVG file into `anime.html`, replacing the comment `<!–SVG CODE GOES IN AT THIS POINT -->` in its entirety.

6. Take a careful look at the SVG code – you should see this line, near the start of the markup; remove it, including the `<style>` tags

    ```
    <style>.st5{fill:#1a1a1a}.st9{fill:#881b30}.st30{fill:#627c55}.
    st39{fill:#a09830}</style>
    ```

7. Go ahead and save the file; we can close it for now.

At this stage we now have most of our markup in place, but no JavaScript – that comes momentarily. This demo is a little fiddly, so now is a good time to pause for a few moments; go make yourself a cup of tea (or coffee?) and relax.

DRAWING SHAPES WITH ANIME: PART 2

The next part is where the fun really starts – we're going to add in our JavaScript. If you're ready to make a start, then let's move on and finish our demo:

1. We'll begin by creating a new file, then saving it as `script.js` in the `js` subfolder – go ahead and copy then paste in the following code:

    ```
    var capsText = anime({
      targets: '.capsText',
      strokeDashoffset: [anime.setDashoffset, 0],
      easing: 'easeInOutCubic',
      duration: 3000,
      complete: function(anim) {
        $(".capsText").css("fill", "#1a1a1a");
    ```

```
  },
  autoplay: true
});
```

2. Repeat step 1 three more times, but in each instance, replace the highlighted values from step 1, with the values as indicated in Table 9-1.

Table 9-1. *Values for the Anime Exercise*

Instance Number	Property	Value
2	var	redText
	targets:	.redText
	fill:	#881b30
3	var	lineDrawing
	targets:	.lineDrawing
	fill:	#627c55
4	var	swirls
	targets:	.swirls
	fill:	#a09830

3. Save the file, and close it.

4. Now, revert back to our SVG image file – we need to edit our SVG, to add in stroke effects. For this, do a search for each instance of st5, then alter the code as indicated:

class="**capsText**" stroke="**#1a1a1a**" stroke-width="**1**"

5. Repeat step 3, but this time look for st9, and add in this code, as before:

class="**redText**" stroke="**#881b30**" stroke-width="**1**"

6. We have two more to update – the next one to look for is st30, and this time alter the code as shown:

class="**lineDrawing**" stroke="**#881b30**" stroke-width="**1**"

7. The last one to look for is each instance of `st39` – go ahead and update the code as indicated:

   class=**"swirls" stroke="#881b30" stroke-width="1"**

8. Last but by no means least, go ahead and add a space after `viewBox="30 90 432 432" in line 1`, then add this in – this is to help keep the SVG to a more reasonable size:

   id="Calque" width=432 height=432

9. Go ahead and save the file, then preview the results in a browser –if all is well we will see our SVG design being drawn.

Phew – that was some exercise! We've covered a lot of steps; our demo has highlighted a useful technique we should master when working with SVG. The art of animated drawing looks complicated, but in fact is based on one simple key point – let's take a moment to find out what that is, and what impact it has on our demo.

Dissecting Our Demo

There is something to be said for relaxing after a long day coding, in front of a log fire, with a nice glass of red wine – it sure takes a lot of beating! It's perhaps no wonder that I would choose to animate an SVG centered on my favorite alcoholic beverage; it doesn't matter though what the image looks like, as the same principles we used in the last two exercises can be applied to any SVG image.

The keen-eyed among you will likely spot that we're revisiting an effect we touched on in the Vivus demo – I suspect you might be (rightly) asking the reason for this, and there is a good one:

Although we're using the same effect in both cases, the tools we've used are different – Vivus is designed for animating SVGs, whereas anime.js is a JavaScript animation engine that can be used to animate all kinds of elements, including but not limited to SVGs. This is a perfect way to show just how different libraries can achieve the same effect, and that it is incumbent on us to choose the most appropriate one for our needs.

In both cases, the libraries depend on one property being present, as a minimum: stroke. Put simply, this can be seen as the SVG equivalent of border: 1px solid XXXXXXX (where XXXXX is our chosen color). We can of course also add a stroke-width value to specify the thickness of our "border," or a stroke-dasharray to give our border a dashed effect, although these are not obligatory for the effect to work.

In the first part of this mega-exercise, we prepared our content – the first step was to optimize the image (which should become de facto when working with SVG), before exporting some inline styles to a separate window in Codepen. In the second part, we then dropped in four configuration objects, one each to represent the four classes that we've applied to the various paths specified in our code. We then finished off by adding in suitably colored `stroke` properties for each of the paths specified in our code, which were used by the Anime library to create the final solution.

Okay – let's change tack and move on: Remember from earlier in the book, where we created some interesting effects using SVG filters? Well, for our next demo, we're going to continue that theme, but take a different look at how we create our filters...this time using JavaScript!

Taking a Different Look at Filters

Cast your mind back, if you will, to Chapter 5, "Applying Filter Effects" – remember how we explored using CSS filters?

We saw how these were in reality just shorthand names for more exotic-sounding names such as `feImage` or `feBlend`; we can easily create a variety of different custom filters, but would typically apply them using standard CSS rules.

Is this the only way we can apply them? Of course not – we could if we wanted to, use JavaScript; this might involve changing classes, or applying them directly in code. Sure, this will work, but it's not the *cleanest* way: is there an alternative? Absolutely – for those occasions where we might need to use JavaScript, there are a few libraries available that are dedicated to managing SVG filters; these include:

- Filter Effects library – available from `https://github.com/mkaemmerer/filter-effects`, this library takes some of the manual grunt work out of creating the SVG markup, by using JavaScript to apply the core values and let the library compile these into fully fledged filter effects.

- SVG-Filter – downloadable from `http://mathisonian.github.io/svg-filter`, this D3-based filter library allows us to apply filter primitive effects such as `feTurbulence` directly to an element; this gives us a really fine level of control over how an element is styled.

- Philter – hosted at `http://specro.github.io/Philter/`, this one takes a different approach; this allows us to control CSS filters using `data-*` tags, which are applied during post-processing.

- Tiltshift.js – this library replicates a tilt-shift effect using data-* tags and standard CSS filters. It can be downloaded from `http://www.noeltock.com/tilt-shift-css3-jquery-plugin/`.

One question I hear you ask though, which is why would we use such a library, when CSS works just as well? Ordinarily I would agree that CSS is a preferred option, but there may be instances where using a filter library might be more suited:

- If you're using an existing technology, such as D3, then at least one of the options in the list requires D3 as a dependency – you might prefer to simply extend the library;

- Applying CSS filters will only show the shortcut names in our style sheet – some of these libraries show the full SVG filter markup, which gives us more control;

- You may prefer to simply concentrate on applying markup to your content, and deal with styling as part of post-processing for your project. In this case, we could use the Philter library, which is designed for this purpose, rather than worrying about which CSS filters to apply.

There is one other library we've not mentioned in our list of possible options – that library is SVG.js. This has a filter plug-in that comes with the library and allows us to apply all manner of SVG filter effects, using a simple JavaScript syntax. To see how easy it is to apply, let's knock up a quick demo using the plug-in – we'll use it to apply a standard Gaussian blur effect to an image, as part of our next demo.

APPLYING FILTERS USING JAVASCRIPT

For our next demo, we will apply a simple Gaussian blur filter over an image from the Unsplash image library, which you can view at `https://unsplash.com/photos/uwbajDCODj4`. It's a very peaceful one of a Stockholm archipelago, taken by Anders Jildén – the principle we will use though can be applied to any image we need to use in our projects.

Let's make a start on our demo:

1. We'll begin by extracting a copy of the `filter` folder that is in the code download that accompanies this book; save this to our project folder.

2. Next, go ahead and create a new text file, saving it as `filter.js` in the `js` subfolder – add in the following code:

```
var draw = SVG('drawing').size(500, 500);

var image = draw.image('https://images.unsplash.com/
photo-1498550744921-75f79806b8a7?fit=crop&fm=jpg&h=500&
q=75&w=800')
.size(500, 500);

image.filter(function(add) {
  add.gaussianBlur(3, 0)
});
```

3. Save the file – if we preview the results, we should see a very blurry photo, similar to the one shown in Figure 9-5.

Beginning SVG: Applying Filters using SVG.js

Figure 9-5. *Applying a Gaussian filter*

This was a really simple demo, to give you an idea of how easy it is to apply filters using the SVG.js filter plug-in. We could easily take it further by chaining together multiple filters, in much the same way as we might be using standard CSS. That aside, using JavaScript does afford us a couple of advantages, so without further ado, let's take a look at the code in more detail.

Exploring the Code in More Detail

Although our code at first glance appears to be very simple, it hides a lot of the grunt work required to configure an SVG filter. To see what I mean, take a look at the code from our demo using a DOM inspector, and you will see something akin to the extract shown in Figure 9-6.

```
▼<svg id="SvgjsSvg1001" width="500" height="500" xmlns="http://www.w3.org/2000/s
  xmlns:xlink="http://www.w3.org/1999/xlink" xmlns:svgjs="http://svgjs.com/svgjs">
  ▼<defs id="SvgjsDefs1002">
    ▼<filter id="SvgjsFilter1009">
        <feGaussianBlur id="SvgjsFeGaussianBlur1010" stdDeviation="3 3" result=
        "SvgjsFeGaussianBlur1010Out" in="SourceGraphic"></feGaussianBlur>
    </filter>
  </defs>
```

Figure 9-6. *Our Gaussianblur filter under the microscope*

All of that markup was added from one line of code in our demo! It's easy to see why using a library such as SVG.js is useful; we can concentrate on using the core effects such as Gaussian blur to re-create the effect that we need, without worrying about the markup. If you remember back as far as Chapter 5, "Applying Filter Effects," we had to create the SVG filter manually; this way, we can focus on creating the effect, then copy and paste the resulting markup into our code (and remove the plug-in) once we've achieved the desired effect.

The code we've used is very simple – we start with defining a new SVG object to the draw variable; this is used to create the SVG container we saw in Figure 9-6. Next up, we then draw our chosen image (in this case, the background image from the Unsplash library), in our SVG container, setting it at a size of 500px square. We then finish by applying a filter effect of GaussianBlur, using a (stdDeviation) value of 3.

The real beauty of this though is that we can manipulate the effects at a DOM level using JavaScript – if we were using plain CSS, then all we would be able to do is override an existing rule with a new one. If we were using JavaScript, we could run code such as this example:

```
var blur = document.getElementById("blur");
blur.setAttribute("stdDeviation", "5");
```

...if we wanted to dynamically change our filter effect at the point of triggering an event such as clicking a button or hovering over an image.

Thinking further afield though – SVG.js' filter plug-in is perfect for creating some more advanced filter effects; one that comes to mind is the backdrop filter. It's a great effect for removing some of the distraction if you have text overlaid on a busy image, for example – you can see it in use in a Codepen example I've created at `https://codepen.io/alexlibby/pen/BxwzQb`.

A word of warning – support for this filter is patchy with only Edge and Safari supporting it without requiring some form of flag to be enabled. Chrome will support it if the Experimental Web Platform features setting is enabled; Firefox doesn't support it at present, but this is likely to change. It's a good reason why SVG filters can be used to create this effect – the developer Vincent de Oliveira has created an example at `https://codepen.io/iamvdo/pen/VLOGdw`, which I think could be achieved using SVG.js!

If you want to really experiment with filters, then try installing the CSS filters console tool extension for Chrome: it's available from `https://github.com/spite/css-filters-devtools-extension` and allows us to tweak filter settings directly in the browser.

Summary

When working with SVG as a medium, we can achieve a great deal using nothing more than a text editor and a little imagination; there are occasions though when we may need to resort to using a library to give us a little helping hand. Throughout the course of this chapter, we've touched on a few examples of what is available; let's take a moment to review what we've learned.

We kicked off with a quick discussion on the merits of choosing a library, before taking a look at some of the options available and understanding why it pays to choose carefully. We then dived into a number of demos, starting with learning how to draw images using the Vivus library. We then explored how to create bubble charts using D3, before getting animated with the Anime.js library, and finally finishing with a different take on creating SVG filters using JavaScript.

Phew – it doesn't seem a great deal, but we've certainly explored a few options! Our journey through the world of SVG continues apace; in the next chapter we will take things up a notch, by exploring some more real-world examples of what can be achieved using SVG.

CHAPTER 10

Taking It Further

We're almost at the end of our journey through the world of SVG in the browser – question is, what next? Where can we go from here? Well, that's easy to answer: over the course of this chapter, we'll work our way through some more involved examples, to give you, the reader, a flavor of what is possible, and why it is worth making the transition to using SVG within your web projects.

Manipulating SVG with JavaScript

Throughout the course of this book, we've made use of a number of libraries to help create and manipulate SVG graphics – after all, if it helps make it easier to create a custom animation effect, or that stunning piece of artwork, when time is against us, then using a library will clearly help save time.

However, what if for some reason this wasn't possible? If for example you're working on a code-heavy site where site speed is super critical, we may be forced to go native (so to speak), and edit our SVG content manually.

Thankfully this is easy enough to do using standard JavaScript – it can be quite refreshing to not have to use a library for once! To see how easy it is, I've created a very rough and ready demo in CodePen – trust me: it won't look perfect, but it's about the *process*, and not just the final answer.

MANIPULATING SVG IMAGES USING JAVASCRIPT

Let's make a start on setting up our code, before exploring what each part does in more detail:

1. We'll begin by extracting a copy of the `vanilla` folder and save it to our project area.

2. Next, go ahead and browse to `https://codepen.io`, then hit Create | New Pen, and copy the contents of `markup.txt` file into the HTML pane.

© Alex Libby 2018
A. Libby, *Beginning SVG*, https://doi.org/10.1007/978-1-4842-3760-1_10

3. We need to add a little styling, so let's add the style rules from `styles.txt` in the CSS pane of our session.

4. Finally, let's add in the script that provides the magic that makes it all work – copy and paste the contents of `script.txt` into the JS pane of our CodePen session.

5. Go ahead and save your work – you can save it as Anonymous or under your own account, if you have an existing login for CodePen.

6. If all is well, we should see something akin to the screenshot shown in Figure 10-1.

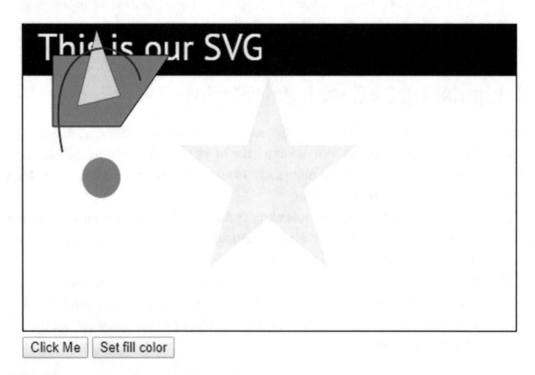

Figure 10-1. *Playing with SVG and JavaScript...*

Well, I'm sure you will agree that it is no masterpiece, but don't say I didn't warn you! Our demo was all about having a bit of fun, with no expectation that it would be perfect, but more about learning the process involved in creating our shapes. This said, the demo exposed a number of key principles, so let's explore these in more detail.

Dissecting the Markup Code

If we are not able to make use of a library, then clearly we need to add code to manage functionality otherwise taken care of by the library. One might be forgiven for thinking that we are between a rock and a hard place – what we gain in site speed (from not calling extra resources), we risk losing when adding additional code! Granted, we won't be adding so much, but it is a risk we still need to manage carefully.

Keeping this in mind, let's take a look at the code we used in more detail – we will split this into two parts, starting with creating each object used in the demo:

The markup we've used is nothing new – we set up an initial `<div>` to act as our container, inside of which we create an SVG element. We add in a number of shapes – it starts with a standard `<rect>`, followed by a `<circle>`, then `<text>` and `<polygon>` objects:

```
<div id="container">
  <svg id="site" xmlns="http://www.w3.org/2000/svg" height="300"
  width="500" preserveAspectRatio="xMidYMax meet">
    <rect x="0" y="0" width="100%" height="50" />
    <circle id="btn" cx="80" cy="150" r="20"/>
    <text x="15" y="35" fill="white">This is our SVG</text>
    <polygon id="square" points="100,30 180,30 180,100 100,100" fill="grey"
     stroke="#000">
      <animate begin="square.click" id="movepoint" begin="indefinite"
       fill="freeze" attributeName="points" dur="500ms" to="30,30 150,30
       100,100 30,100" />
    </polygon>
```

`</svg>`This is where things get a little more interesting – we've implemented two event handlers: one to animate the polygon object:

```
<br>
<input type="button" value="Click Me" />
```

… with the second used to change the color of the polygon object defined with an ID of square:

```
<input type="button" value="Set fill color" onclick="setFillColor()"/>
</div>
```

We now come to the crux of our code – the JavaScript used to create and manipulate additional shapes used in our demo. We kick off with setting a number of variables that are used in our code:

```
// define variables
var svg, svgStar, rotation = 0, a = 0;
var svgns = "http://www.w3.org/2000/svg";
var circleBtn = document.querySelector("#btn");
var svgBox = document.querySelector("#site");
var circleBtn = document.querySelector("#btn");
```

We then create the first of our additional shapes – a polygon, which will be displayed as a triangle on screen. We've used the `createElementNS` method to construct it, passing in the SVG namespace.

It's important to note that when creating SVG objects in code, we should use this to construct our shape, when we might otherwise have used `createElement`.

Why? There is a valid reason for this – using `document.createElement` is the standard method for creating elements within JavaScript. However, SVG as a format uses **namespaces**; we can separate common elements or objects that are on the same page but were created using different sources. If we use `createElementNS`, this simply allows us to group common elements together with a common namespace (or identity tag), so that we can style only those elements that should be styled.

We then set the various points of our shape, before appending it to the main SVG specified in the HTML pane of our demo (under the ID of #site):

```
// Create SVG polygon shape in code
var polygon = document.createElementNS(svgns, "polygon");
polygon.setAttributeNS(null, "points", "150,10 200,140 110,160");
svg = document.getElementById('site').appendChild(polygon);
polygon.id = "triangle";
```

It's worth noting that you can get away with using `.setAttribute` but ideally should use `.setAttributeNS` for the same reason. Take a look at the code coming up for the Bezier curve – you will see both formats in use, although the latter is preferable!

Moving on, we can create other objects using similar code – this example is for the star within the demo:

```
// Create SVG star and fill it in code
var star = document.createElementNS(svgns, "polygon");
star.setAttributeNS(null, "points", "100,10 40,198 190,78 10,78 160,198");
star.setAttributeNS(null, "fill", "gainsboro");
svg = document.getElementById('site').appendChild(star);
star.id = "star";
```

Now you may think that creating a Bezier curve might require something more complex – this isn't the case: we can use the same format here too:

```
var bezier = document.createElementNS(svgns, "path");
bezier.setAttributeNS(null, "d", "M40,125 C15,5 110,5 120,55");
bezier.setAttribute("fill", "none");
bezier.setAttribute("stroke", "#333");
bezier.setAttribute("stroke-width", "2");
svg = document.getElementById('site').appendChild(bezier);
```

bezier.id = "bezier"; At this point, all of our objects have been created – I profess that they haven't all been positioned in ideal locations onscreen, but then this is all part of experimenting with code! Let's move on and take a look at the second part of the code we've used in this demo, beginning with moving our viewBox dynamically.

Dissecting Our Code – the Functions Used

Although much of our code caters for creating the additional SVG objects, this is only part of the story – we've added in a handful of functions to illustrate how we might manipulate these SVG objects using nothing more than plain JavaScript.

Our first example takes care of moving the visible area of the SVG, by updating the values set for our viewBox:

```
// Move viewBox on click of circle
circleBtn.addEventListener('click', moveSVG, false);

function moveSVG() {
  a-= 10;
  svgBox.setAttributeNS(null, "viewBox", a + " " + a + " 200 150");
}
```

We can clearly see that the code used is standard JavaScript, but with one exception – we've used the setAttributeNS method to recalculate the position of our viewBox. If you remember from the previous section, we talked about the fact that SVG is a format that relies on the use of namespaces, so specifying it here avoids the risk of collision with other code on the page intended for other applications.

The second function we created is a very simple click-based event handler – for this, we simply put an alert on screen to confirm that a user has clicked on the star:

```
// Show message on click of star
star.addEventListener('click', click, false);

function click(e) {
  alert("star clicked!");
}
```

The third and final function is a little more complex but nothing complicated; here the setFillColor function is fired as soon as we click on the square SVG. This time around, we're changing the color to a shade of light gray:

```
// Fill a shape with random colors
document.querySelector("#triangle").addEventListener('click', setFillColor,
false);

function setFillColor() {
  var triangle = document.getElementById('triangle');

  var r = Math.floor(Math.random() * 255);
  var g = Math.floor(Math.random() * 255);
  var b = Math.floor(Math.random() * 255);
  triangle.style.fill = 'rgb(' + r + ', ' + g + ' , ' + b + ')';
```

Our demo isn't complete though – we've also specified a handful of style rules to add some color (yes, even in black and white print!) to our demo, and a simple animation effect when hovering over the square SVG:

```
@import url('https://fonts.googleapis.com/css?family=PT+Sans');

body { font-family: "PT Sans", sans-serif; color: antiquewhite; }

#container { margin: 6rem; }
```

```
svg { border: 1px solid #000; font-size: 36px; }

circle { fill: slategrey; cursor: pointer; }

#triangle { fill: darkgrey; stroke: black; stroke-width: 1;
  transform: scale(0.5); width: 150px; cursor:pointer; }

#star { fill: antiquewhite; transform: translate(150px, 40px);
  cursor: pointer; }

#btn {
  cursor:pointer;
}
```

Phew – that was one monster deconstruct! That aside, it shows that we can manipulate SVG elements using nothing more than plain JavaScript, although one must weigh up whether it is worth the effort required if your project demands anything more than a simple effect using SVG. It is always worth considering if your solution can be achieved using plain JavaScript, although the pressures and demands on your time and project may mean that using a library is the most effective and practical option!

Animating Borders Using SVG

Although we may want to use JavaScript to manipulate our SVG graphics, I'm a great believer in the KISS principle ("Keep it Simple,…" – you get the idea!). There are occasions where creating something simple can have just as much (if not more) impact than a more complex affair.

To see what I mean, and for our next exercise, we're going to create a simple, if somewhat unusual, effect. Let's say you hover over an image which could be expanded - you would expect something to happen to indicate this, such as the level of opacity increasing, right? Or perhaps a border that shows or hides when hovering…?

This sounds pretty straightforward, right? We could easily create something in our sleep – nothing difficult here! But – what if we were to use animation to create something a little different? Sure, our border will still appear, but let's just say that it won't be quite what you might expect…

ANIMATING BORDERS WITH SVG

Intrigued? Let's get cracking on our code:

1. We'll start by extracting a copy of the `pyramid` folder that is the code download that accompanies this book – go ahead and save it to our project folder.

2. Next, we need to set up our base markup – for this, go ahead and open `pyramid.html`, then add the following lines of code immediately after the `<h2>` element:

```
<svg height="490" width="655" xmlns="http://www.w3.org/2000/svg">
  <rect class="shape" height="490" width="655" />
  <div class="content">
    <img src="img/pyr.png">
    <p>Pyramids at Giza, Eygpt</p>
  </div>
</svg>
```

3. If we run our demo now, we clearly won't see anything of real interest, save for a picture of the Pyramids! Clearly, we need to add some animation, so go ahead and create a new file called `pyramid.css` in the `css` subfolder.

4. There are a few styles required, although nothing too heavy – we will add them block by block, starting with some rules to style the original markup and position our image:

```
@font-face { font-weight: normal; font-family: 'pt_sansregular'; src: url
('../font/pt_sansregular.woff') format('woff'); font-style: normal; }

html, body {text-align: center; height: 100%; overflow: hidden;}

body { font-family: 'pt_sansregular', sans-serif; padding: 2rem;
  font-size: 1.125rem; }

img { position: relative; filter: sepia(10); }
```

5. In order to facilitate the required animation effect, we will make use of a container – for this, add the following code, leaving a line blank after the previous rule:

```
.container { position: relative; top: 0.625rem; margin: 0
auto;  width: 40.9375rem; }
```

6. This next block of code takes care of hosting our image – for this, we're creating a `<rect>` element and applying a standard CSS transition on three elements:

```
rect { stroke-dasharray: 150 210; stroke-dashoffset: 0; stroke-width:
3px; fill: transparent; stroke: #b491a1; border-bottom: 0.3125rem
solid black; transition: stroke-width 1s, stroke-dashoffset 1s,
stroke-dasharray 1s; }
```

7. For the animation to kick in, we need to apply a `:hover` – add the following rule to take care of this for us:

```
.container:hover rect { stroke-width: 0.375rem; stroke-dashoffset: 0;
stroke-dasharray: 2560; }
```

8. These last two rules deal with styling our text, and positioning it as desired within our SVG:

```
.content { font-size: 1.375rem; line-height: 2rem; letter-spacing:
0.5rem; color: #fff; top: -29.875rem; position: relative; color:
#b491a1; }
```

```
.content p { margin-top: 0.3125rem; }
```

9. At this point, go ahead and save the file – if we preview the results of our work, we should see something akin to the screenshot shown in Figure 10-2.

Beginning SVG: Animating Borders

Pyramids at Giza, Eygpt

Figure 10-2. Animating border trick

Hopefully you will agree that this is something different – the style may not appeal to everyone, but then again, I've not always been one for conforming to the norm! Although there is nothing in this code that we not seen before, it's worth taking a few moments to review it in more detail, to understand exactly how it works.

Dissecting the Demo

If we take a look at the markup for our demo, we can see the bulk of our demo is contained within a standard SVG object that sits inside the `.container` div. Inside this SVG we use a `<rect>` that provides the border effect, along with the content div that houses both the image and image label.

The key to making it work lies in the style rule applied to the `<rect>` element and the associated hover event. In this case, we've applied three stroke values, namely `stroke-dasharray`, `stroke-dashoffset,` and `stroke-width`. The first controls the length of each dash around the image, interspersed with the whitespace; `stroke-dashoffset` controls at what point we start the border, and stroke-width for the thickness of this border.

We start by setting dashes of 150 units, followed by spaces of 210 units wide; we want this to start from point zero, so `stroke-dashoffset` is not needed and therefore set to zero. At the same time, our border is set to `0.1875rem`, or 3px thick.

When hovering over the .container element, this is set to inherit child elements, so it includes the image and text; the border thickness increases to `0.375rem` or 6px. At the same time, we no longer want our border to have gaps, so set it to 2560; this has the effect of showing one long dash around the entirety of the image.

Okay – let's move on: time for something different, methinks! I don't know about you, but I've lost count of the number of sites that use the same format for navigating around the site. Sure, it might be the classic hamburger approach for mobile or responsive sites, but in many cases, it is likely to be the typical linear affair. I think it's time to change that and go for something a little more unusual...

Creating Menus Using GSAP and SVG

Hopefully that last comment has left you a little intrigued – if so, let me explain all:

What if we could create the basis for a menu, but this time use animation to blow it up like an expanding circular overlay, over our main text? Fortunately, one kind soul has already created something that shows off the power of SVG; it uses the GSAP animation library (available from `https://www.greensock.com`).

That kind soul (and where credit is due), is Breno Thales; you can see his original version at `https://codepen.io/brenothales/pen/MKaxaq`. Our version will use a slightly different color scheme, but the functionality will remain unchanged.

CREATING MENUS USING GSAP

Before we get started, it's worth nothing that our next demo will be created using the MorphSVG plug-in, from the GSAP suite. As this plug-in is a commercial offering, we'll be using a trial version, which will only work in certain URLs such as Codepen.

With this in mind, let's make a start with our code:

1. First, we need to extract a copy of the `menu` folder from the code download that accompanies this book – go ahead and save it to our project folder.

2. To create our demo, we need to browse to `https://codepen.io` in your usual browser – once there, click on Create | New Pen.

3. We're making use of three external libraries for this demo, so click on Settings | JavaScript, and add each of the following links into the boxes at the bottom, underneath `External Resource search...`

    `//cdnjs.cloudflare.com/ajax/libs/jquery/2.1.3/jquery.min.js`

    `//cdnjs.cloudflare.com/ajax/libs/gsap/1.18.0/TweenMax.min.js`

    `//s3-us-west-2.amazonaws.com/s.cdpn.io/16327/MorphSVGPlugin.min.js?r=182`

4. From the code we downloaded in step 1, copy and paste the contents of the `markup.txt` file into the HTML pane.

5. Next, go ahead and copy and paste the contents of the `styles.txt` file into the CSS pane within Codepen.

6. We're almost done – to tie everything together, and make our menu operate, we need to add our script. For this, copy the contents of the `script.txt` file into the JS pane.

7. At this point hit the Save button – you can either save it as Anonymous, or under your own account if you already have one with Codepen.

If all is well, we should see something akin to the screenshot in Figure 10-3.

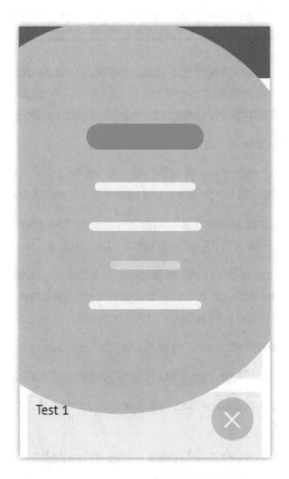

Figure 10-3. *Our finished menu using GSAP*

Hopefully you will agree that this could prove to be a more interesting way to display our content! The real beauty is that we could potentially use this effect elsewhere – how about as an image overlay?

It would certainly be a more unusual option, but who says the rule book can't be broken sometimes? That aside, this demo contains some useful tips, particularly when animating content with the GSAP library – let's dive in and take a look at our code in more detail.

Understanding How It Works

If we take a closer look at the code we put together in our Codepen demo, it might at first glance look a little complex. However, this example relies on one simple trick – we're animating content from one state to another but doing it in stages (just like a bus travels from point A to B via C).

A large part of our markup forms the background container, inside we start with an empty placeholder for our circular menu (#menu). We also specify some simple markup to create a series of blocks (within the `.navbar` class), which will act as our background content. The real meat of our markup though is in two SVG group elements, inside of which are a number of SVG paths: the `animgroup` takes care of animating the circular menu, while the `linegroup` creates the fake menu entries.

To make our demo work, we've used the `morph.to` method from the morphSVG plug-in, to animate the content. This sets the starting point as #state1, which we then morph to #state2 using a `Sine.easeIn` easing effect. We then immediately jump back to #state1 and morph through to #state3, this time using an `Elastic.easeOut` easing effect. We then finish off the demo with two event handlers, which check to make sure we are at point zero (i.e., can animate to the circular menu) or reset the code so that the animated menu can reverse direction and be closed back to our original content.

Okay – let's change tack and move onto something completely different: lazy loading. I'm sure you will be familiar with the principle of placeholders that are subsequently replaced with the real image, right? Well, instead of inserting lots of lo-res images as placeholders, how about using SVG to create something similar?

Lazy Loading with SVG

As a principle, Lazy loading is nothing new – it's been around since at least 2003; it's a useful technique to delay loading of image content until the last possible moment. It's particularly important in an age where mobile usage is becoming more popular than normal desktop usage, and removing bottlenecks in loading pages is an essential part of any designer's work.

The challenge we have though is that we clearly need something to act as a placeholder for each image. Ordinarily we might use a low-resolution image – this would work, but calling another image as part of the solution defeats the purpose of what we're trying to achieve!

Instead, why not use SVG? It might not seem obvious, but as a format it lends itself really well to this technique:

- We can scale it to any size without loss of quality;

- It can be stored inline as markup, without the need to call a separate resource;

- It can be reused throughout the site, avoiding the need to create or manage multiple low-res placeholder images.

There are a couple of ways we can create a lazy loading effect that makes use of SVG – in both cases, we use SVG as the placeholder. The image can then be introduced once a random timeout value has passed, or we use a `window.onload()` to prevent loading until everything else is in place. To see how it works, let's dive in and take a look at some example code in more detail.

LAZY LOADING WITH SVG

For our next demo, we'll use the first of the two methods – we'll load an image once a randomly set timeout value has passed (more on this later). This is to simulate the time it might take for other content to appear, which may vary; once done, the image can then be displayed in all its glory. The image we will use is from the Unsplash image library; it is one of a vintage camera, and it is available from `https://unsplash.com/photos/1oke6gf5vKo`.

This example works very well when run locally or in a Codepen – see my version online at `https://codepen.io/alexlibby/pen/ELrXYz`. Note though, that it will take a few seconds for the image to appear – it pays to be patient!

Let's crack on with creating our demo:

1. First, go ahead and extract a copy of the `lazyload` folder that is in the code download that accompanies this book; save it to our project folder.

2. Next, we need to add in our SVG markup – for this, copy and paste the contents of the `markup.html` file in just below the opening `<body>` tag and comment in our file.

3. We need a little styling to position the image – for this, add the following rules
    to a new file, saving it as `lazyload.css` in a `css` subfolder:

```css
@font-face { font-family: 'pt_sansregular'; src: url('../font/pt_
sansregular.woff') format('woff'); font-weight: normal; font-style:
normal; }

body { margin: 2rem; font-family: 'PT Sans', sans-serif;
  font-size: 1.125rem; }
.imageContainer { float: left; height: 0; padding-bottom: 33.33%;
position: relative; width: 50%; }
svg, .image { height: 200%; left: 0; position: absolute;
  width: 100%; }
.image { opacity: 0; transition: opacity 300ms; background-size:
cover; }
.image-displayed { opacity: 1; }

@media all and (max-width: 480px) {
  .imageContainer { padding-bottom: 66.67%; width: 100%; }
}
```

4. To finish it all off, there a little JavaScript we need to add to provide the final
    effect – for this, go ahead and copy and paste the contents of `script.js` into
    a new file in the js subfolder, saving it as `lazyload.js`:

```javascript
setTimeout(() => {
  var elem = document.querySelector('.image');
  elem.style.backgroundImage = 'url(https://images.unsplash.com/photo-
  1510141365970-ac1f0f80b1a5';
  elem.classList.add('image-displayed');
}, Math.random() * 2000 + 500);
```

For the purposes of this demo, we've set a random time, to simulate the fact that
resources do not always load in the same order consistently. I would recommend
though that in production use, the time taken to load should be tested, and that a
value to cover this plus some leeway, be used instead.

5. Save the file as `lazyload.html` – if we preview the results in a browser, we
    should see something akin to the screenshot shown in Figure 10-4.

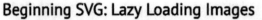

Figure 10-4. *Lazy loading an image*

For such a useful effect, this surely has to be one of the simplest ones to implement! If we examine our code in detail, it might look like we have a fair amount in use, but much of this is for the SVG placeholder. The real crux of the code is in the small amount of JavaScript that we use – let's take a look to see how it works in more detail.

Breaking Apart Our Code

We begin first with setting a div with a class of `imageContainer`; this is purely to group the two parts of our demo together. The first part of our code is our SVG image; we've used a random one in our code, but this could easily be a company logo or motif. It doesn't really matter what we use, although I would recommend keeping it simple. The more complex our SVG, the more code it requires; we're not going to see it for too long, so detail will be redundant.

The second part of our demo is really simple – we include a single div (with a class of image) as a placeholder for our final image. This is loaded using a plain vanilla script; in this, we get a reference to the aforementioned div, then set our picture from the Unsplash library as the background image. We then add a class of image-displayed; it's not used in our demo but would act as a trigger to confirm that the image has been loaded on the page.

Note   If you decide to try this in a Codepen demo, then you may want to replace the font declaration with this line, to allow it to work in the same way as our offline demo: @import url('https://fonts.googleapis.com/css?family=PT+Sans');

I hope you're suitably rested after that mini demo, as I have a real corker of an exercise coming up for you! For our next demo, we'll be revisiting a subject we've already touched on earlier in the book. – creating charts. Remember how we created various types, such as bar and pie charts? They were easy enough to do; this time though, we'll put a whole new spin on things, and incorporate a simple pie chart into a template-based framework.

Creating Template-Based Charts

Back in the day, we didn't have that – we had to do it by hand…

A phrase that often comes to mind when working with template libraries – it serves as a reminder that the days of cranking code markup have long since gone! (Although I still think that sometimes it would be nicer to be able to get back to grassroots, so to speak – but I digress…)

Anyway – enough reminiscing: our next demo will focus on using a template library to create an SVG chart. However, we're not going to use one of the "big boys" like Angular or React, but something different: Ractive. Created by the IT team at the Guardian newspaper here in the UK, it's a lightweight framework that operates in much the same way as its bigger cousins, but without all of the overhead or baggage that come with the larger libraries.

If you are interested in learning more about Ractive, then I would recommend perusing my book, *Beginning Ractive.js* (Apress, 2017).

For the demo, we're going to use Ractive to create a standard pie chart that displays population counts for five countries, namely Italy, Mexico, France, Argentina, and Japan. We'll add in our data from a JSON source using AJAX and use a couple of libraries to create a color scheme for our chart, based on two given colors. Our demo is based on a version created by Marcello la Rocca; I've simplified some of the functionality, reduced the data files in use, and updated both Ractive and jQuery to more recent versions.

CREATING TEMPLATE-BASED CHARTS – PART 1

Before we go ahead with developing our code, there is one small thing we need to do, and that is set up a local webserver. Unfortunately, JSON files can't be loaded from the file system – the only way to do this is under the HTTP protocol.

For this, we can use any local web server, such as XAMPP (`https://www.apachefriends.org`), or even the simple HTTP-Server available from NPM at `https://github.com/indexzero/http-server` is perfectly fine for this purpose.

Assuming we have a local working server installed, let's make a start on our code:

1. We'll begin by extracting a copy of the `ractive` folder from the code download that accompanies this book – go ahead and save it to our project area.

2. Next, go ahead and open `ractive.html` – we now need to add in our markup. There is a fair bit to add in, so we'll go through it block by block, starting with the container pie `<div>` and opening `<script>` tag:

   ```
   <div id='pie'></div>

   <script id='myTemplate' type='text/ractive'>
   ```

3. We can now add in our opening tags and title:

   ```
   <div class="panel panel-default">
     <div class="panel-heading">
       <h2 class="panel-title">Beginning SVG: Creating Population Charts</h2>
     </div>
   ```

4. Next in comes the main part of our SVG – this first block takes care of creating the base pie chart:

```
<div class="panel-body">
  <svg width=375 height=400>
    <g transform="translate(180, 200)">
      {{# Pie({center: center, r: r, R: R, data: countries, accessor:
      accessor, colors: colors}) }}
        {{# curves:num }}
          <g transform="translate({{ move(sector.centroid,
          expanded[num]) }})">
```

5. Our demo uses a gradient effect to add some styling to each tranche in the pie chart; this is taken care of by this block:

```
<linearGradient id = "grad-{{ num }}">
  <stop stop-color = "{{ color_string(color) }}" offset = "0%"/>
  <stop stop-color = "{{ lighten(color) }}" offset = "100%"/>
</linearGradient>
<path d="{{ sector.path.print() }}" fill="url(#grad-{{ num }})" />
```

6. We can't have a pie chart without some form of labelling – we add the details using this `<text>` element:

```
<text text-anchor="middle" transform="translate({{ point(sector.
  centroid) }})">{{
  item.name }} ({{ item.population }}m)</text>
</g>
```

7. Last but by no means least, we need to close out our demo with a handful of tags, including one to indicate that our population figures are in the millions:

```
        {{/ curves }}
        {{/ end of pie}}
      </g>
    </svg>
    <p class="tagline">Numbers shown in millions</p>
  </div>
</div>
</script>
```

8. To tie it all together, we need to place a call to Require.js, to reference each script module as needed:

```
<script data-main="js/demo" src="js/require.js"></script>
```

At this point, save your work and take a breather for a moment – we have our markup in place, but it won't come to life until we add in our JavaScript code.

Ractive works on the basis that data is stored away from the markup in one big configuration object; for now, let's add that block in, before we go through it in more detail at the end of this next exercise.

CREATING TEMPLATE-BASED CHARTS – PART 2

In the second half of this project, we're going to concentrate on the JavaScript code that is required to make our demo work – it might seem like a lot, but a good chunk of this takes care of calling in each script library as needed, along with loading our data from JSON files using AJAX.

As before, we'll go through it in more detail at the end of this exercise, but for now let's get it up and running:

1. We'll start by opening a new document in your normal text editor, saving it as demo.js in the js subfolder of our `ractive` folder.

2. Next, go ahead and add in each block in turn – this first one configures Require.js, to point it to the relevant libraries that we will make use of in our demo:

```
requirejs.config({
  "baseUrl": "js/dist/amd/",
  "paths": {
    "jquery": "../../jquery.min",
    "ractive": "../../ractive",
    "Colors": "../../colors",
    "util": "../../util",
    "pie": 'pie'
  }
});
```

3. With Require.js configured, next comes the call to each library:

```
require([
  'jquery',
  'ractive',
  'pie',
  "Colors",
  "util"
], function($, Ractive, Pie, Colors, util) {
```

4. We now start the core part of our code – the first step is to set the use
    strict statement, to help enforce better error checking in the browser. We
    then follow this with a function to load the data from a JSON file (this could
    easily be extended to use multiple files):

```
"use strict";
function loadCountries(dataset) {
  $.ajax({url: dataset, headers: {'Content-Type': 'application/json'},
  processData: false})
    .done( function ( data ) {
      data = JSON.parse(JSON.stringify(data));
      ractive.animate('countries', data);
    })
    .fail(function (err) { console.log("ERROR LOADING JSON", err);
  });
}
```

5. Our pie chart of course needs some color – for this, we're using the Colors
    library to mix up each color in turn, based on two given colors (a shade of dark
    gray-blue and light gray-orange):

```
var palette = Colors.mix({r: 112, g: 128, b: 144}, {r: 250, g: 235,
b: 215});
```

6. Next in comes the core of our code – the Ractive object; here we initialize
    Ractive with each of the various sections, beginning with the target location and
    template to use:

```
var ractive = new Ractive({
  el: 'pie',
  template: '#myTemplate',
```

7. We need to specify a data block – this covers a number of different pieces of data, such as specifying our pie chart, center of our chart, the radius and size, along with the dataset to use:

```
data: {
  Pie: Pie,
  center: [0, 0],
  r: 20,
  R: 150,
  countries: [],
  expanded: [],
  datasets: [{label: "Mixed", filename: "json/countries.json"}],
  accessor: function (x) {
    return x.population;
  },
  colors: util.palette_to_function(palette),
  move: function (point, expanded) {
    var factor = expanded || 0;
    return (factor * point[0] / 3) + "," + (factor * point[1] / 3);
  },
  point: function (point) {
    return point[0] + "," + point[1];
  },
  lighten: function (color) {
    return Colors.string(Colors.lighten(color));
  },
  color_string: Colors.string
  }
});
```

It is worth noting that our data block also includes functions to create the color scheme used, along with positioning each data label in our chart.

8. We finish with placing a call to the loadCountries method, to get and load our JSON data file:

```
loadCountries(ractive.get('datasets')[0].filename);
});
```

9. At this point, go ahead and save the file – if all is well, we should see the screenshot shown in Figure 10-5 when previewing the results in a browser:

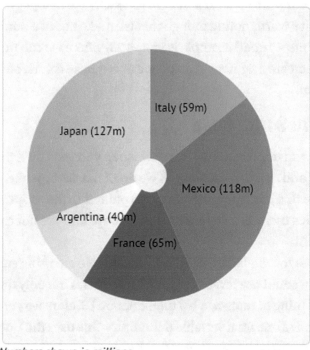

Figure 10-5. *Our finished chart, displayed using Ractive*

Dissecting the Code

If you were asked to write a summary of this demo, you might be forgiven for thinking where it is that one would start to explore how it works, there is so much code! Our demo looks complex, but in reality, it is simpler than it looks: a good chunk is there to support Require.js and the loading of data. The crux of our demo centers around two files – ractive.html and demo.js; these contain the markup and script required to make our demo operate. Let's take a look at the code in more detail, starting with ractive.html.

If you open up ractive.html, a large chunk of it contains standard HTML markup; you will notice that much of this code has been wrapped in a <script> block. The difference here is in the use of the <....type="text/ractive"> tag; this is used by Ractive to define the template in our demo (more on this shortly).

Take a closer look at the code though, and you will see several examples of {{...}} in the code. These are used as placeholders for our content – take, for example, the item.name and item.population values in line 27.

These correspond to the name and population values in our JSON file; the {{# curves: num }} loop runs through each item in the JSON file and populates the values in our markup. It's worth noting though that we make use of a number of functions in our placeholders – a good example is in line 23, where we call the function {{ lighten(color) }} to create a lighter shade of one of our base colors, before inserting it into our markup.

Exploring the Ractive Script Code

Although the markup plays an important role, it's only when you view the script does it all begin to come together and make more sense. If we open the demo.js file, we can see two blocks at the start – the first configures Require.js to point it to the script libraries we will use. The second initiates them as a dependency; the script files are not called until they are needed in the script.

Next up comes a request to load in our JSON file – for this we are using standard jQuery for convenience; we could use JavaScript (and given this is the only time it is used, it might be no bad thing to remove a big dependency!). Before we get to our Ractive script though, we have one final variable definition – this uses the Colors library to mix two colors to help create our color scheme for the chart.

With these definitions out of the way, we now move onto our Ractive object – this is made up of three elements, namely el, template, and data. The first, el, is our target for where the compiled template will be inserted – in this case, the div with an ID of pie. The template attribute corresponds to the template we will use; remember the script block we created in our markup file, which has the ID of myTemplate? This is what we will use to generate our final markup.

The third and final section is data – this contains all of the functions and attributes used in our markup. This can contain all kinds of content; this might range from simple values such as r or R (used to specify the radius of our pie chart), through to datasets (used to specify which data files to use) and colors, where we create our palette based on the two defined base colors.

We also have a couple of extra functions of note – move and point handle the location of each label, while lighten is used to create a lighter shade of color for our palette. We then round out our demo with a call to loadCountries, to initiate our Pie chart with the appropriate data from the JSON file.

I would strongly recommend taking a look at the compiled code from within your browser's DOM inspector – the compiled version will look something like the screenshot shown in Figure 10-6. It will help you to understand how the source code has been transformed into the final solution.

```
▼<div id="pie">
   ▼<div class="panel panel-default">
      ▶<div class="panel-heading">…</div>
      ▼<div class="panel-body">
         ▼<svg width="375" height="400">
            ▼<g transform="translate(180, 200)">
               ▼<g transform="translate(0,0)">
                  ▶<linearGradient id="grad-0">…</linearGradient>
                   <path d="M 0 -150 A 150 150 0 0 1 118.0911855!
                   fill="url(#grad-0)"></path>
                  ▶<text text-anchor="middle" transform="translat
                  </g>
               ▶<g transform="translate(0,0)">…</g>
               ▶<g transform="translate(0,0)">…</g>
               ▶<g transform="translate(0,0)">…</g>
               ▶<g transform="translate(0,0)">…</g>
               </g>
            </svg>
```

Figure 10-6. *The compiled Ractive code*

It might seem a lot of code, but this is a fairly in-depth example – partially to show off that complexity should not be an issue when using SVG, but also to show a real-world example of how SVG can be incorporated into sites written using frameworks such as Ractive. It is worth spending time understanding how this is put together – you may not use Ractive (although it is a great tool to use), but many of the principles also apply to the bigger versions such as Angular or React.

Okay – let's move on: we're almost at the end of our journey through using SVG, but to help round out our adventure, we will finish with some smaller, but equally interesting examples, of how we might use SVG in a more practical context in our projects.

A Parting Shot

Phew – that last demo was a real monster! Time for something a little lighter, methinks…!

Throughout the course of researching for this book, I've come across a fair few examples of using SVG in a practical context; this included very simple to examples to some more detailed solutions. There are a few that I thought were worthy of a mention – they show that with a bit of ingenuity, it's possible to produce some really original effects. Let's take a look at each of them in turn, beginning with an example that is perfect for a restaurant or food outlet.

Tilting UI Effect

Our first example comes courtesy of the developer Neil Pearce – he's used a mini library called Tilt.js. Created by Gijs Rogé, the library itself can be downloaded from `https://gijsroge.github.io/tilt.js/`.

Neil has put this library to great use, by creating two cards that display information from a mocked-up page that wouldn't be out of place on a hotel website. You can see the demo on Codepen at `https://codepen.io/2975/pen/WJwxYv` – try hovering over each card in turn: notice how it tilts slightly as you move the mouse over each (Figure 10-7):

Figure 10-7. *Making use of tilt.js*

In this instance, the demo illustrates how we can make use of other libraries to manipulate SVG elements with little difficulty; the animation effect is managed within the SVG, while the tilting effect comes from the Tilt.js library.

Panning and Zooming Images

This next example features a simple take on an age-old problem – viewing images close up, particularly those with lots of detail.

The developer Anders Riutta has created a library that enables anyone to pan or zoom in on an SVG image for this purpose; it can be downloaded from GitHub at `https://github.com/ariutta/svg-pan-zoom`. We can see it in use with one of the demos provided on the main website; as an example, Figure 10-8 shows an inline SVG image of a tiger in close-up.

Figure 10-8. *Panning and zooming an SVG image*

This is just one way of navigating around SVG images – the library offers support for a host of different options, such as embedded SVGs, custom events, animation, and using custom controls.

You can see the original demo on the main website at `http://ariutta.github.io/svg-pan-zoom/demo/inline.html`.

Tracking Progress

Our final example makes use of one of SVG's key strengths – the ability to use the `<path>` element to create any kind of shape, simply by providing suitable coordinates.

This is put to good use in the Progressbar.js library; created by Kimmo Brunfeldt, this library can be downloaded from `http://kimmobrunfeldt.github.io/progressbar.js/`. It's designed for use in modern browsers, released within the last two to three years; this includes IE10 and 11! The library produces a clean and slick design – we can see it in action in a screenshot shown in Figure 10-9.

Beginning SVG: Creating a Circular Progressbar

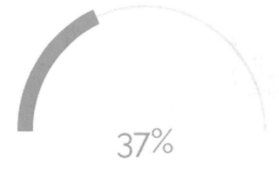

Figure 10-9. *Animating a SVG progress bar*

To really understand how SVG plays its part in this library, I would recommend taking a peek at the code behind this example; Figure 10-10 shows what the SVG code looks like from our example.

```
▼<svg viewBox="0 0 100 50">
   <path d="M 50,50 m -47,0 a 47,47 0 1 1 94,0" stroke="#eee" stroke-width="1" fill-opacity="0">
   </path>
   <path d="M 50,50 m -47,0 a 47,47 0 1 1 94,0" stroke="rgb(112,128,144)" stroke-width="6" fill-
   opacity="0" style="stroke-dasharray: 147.708, 147.708; stroke-dashoffset: 0;"></path>
</svg>
```

Figure 10-10. *An example of how Progressbar.js is used*

The great thing about this library is that we don't even have to provide the path coordinates to use if we want to use a standard shape; Progressbar.js provides a number of pre-built options such as circle or line. If though we want to push the boat out (so to speak), we can of course provide our custom path coordinates in the markup and let the library take care of the rest...!

Summary

SVG as a format is hugely versatile – unlike images or other graphic formats, we can manipulate elements within with ease, using nothing more than standard JavaScript (or libraries), and plain CSS styling. Over the course of this chapter, we've worked through a number of examples to illustrate how we might use SVG in a real-world example; let's take a moment to review what we have learned.

We kicked off with a quick tour on how to create or manipulate SVG objects using vanilla JavaScript – some might argue that this should be nearer the start of the book, but we quickly learned how much extra code (and time) is required to add in simple shapes - which could indeed put beginners off! Making use of a library will frequently be a more efficient use of time and resources.

Next up came a look at an interesting take on animating borders using SVG – this illustrated a perfect means of animating a simple change that adds a certain edge to an otherwise plain image, using nothing more than standard SVG animation.

Our next demo took animation up a notch and explored part of the Greensock GSAP animation library; we saw how the morphing tool can provide an original solution, which stands apart from other menus you may have seen online.

We then moved onto exploring a time-honored technique of lazy-loading images – this is nothing new, but our version swapped in SVG images as placeholders for what would otherwise be low-resolution images. We covered how this reduces the number of calls for extra resources, so it ultimately reduces the load on the server and helps retain page speeds.

Our final large demo explored how we might create template-based charts using a framework such as Ractive; we learned how we can use such a library to swap in data and text to a standard chart, so that ultimately our chart can be set as a reusable template for future projects. We then rounded out the chapter with some smaller examples of how SVG can be used in a practical context; this was to show that SVG is a versatile format, and that you are really only limited by your imagination!

Phew – well, all good things must eventually come to a close, as we reach the end of this book; I hope you've enjoyed our adventure through the world of SVG as I have writing this book.

Index

© Alex Libby 2018
A. Libby, *Beginning SVG*, https://doi.org/10.1007/978-1-4842-3760-1

Printed in the United States
By Bookmasters